Experiences in Teaching Business Ethics

D1715789

A volume in
Contemporary Human Resource Management:
Issues, Challenges, and Opportunities

Series Editor:
Ronald R. Sims, *College of William and Mary*

Contemporary Human Resource Management: Issues, Challenges, and Opportunities

Ronald R. Sims, Series Editor

Human Resource Management:
Contemporary Issues, Challenges, and Opportunities (2006)
edited by Ronald R. Sims

Reforming (Transforming?) a Public Human Resource Management Agency:
The Case of the Personnel Board of Jefferson County, Alabama (2010)
by Ronald R. Sims

Experiences in Teaching Business Ethics (2011)
edited by Ronald R. Sims and William I. Sauser, Jr.

Experiences in Teaching Business Ethics

edited by

Ronald R. Sims
College of William and Mary

and

William I. Sauser, Jr.
Auburn University

Information Age Publishing, Inc.
Charlotte, North Carolina • www.infoagepub.com

Library of Congress Cataloging-in-Publication Data

Experiences in teaching business ethics / edited by Ronald R. Sims and
William I. Sauser.
    p. cm. — (Contemporary human resource management)
    Includes bibliographical references.
    ISBN 978-1-61735-469-4 (paperback) — ISBN 978-1-61735-470-0 (hardcover) —
ISBN 978-1-61735-471-7 (e-book)
    1. Business ethics—Study and teaching. I. Sims, Ronald R. II. Sauser,
William I.
    HF5387.E98 2011
    174'.4—dc22

                                                              2011016282

Printed in the United States of America

CONTENTS

Preface .... *vii*

Acknowledgments .... *xiii*

1. Too Bad for Kant: Lessons of Experience With the Three
   Questions Foundational to Teaching Business Ethics
   Steven Olson *1*

2. Business Ethics Curriculum Development: Balancing
   Idealism and Realism
   Johannes Brinkmann and Ronald R. Sims *27*

3. Business Ethics Teaching: Working to Develop an Effective
   Learning Climate
   Ronald R. Sims *53*

4. Putting Career Morality on the Agenda of Business
   Students: How One Could Use a Play and Survey Results
   for Triggering Moral Reflection
   Johannes Brinkmann *83*

5. Teaching Business Ethics via Dialogue and Conversation
   Ronald R. Sims *97*

6. Once More With Feeling: Integrating Emotion in Teaching
   Business Ethics—Educational Implications from Cognitive
   Neuroscience and Social Psychology
   Christopher P. Adkins *123*

7. Using Writing to Teach Business Ethics: One Approach
   Ronald R. Sims *143*

8. Reflection Through Debriefing in Teaching Business
Ethics: Completing the Learning Process in Experiential
Learning Exercises
Ronald R. Sims and William I. Sauser, Jr. *171*

9. Auburn University's Management Ethics Program
Achilles A. Armenakis *205*

10. Teaching Business Ethics at a Distance to Executive MBA
Students
William I. Sauser, Jr. *217*

11. Rethinking Ethics Training: New Approaches to Enhance
Effectiveness
John C. Knapp *231*

12. Beyond the Classroom: Business Ethics Training Programs
for Professionals
William I. Sauser, Jr. *247*

About the Authors *273*

PREFACE

Since the fall of Enron and other scandals in both the private and public sectors in which managers have enriched themselves and defrauded others, increasing attention has been given to business ethics. Many stakeholders place heavy blame for the corporate and organizational climates that produced these scandals at the feet of management education. These stakeholders contend that while business schools are effective in teaching techniques of analysis and decision making, they have failed to teach with equal effectiveness values and accountable management behavior.

One result of this criticism has been a reexamination of the role of business ethics in the teaching of management. These concerns have spawned new courses on ethics and even majors in the area. Some schools have even declared that ethics is now at the forefront of their management teaching.

No agreement exists on what is the most effective way of teaching business ethics. Historically teachers of ethics started with the classical thinkers and writings on ethics, primarily from the fields of philosophy and theology, and asked students to wrestle with the relevance of the content of classical thinking to the practices of management. Today it is much more common for teachers of ethics to begin with the actual practices of management and then move the discussions back to exploring the bases and foundations of one's ethical thinking and decision making.

The primary purpose of this book is to stimulate dialogue and discussion about the most effective ways of teaching business ethics. Contributors to the book focus on approaches and methodologies and lessons learned that in their

Experiences in Teaching Business Ethics
pp. vii–xi
Copyright © 2011 by Information Age Publishing
All rights of reproduction in any form reserved.

experience are having an impact in leading students to confront with account-ability and understanding the bases of their ethical thinking, the responsibili-ties they have to an enlarged base of stakeholders (whose needs and interests often are conflicting), and their stewardship to use their talents responsibly not only in fulfilling an organization's economic goals but also in recognizing the impact of their actions on both individuals and the larger society.

In chapter 1, "Too Bad for Kant: Lessons of Experience With the Three Questions Foundational to Teaching Business Ethics," Steven Olson uses James Rest's four-component model of ethical behavior to answer what he suggests are the three foundational questions in teaching business ethics: (1) What does it mean to teach ethics in general and within the domain of business?; (2) What are the specific challenges con-fronting students who would learn business ethics?; and (3) How is stu-dent learning to be assessed? Olson argues that the learning challenges for novice and advanced beginner students differ from those of compe-tent and proficient students and offers examples of effective teaching techniques for both groups. The chapter contrasts the author's perspec-tive with traditional philosophical approaches to teaching business ethics, typified by Kantian approaches, and suggests that they are wanting because they overemphasize one component of ethical behavior, namely, ethical judgment, and assume a disembodied account of practical reason that is inadequate to the challenges that ethical issues present in the domain of business management.

In chapter 2, "Business Ethics Curriculum Development: Balancing Idealism and Realism," Johannes Brinkmann and Ronald R. Sims discuss three critical components to successfully teaching business ethics. The chapter first focuses on the targeted learning goals of teaching business ethics. Next, the chapter takes a look at the working conditions of an ini-tiative to teach business ethics. Finally, the third component of the tradi-tional threefold distinction in teaching pedagogy—curriculum design—is addressed and discussed.

In chapter 3, "Business Ethics Teaching: Working to Develop an Effec-tive Learning Climate," Ronald R. Sims describes efforts to develop a learning environment that facilitates learning in his business ethics courses. The chapter offers answers to the following questions: What is the appropriate context or learning environment to foster? What is the process or conduct or model to use in developing, attending to and man-aging the learning environment? What is the character of the role of the business ethics teacher given the classroom learning environment? What are the process issues that must be attend to and managed throughout the business ethics course that support a learning environment that promotes respect, student involvement, clear expectations and rigor? The chapter also presents a model that can be used to manage the business ethics professor's and students' expectations and contributions during the business ethics courses.

In chapter 4, "Putting Career Morality on the Agenda of Business Students: How One Could Use a Play and Survey Results for Triggering Moral Reflection," Johannes Brinkmann discusses the design of a teaching unit which addresses the students' (heterogeneous) career visions, ambitions and strategies in an ethical reflection perspective. The chapter consists of three somewhat independent parts, with career strategy and morality as a common denominator. First a theater piece is presented, about what one might call career strategy. Then parts of a previous pilot survey are summarized, where business students and marketing professionals were asked questions about career visions, strategies, and morality. Finally, Brinkmann offers suggestions on how one could invite serious reflection about these important topics among business students.

In chapter 5, "Teaching Business Ethics via Dialogue and Conversation," Ronald R. Sims discusses the importance of dialogue, good moral conversation, and more particularly conversational learning to teaching business ethics courses for effective learning. The chapter first describes how the author recognized that introducing dialogue and conversations within the classroom when teaching ethics was important to effective teaching and learning. Next, attention turns to a brief discussion of dialogue and good moral conversation before focusing on conversational learning and its use in business ethics courses. Special attention is then given to how Sims views his role as the teacher in using conversational learning in a business ethics course. Finally, further reflection using conversational learning and dialogue in teaching business ethics is offered for the reader.

In chapter 6, "Once More With Feeling: Integrating Emotion in Teaching Business Ethics—Educational Implications From Cognitive Neuroscience and Social Psychology," Christopher P. Adkins argues that the teaching of business ethics has focused primarily on the cognitive domain, based on the assumption that moral reasoning is the pathway to moral development and thus moral behavior. Adkins suggests that in contrast, research in cognitive neuroscience and social psychology suggests that emotion fuels our first intuition in ethical situations, and in turn influences our reasoning, motivations, and actions. This chapter builds on this current research and explores how faculty can incorporate discussions of emotional influences on ethical decision making within business contexts. The educational implications of these findings are also discussed, including suggestions for modifying course design, learning exercises and pedagogical approaches.

In chapter 7, "Using Writing to Teach Business Ethics: One Approach," Ronald R. Sims describes his experience in incorporating writing via journals in business ethics courses. The advantages and disadvantages of using journals in teaching business ethics are discussed and practical suggestions or recommendations are offered based upon the author's experience in using journals in teaching business ethics in an undergraduate business and society course.

In chapter 8, "Reflection Through Debriefing in Teaching Business Ethics: Completing the Learning Process in Experiential Learning Exercises," Ronald R. Sims and William I. Sauser, Jr., offer an up-to-date view on the role that reflection and debriefing can and should play in the effective teaching of business ethics. The chapter first focuses on the process of reflection and debriefing and the postexperience analysis of experiential learning exercises in business ethics education. The chapter then provides a conceptual model for debriefing using Kolb's (1984) experiential learning cycle and model of the learning process in teaching business ethics. Next, practical ideas are offered for applying the model to reflecting on and debriefing experiential learning exercises used in business ethics courses. Special attention is given to a brief discussion of experiential learning exercises as a teaching tool, the importance of the business ethics teacher's role in providing structure, ambiguity and a climate for learning in experiential exercises so that learners can personalize the learning. Before concluding the chapter the authors discuss mistakes to avoid in debriefing experiential learning exercises in teaching business ethics.

In chapter 9, "Auburn University's Management Ethics Program," Achilles A. Armenakis describes how Auburn University contributes to the diffusion of knowledge about what is ethical and unethical in business through two programs. Armenakis first focuses on a speakers' program in which executives, researchers and professors who have distinguished themselves through some positive act are invited to share their experiences with students in credit and noncredit courses. The chapter discusses how undergraduate students as well as graduate students enrolled in MBA, executive MBA, and physicians' executive MBA programs participate in learning exercises directed by these speakers. The chapter next describes a research program with the mission of developing a methodology that can be used to assess the extent to which organizational cultures are ethical. This chapter summarizes both programs.

In chapter 10, "Teaching Business Ethics at a Distance to Executive MBA Students," William I. Sauser, Jr., describes the goals and content of the most recent (fall semester, 2009) one-semester-hour required version of the Auburn University Executive MBA program's business ethics course taught at a distance, the methods by which it was delivered to the students, efforts to maintain continuing contact among the professor and students despite asynchronous delivery across state and national borders, required graded student deliverables, and student reactions to the course.

Sauser also discusses from his point of view the challenges and joys of teaching such a course at a distance and offers recommendations to other faculty members who may be considering a similar endeavor.

In chapter 11, "Rethinking Ethics Training: New Approaches to Enhance Effectiveness," John C. Knapp considers how training programs can engage employees more effectively and contribute to a culture where conversations about ethics are commonplace and positive, not sporadic, off-putting or threatening. The chapter explores trends in compliance management, including legal developments, and identifies some emerging best practices to enhance learning about ethics in the workplace. Three key factors are discussed in the chapter: (1) *Strategic orientation*: a values focus vs. a compliance focus; (2) *Contextual learning*: training led by managers and supervisors; and (3) *Functional relevance*: aligning training with the risks and opportunities pertinent to each employee.

In chapter 12, "Beyond the Classroom: Business Ethics Training Programs for Professionals," William I. Sauser, Jr., focuses on stimulating discussion on questions like the following which are of interest to business ethics professors, business leaders, and others: How should such programs be structured, and how can employees become meaningfully engaged in program development and delivery? What kinds of programs foster strong employee participation and lead to meaningful learning and implementation of ideas? The chapter begins with a definition of the corporate "culture of character," and describes the importance of ethics training as a step in the creation of such a culture. Research relating to elements of an effective ethics training program is then briefly reviewed. Three examples of ethics training programs designed and provided by the author are then described, one for municipal employees, one for university employees, and one offered at a distance to professional engineers. The chapter concludes with some reflections on the role of the business ethics professor in providing ethics training "beyond the classroom."

The primary audiences for this book are those individuals responsible for teaching management or leadership, especially those with responsibilities for teaching business ethics.   But the book is also designed for practicing managers, for these managers have among their most important responsibilities the development of people in their organizations who have the integrity, values, and competence to be effective managers of economic resources while at the same time recognizing the roles of their organization in shaping society.

REFERENCE

Kolb, D. A. (1984). *Experiential learning: Experience as the source of learning and development*. Englewood Cliffs, NJ: Prentice-Hall.

ACKNOWLEDGMENTS

A special thanks from Ronald Sims to Bill Sauser, my coeditor (and nearly 30-year colleague and friend) during our first coedited book journey. The administrative support of the Mason School of Business at the College of William and Mary is acknowledged.

Thank you goes to Nandi, Dangaia, and Sieya, who have supported me once again during my work on this book. A special thank you and appreciation goes out to Kani, Ronald, Jr., Marchet, Vellice, Shelley, and Sharisse.

William Sauser wishes to thank his friend and coeditor, Ronald Sims, for his invitation to join him in this project; our colleagues for contributing interesting and informative chapters; his students and workshop participants for willingly wrestling with tough ethical issues; and his wife Lane for her constant encouragement, support, and love.

We are indebted to George Johnson, president and publisher of Information Age Publishing for his support in this project. We are grateful to our group of contributors who graciously took the time from their very, very busy schedules to assist us in this project. Their collective insights and wisdom as educators, practitioners and theorists on ethics and business ethics in particular will be quite evident as you read through the impressive words of wisdom and the content of their chapters. We believe that their work has made a significant contribution to the ongoing dialogue on teaching business and ethics, and we are truly indebted to them all as colleagues and friends. Without their efforts and insights, this book would not exist. We hope we'll get to work with all of you again in the future.

CHAPTER 1

TOO BAD FOR KANT

Lessons of Experience With the Three Questions Foundational to Teaching Business Ethics

STEVEN OLSON

INTRODUCTION

I will never forget my college encounter with Hegel's critique of Kant's ethics. As I sat in the upper-course philosophy class I thought, "Finally, I can recognize my own life experience in a philosophical account of what it means to lead an ethical life."

Before entering college, I spent a year collecting past due credit card accounts for Sears & Roebuck. Each day, it seemed, I was confronted with ethical dilemmas about which I had to make instantaneous judgments and for which I was certain that Kant, in his deontological rigor, would have only condemned me. Hegel helped me appreciate the ethical difficulties I was struggling with and gave me a sense of how I might chart moral progress in the face of them. I decided then and there that if Kant could not help me understand the richness of my moral experience and

Experiences in Teaching Business Ethics
pp. 1–25
Copyright © 2011 by Information Age Publishing

1

improve it in realistic ways, then too bad for Kant. Too bad for any theory that could not help me advance the lessons of my own experience.

I have carried this spirit with me toward all theories of ethics and ethical justification. It informs this essay mightily because it has led me to answer the three foundational questions of teaching business ethics in a way that would be scarcely recognizable to most of the professors who taught me ethics.

THE THREE FOUNDATIONAL QUESTIONS

My experiences in teaching business ethics for 18 years, mainly in business schools and corporations, have convinced me that one must answer three foundational questions in order to know what successful teaching is and how to achieve it. First, what does it mean to teach business ethics? Answering this question entails establishing an intellectually defensible viewpoint on what it means to teach ethics in general, as well as within the domain of business education. Second, what are the specific challenges confronting students who would learn business ethics? Answering this question requires an understanding of ethical development and of the educational processes that support it. Third, how is student learning of business ethics assessed? Answering this question requires an understanding of the evaluative methods that match the educational challenges as conceived in questions one and two. All education involves teaching processes and assumes concomitant views regarding the criteria for evaluating student learning (Biesta, 2010). It behooves an instructor of ethics in general, and of business ethics specifically, to develop explicit processes for the learning of business ethics and clear evaluative criteria for assessing students' use of the process and the results they produce. Research into behavioral domains consistently demonstrates that people learn more not only when they understand the criteria by which their performance is to be evaluated, but also when they receive feedback on the processes they used in achieving their results, rather than just on the results alone (Klein, 2009).

A LITTLE CHICKEN BEFORE SOME EGG: WHAT METHOD? FOR WHOM?

In this chapter, I relate my lessons learned in teaching business ethics using a range of methods—case-study analysis, simulation, consultation on dilemmas (past or present), case-in-point analysis, and structured role-play. But answering the question, "What method to use?" depends upon your answer to the three foundational questions that I haven't answered yet. So let me serve up a little chicken before we examine the egg from which it hatched by exploring the related question of audience. To whom are you teaching business ethics? I will focus on two groups of students distinguished by their different levels of knowledge and know-how, (1) "novices" and "advanced beginners" and (2) "the competent" and "the proficient" (Dreyfus & Dreyfus, 1986). I focus on these two groups because they comprise the vast majority of business students (novices and advanced beginners) and corporate managers (the competent and the proficient) to which I have taught business ethics. The learning needs and resources of these two groups differs significantly with regard to ethics—a difference that makes all the difference.

Lacking experience in the topics under study, both novices and advanced beginners necessarily rely on explicit rules in order to learn a subject matter. Both types of learners approach the subject matter from a generalized, detached perspective and an analytical interest. Novices rely heavily on context-free rules which allow them to accumulate experience and assess their performance. With the accumulation of experience in a variety of different situations, the novice's strict reliance on context-free rules gives way to the advanced beginner's ability to recognize situational elements, which cannot be objectively defined or recognized in terms of context-free features. Once students have accumulated enough experience to distinguish between situational rules and context-free rules, their learning challenges become more nuanced. But neither novices nor advanced beginners possesses enough experience to adopt the realistic, engaged perspective of a competent or proficient practitioner.

Competent and proficient practitioners also rely on context-free and situation specific rules, but they do so from realistically embodied and practically engaged perspectives which generate decisions that are both analytical, professional and personal. Competent, knowledgeable students approach a situation with specific, embodied goals in mind, having executed decisions in a wide variety of similar situations. Competent learners draw on those analogous situations to make sense of the current situation. Furthermore, rather than viewing the situation as an assemblage of facts, as novices and advanced beginners do, competent students interpret the situation based on their recognition of the specific facts or features that are present or absent. Competent students have learned that situations vary according to the constellation of facts and features present and they have learned from experience to recognize those constellations as well as the types of questions, expectations, decisions, and possible actions such constellations suggest.

Proficient students use their vast experience base to dive into analysis of a specific situation with a deep involvement that enables them to intervene into and shape the situation in anticipation of both key points of leverage that can enable the attainment of higher than expected outcomes and in anticipation of key points of challenge or breakdown that can stymie such attainment. In terms of ethics, proficient students know through experience that specific forms of intervention, probably not seen or not even imagined by novices or advanced beginners, can change one's outcomes decisively, making the difference between merely "justifiable" outcomes and ethically exemplary outcomes. The proficient also know what lines of action are needed to get those ethically exemplary outcomes, even if they don't have all the know-how needed to execute those actions themselves.

The "recognition-primed decision making" (Klein, 1998) of both the competent and the proficient exceeds the analytical decision making of novices and advanced beginners because it combines varying amounts of detached analysis and understanding, involved interpretation of expected or emergent dynamics, and context-specific evaluation and judgment of both "means" and "goals." As competence increases to the point of proficiency, students operate ever-more fluidly within the nonlinear aspects of recognition-primed, naturalistic decision making, so my teaching focuses increasingly on ethical "sensemaking," that is, developing a nuanced understanding of what led up to the events that are happening and anticipating how one's actions are likely to influence future events (Klein, 2009).

My goal in teaching business ethics is to get novices and advanced beginners to the level of competence and, by teaching them how to learn in this domain, to support their development toward proficiency. For learners that are already competent or proficient, I aim to equip them with tools and concepts for the journey toward expertise. I find that case studies, reflections on past failures, and simulations are particularly effective for teaching business ethics to novices and advanced beginners, while consultation on current dilemmas, case-in-point analysis, structured role-plays, and case-study storytelling by experts are particularly effective for teaching competent and proficient students. I will relate the lessons of my experience in teaching ethics to both groups in relation to each of these methods.

I focus on the case-study method for novices and advanced beginners because it is the most commonly used method of business instruction and because case-based reasoning appears best suited to analyzing the ethical problems of management where actions cannot be deduced from or based on theoretically rigorous, explanatory principles (Kolodner, 1993). Case studies can generate inductive, experientially derived generalizations that vary in their scope and "rigor" according to the nature of the situations from which they arise or to which they apply. Case studies are excellent vehicles for teaching novices the specific steps in the application of context-free rules for any business discipline. Case studies also provide the instructor with a vehicle for helping students to develop into advanced beginners by teaching them situation-specific rules and the array of structures, pitfalls, and heuristics involved in a practical analysis of specific situations. Furthermore, defining words, concepts and rules using specific case examples—the process of "ostensive definition"—creates a common ground among students that aids learning. Students and teachers unavoidably freight the words and concepts of ethics with the content and emotional valence of their individual life experiences. Case studies provide a common point of reference against which differences in definition, meaning and valence can be explored and appreciated.

In contrast to case studies, simulations confront students with specific, uninterpreted situations that require them to assemble the facts and features of their "live" situation and to generate and enact specific, embodied courses of action. In essence, simulations "simulate" the conditions that require competence and proficiency. These conditions reveal to students what they still don't know but were not aware that they lacked until they were confronted with the limits of their own success or failure. Of course students learn more when they fail, so I like to give them very difficult simulations to ensure that their experience in the simulation will provide a plethora of "teachable moments."

The alert reader will note that I have already begun to tip my hand regarding my answers to the three foundational questions of business ethics education. It could not be otherwise (Biesta, 2010). My own theoretical commitments necessarily inform my view of what it means to teach business ethics. I adopt a developmental and practical-reason perspective to the teaching of business ethics (Kegan, 1982, 1994; Klein, 1998; MacIntyre, 1984; Rest, 1999; Solomon, 1992; Varela, 1999).

The terms "teaching" and "learning" cover a vast range. We can teach, and students can learn, skills, sensitization, mental models, patterns, typicality, habituation, categories, concepts, object recognition, metacognition (learning about and assessing one's self and one's own performance), instances (episodic learning), declarative knowledge (facts), attention management, spatial mapping, generalization, discrimination, tool learning, decentering (taking the perspective of someone else), emotional control, statistical methods, analytical methods, and sequencing of tasks (Klein, 2009). Each type of learning potentially involves different teaching processes and different evaluative criteria. Only a small subset are applicable to business ethics and amenable to case-study analysis, simulation, case-in-point analysis, dilemma consultation, and structured role-play. I emphasize the development of the practical concepts and skills for learning to conduct business ethically in order to highlight what, in my

experience, has been effective and ineffective in teaching my two principal student groups, novices and advanced-beginners and the competent
and the proficient.

In the next sections, I will unpack the lessons of my experience in
teaching business ethics and how I have come to answer the three foundational questions of teaching business ethics. I will give examples throughout that illustrate these lessons. I will conclude with some remarks about
the most effective means of teaching business ethics.

WHAT DOES IT MEAN TO TEACH BUSINESS ETHICS? ADDRESSING THE FOUR COMPONENTS OF ETHICAL BEHAVIOR AND MICROECONOMIC THEORY'S CHALLENGE TO ETHICAL SENSITIVITY

The answer to the first foundational question—What does it mean to
teach business ethics?—presupposes a view regarding the determinants of
moral behavior. The literature treating moral behavior covers a vast range
of disciplines and topics. Principally, the disciplines of philosophy, sociol-
ogy, organizational theory, social psychology, developmental psychology,
social learning, behavioral psychology, psychoanalytic psychology, and
neuropsychology are utilized to examine topics ranging from the perception and judgment of ethical issues to the structuring, valuation and prioritization of goals and means, emotional control, prosocial and antisocial
behavior, justification, rationalization and self-deception, role-modeling,
role-taking, social influence, situation or "domain" influence, identity or
"self-structure," skills, and competence. Following James Rest (1994), I
organize this vast array into four component processes:

1. moral sensitivity—interpreting the situation for the ethical issues
    at stake;
2. moral judgment—judging which action is morally right/justified;
3. moral motivation—prioritizing the moral value relative to other
    values; and
4. moral implementation—having courage, persistence, and skills to
    overcome obstacles in enacting moral judgments.

While these four components are decidedly psychological in their con-
struction, the processes they encompass can include more than just psychological determinants. The psychological bias, however, emphasizes
aspects of moral behavior amenable to educational intervention across
various disciplines and professions.

All professional education entails sensitizing students to the issues at stake in situations they will face, forming judgments about which actions are right or more adequate than alternatives, prioritizing among competing goals and demands, and acquiring the skills to act effectively and professionally. Thus, the four-component model seems particularly well-suited to understanding the inherently ethical dimensions of education in general and of professional education in particular. Business education proves no exception to the four-component model, though it does present an instructor with some unique issues. I will explicate the content of each of the four components by articulating my view of what each component entails for business education and its unique issues.

Teaching ethical sensitivity involves conveying concepts, categories and analytical methods that enable students to perceive and interpret social situations regarding the issues involved, the parties involved, their interests, needs and goals, the possible actions that are feasible in addressing the situation, and the likely consequences and impacts of the possible actions upon the parties and issues. Business case studies typically contain a host of actors and agents, numerous issues, interests, needs and goals, and a variety of possible actions available to specific actors. Business case instruction aims to assist novice and advanced-beginner students in perceiving, interpreting, and analyzing the business dimensions of the situation presented in order to develop and evaluate feasible actions.

While business faculty are trained in and comfortable with the perception, interpretation, and analysis of a case's business dimensions—marketing, accounting, finance, et cetera—they are rarely trained in or comfortable with doing the same for the case's ethical dimensions. Undoubtedly many reasons account for this lack of training in or comfort with ethical dimensions, not least of which is the widely-held assumption that the social sciences and the methods which inform the business disciplines are value-free or value-neutral. This assumption is especially operative among finance, accounting, and economics faculty.

For example, Jeffrey Everett (2007) tested the ethical critiques of U.S. business education advanced by Mitroff (2004), Ghoshal (2005), and Swanson (2005), who charged business schools with advancing a distorted view of human nature, outdated notions of ethics, and narrow definitions of management. Everett studied business academics who earned their PhDs in the departments housing the editors of the top-tier journals in accounting and finance. Using Pierre Bourdieu's insights into the subjective cognitive structures that frame perception, cognition, and valuation, and that produce specific social worlds and the symbolic social capital agents employ in them, Everett conducted qualitative interviews with these symbolic-capital rich members of the field in order to understand the meanings that these specific social agents produce in their actions as they engage their social world and help produce it. Everett found a pro-found and disturbing disconnect between the values that these agents personally espouse and the professional actions that they take. While pro-fessors of finance and accounting personally believed ethics to be of great importance, they were appalled and even horrified at the idea of teaching ethics in their finance and accounting courses. Everett argued that this disconnect between personal values and professional action is not due, as many would argue, to a lack of time, materials, encouragement, training, reward structures, a failure of will, or even a breakdown of individual moral process. Rather, the disconnect reflects these individuals' anticipa-tion of the demands of the symbolic market operating within the field of finance and accounting and the prices which that market indirectly sets for certain symbolic goods, in this case, research goods, or the goods of discovery as defined by the deeply rooted episteme, or mental model, of neoclassical economics. Everett concludes that neoclassical economics "systematically divests itself of ethical concern, resulting in an incipient conflict that separates the personal and the occupational identities, or *habitus,* of the field's members" (Everett, 2007). The formidable forces of the field discourage and even penalize acts of individual resistance and render them futile, along with the strategies employed by traditional approaches to ethics, such as virtue ethics, situational ethics, and deonto-logical ethics.

The assumption of value-free methods and analysis severely constricts ethical sensitivity. If one assumes, as most business faculty do, that stu-dents-as-managers are agents acting on behalf of principals (sharehold-ers) with a fiduciary duty to maximize the economic value of the shareholder's equity within competitive markets for products, labor, and capital, then one will perceive, interpret and analyze the situation in terms of the marginal utility to the firm of its various possible actions. The assumption that other actors—consumers, competitors, owners of land, capital and labor (employees)—are also calculating the marginal utility of their own transactions, all within the agreed-upon framework of laws and regulations, limits the interpretation and analysis of interests, needs, goals, possible actions and impacts to one's own (or the firms's) marginal utility. By definition, this view rules out the interpretation and analysis of the interests, needs, goals, and possible actions of other actors, except and insofar as it impinges on the firm or the individual's marginal utility. The price system itself coordinates the use and distribution of resources (Mahoney, 2005).

Note that the sensitivities of this analysis are not nonethical, but ethical in a severely limited way. These are the ethical sensitivities implicit in microeconomic theory (Hosmer, 1987), the dominant mental model of business analysis, most famously stated by Milton Friedman in his essay,

"The Social Responsibility of Business is to Maximize Profits" (Friedman, 2007) and subsequently buttressed by numerous restatements, refinements and elaborations (Mahoney, 2005). The microeconomic interpretative schema analyzes a business case by assuming a complex system of concepts and institutional and social arrangements that "rule in" and "rule out" specific needs, interests, goals and actions. The needs and interests of the self (or household) and firm are ruled in, as are competitive goals and economic value maximizing and law-abiding actions. Ruled out are "other-oriented" needs and interests (social, political, religious, environmental/nonhuman-species, and altruistic), cooperative goals, and actions that balance economic value with other values or which exceed existing laws and regulations. This narrow interpretation gives rise to the simple maxim which every business student can recite, namely, "Act to maximize firm profits within the constraints imposed by law and regulation," or, more simply, "Maximize shareholder wealth." Given this mental model of how business managers ought to operate, is it any wonder that so many firms choose to behave as badly as the law allows?

When my novice and advanced-beginner business students invoke the ethics of microeconomics to justify their decisions, I ask them, "Would you want to be a part of a family in which you did no more for each other or to each other than what the law requires?" The answer, not surprisingly, is no. "How about neighbors who do no more to you or for you than what the law requires?" Again, the answer is "No." "Okay," I say, "then what about a neighborhood where people do to you and for you no more than the law requires them?" Same answer. I then ask, "Would you want to be part of an organization that treated you, your fellow employees, and customers only in terms of the bare minimum that the law requires?" I remind them that the law does not require that we respect each other or show each other courtesy and that the exercise of free speech rights on television every night provides ample evidence of discourteous and disrespectful, commercial behavior. Again, the answer is always, "No." They wouldn't even want to be part of a classroom that merely met the minimum standards established by law. I ask these questions to prompt them into exercising other frames of ethical analysis and to leverage the perspectives that additional roles generate in helping us evaluate the adequacy of an ethical judgment. If I cannot teach my students to expand the range of their ethical sensitivity, then I will have little success in teaching them business ethics.

The foundational disciplines to business case analysis—the microeconomic theory of the firm, transaction cost theory, agency theory, and resource-based theory—purchase their quantitative rigor at the expense of a severely limited definition of a manager's role, responsibility, and perspective. They assert that the manager has one role, namely, as agent acting on behalf of a principal. The manager has one responsibility, to maximize one variable (profit). The manager has one legitimate perspective, namely, firm- or self-interest.

These limitations constrict business case analysis to the point of ethical inadequacy and give rise to very specific educational challenges for teaching business students ethics, because studies indicate that moral sensitivity (component one) operates independently of moral judgment (component two) (Bebeau, 2002). The limitations that microeconomic theory imposes on the consideration of interested parties, their needs, duties and obligations, and the possible courses of action prevents students and managers from making ethical judgments about a wide range of ethical issues present in business cases and situations. Failing to "see" ethical issues in a situation, students and managers who adopt the canonical microeconomic ethical sensitivities never activate their capacities for ethical judgment. This might explain the "What were they thinking?" reaction, in hindsight, to many of the corporate ethics failures and scandals. The actors themselves were trained to exclude the very aspects of the situation that gave rise to the ethical problems they failed to address. It's not that students and managers can't reason ethically and form ethical judgments. They can, but they are taught in business school to turn off or shut down their systems for ethical perception and appraisal when dealing with commercial issues.

The narrowing of ethical attention cannot be accomplished without suppressing a key component of ethical sensitivity, namely, our affective, emotional processes. Ethical sensitivity entails emotional processing, not just cognitive processing. The suppression or limiting of emotional reactions and data, while perhaps necessary for certain analytical operations, constricts the range of parties, needs, interests, issues, and impacts that students and managers will consider. I find that novice students struggle to know what to do, analytically speaking, with their raw emotional reaction to specific issues. Advanced beginners have usually learned from faculty and peers to suppress those emotions and I have to work hard to unearth their emotions so that they can be used to stimulate the recognition of ethical issues. I believe strongly that the treatment of students' emotional reactions to cases should not be dismissed or ignored, but acknowledged and worked with as one would with any other data. Ignoring or suppressing students' emotional responses runs the risk of desensitizing them to the very conflicts that are a source of ethical and professional development (Kegan, 1994).

MBA education, unfortunately, appears to have its own version of the famous "splitting" of identity performed unconsciously by first-year medical students when they begin dissecting cadavers (Lifton, 1986). Medical students split their selves into two parts, the professional self that performs otherwise proscribed behaviors like cutting open bodies and the personal self that behaves according to society's norms and conventions. Having taught clinical ethics to third-year medical students (novices and advanced beginners), I came to recognize that managing this split identity was a decisive factor in advancing students' ethical sensitivity and, therefore, their clinical judgment, to the level of competence or proficiency. The students who were explicitly working toward the integration of their professional and personal identities exhibited a great deal more sensitivity to the ethical issues present in clinical cases. Furthermore, because they were sensitive to a greater range of ethical issues, the more personally-and-professionally integrated students had a head start on others in terms of building skills for dealing with those issues. Students who were more skilled in the types of behaviors needed to address the range of ethical issues that arose in clinical cases also exhibited more sensitivity to the presence of the ethical issues, in contrast to their less-skilled peers who suppressed the issues, sometimes denying that they existed at all or arguing that the ethical issues had no legitimate place in forming their clinical judgments.

The key factor that determines whether students will grow, stagnate or even regress in their ethical sensitivity is, in my experience, the ethical sensitivity modeled by the highest formal authority present, that is, the instructor. I frame the instructor's role as "highest formal authority" for an explicit reason, namely, to highlight the ethical-skewing influence that authority dynamics exercise over ethical sensitivity. The learned suppression of ethical sensitivity imposed by the analytical framework assumed in standard business case analysis gains additional strength from the "authority bias." To teach my novice and advanced beginner students about this bias, I use simulations.

To teach the impacts of authority bias, I use "OmegaSim," an online simulation that is presented to the students as an exercise in business decision analysis, which it is, but which is also an exercise in ethical decision-making and the role that authority dynamics play in skewing or suppressing the ethical dimensions of the situation presented in the simulation. In the simulation, students assume the role of a newly hired vice president of marketing for a holding company with four major brands. They are told that they have to allocate and briefly justify their distribution of their $10 million marketing budget among the four brands using the quantitative and qualitative information presented to them—requested budget, revenue, margin, past year's performance, and so on. Unbeknownst to the students, they have been assigned to one of two groups, the "CEO" (chief executive officer) group or the "personal assistant" group. During the simulation, each student receives a knock on his or her door on the computer screen and opens it to find either the CEO or the personal assistant staring back at them. The students then receive from either the CEO or the personal assistant additional, qualitative information about the four brands and the situations facing them. The information presented by the CEO and the personal assistant is exactly the same, but the ethical effect of the information differs dramatically depending on the status of the information giver, as evidenced by the data regarding the investments and rationales provided by the two groups. The students receiving the qualitative information from the CEO largely suppress, omit, or rationalize away the ethical issues presented by one brand's product—a space heater that is awaiting judgment regarding a possible recall by the Consumer Products Safety Commission for documented incidents of having caught fire and caused harm. Receiving the information from the CEO that "this is a classic case of move that inventory," students overwhelmingly decide to market the product heavily and reap the profits from its high margins before the Consumer Product Safety Committee decides the case and potentially pulls the product from the market. The other half of the class, receiving exactly the same information from their personal assistant, largely use their budget to pull the existing product from the market, to warn consumers about the potential problem, to educate consumers about safe usage, and to implement processes designed to make sure that such flawed products are not produced or marketed in the future.

Confronted with the vastly different investments and rationales of the two groups, but without any explanation regarding the independent variable, I ask the students, "What could account for this vast ethical difference?" Like the experts consulted prior to Milgram's famous obedience to authority experiments, no one even suspects that merely invoking the role of an authority could account for the differences (Zimbardo, 2007). When I reveal the independent variable to the students, they exhibit a range of emotions, from shock and anger to shame, embarrassment, and even denial. I use their emotional responses to explore the role of emotions in constricting or expanding our ethical sensitivity and judgment, which usually leads to a long discussion in which I share my perspective on the "splitting" imposed by business education.

To teach ethical sensitivity toward the human and nonhuman dimensions of environmental issues, I use two simulations, *FishBanks Ltd.* to introduce environmental sustainability and *Transformation: The Green Business Laboratory* to teach corporate strategy for sustainability. *FishBanks* places students in teams to operate fishing companies in an ocean containing a coastal and deep sea fishery. Students immediately launch into commercial operations and decisions, the results of which confront them with the tragedy of the commons (Hardin, 1968; Ostrom, 1990; Senge, 1990, 2008). Confronted by the constraints imposed by a common pool resource, the students' implicit, microeconomic ethic leads them to economic bankruptcy and environmental collapse, just as it does in the real-life examples that are examined in the debrief of the simulation. The deep personal, emotional investment that the students make in running their simulated companies makes the ethical lessons of the tragedy of the commons vivid, painful, and enduring. I don't believe we can begin to improve the mental models that guide our ethical thinking without shaking them loose through such emotionally powerful experiences.

To teach more advanced concepts and skills regarding ethics, environment, and corporate social responsibility, I use *Transformation: The Green Business Laboratory*, which places students in teams where they adopt a specific vice-president role (finance, marketing, human resources, manufacturing, etc.) in a firm producing and marketing "Spheremovers," an automobile-like widget comprised of Knex toy parts (rods, wheels, connectors) that transports ping-pong balls. Students use a web-based, enterprise resource planning-like set of support tools to make decisions about the design, sourcing, manufacturing, marketing, and selling of their Spheremover. Students have information regarding the environmental (pollution, energy consumption) and economic (materials costs, labor costs, etc.) performance of each component across its full life cycle (extraction, transportation, manufacture, customer use, and disposal or recycle or remanufacture), as well as information about customers, markets, employees and employee issues, and a variety of stakeholders (government, nongovernmental, media, investors, local communities, habitats, etc.)

The instructor plays the role of various stakeholders, interacting with the students around specific issues to simulate awareness of the needs and interests represented by each group. Students are evaluated using four sets of explicit criteria regarding (1) product performance (capacity, distance, customer appeal), (2) Stuart Hart's "sustainability portfolio" model of environmentally sustainable value creation, (3) the execution of the students' own explicitly stated strategy, and (4) a model of strategic balance based on the competing values model of behavioral complexity required for leadership (Hart & Milstein, 2003). Students earn market share according to the amount of overall value (economic, social, and environmental) they create, captured in their total score. Selling price is divided by overall value to generate a ratio and firms are ranked accordingly and rewarded with varying percentages of market share. Market share determines sales numbers, which are used to generate a full income statement for each firm as well as pollution and energy consumption reports across the full life-cycle of all components, from extraction and transportation to customer use and disposal, remanufacture, or recycling.

I have used FishBanks successfully with both novices/advanced beginners and competent/proficient. I find Transformation is most successful with advanced beginners, competent and proficient students. Transformation has been used extensively by corporations such as S.C. Johnson, General Electric, and others to train managers in sustainability strategy. Both simulations teach much more than ethical sensitivity, but I introduce them under this topic to underscore the necessity of getting beyond people's heads and into their hearts (emotions, values), skills and action-scripts in order to expand their ethical sensitivity. We do not easily unlearn or revise our mental models because they determine what data will be counted as relevant data and they determine how to interpret the data that we selected. So, simply presenting new data will not suffice because it will either be denied or interpreted in accordance with the receiver's prevailing mental model.

To unlearn one's mental model and thereby expand one's ethical sensitivity, one must have an emotionally powerful experience of the anomalies and contradictions that arise from one's current mental model. In this regard, I find case-study analysis to be a poor vehicle for teaching the "unlearning" of mental models. Overreliance on case-studies stunts or even numbs our students' growth in ethical sensitivity. Simulations prepare learners to make use of the data of their own powerful experiences to revise their mental models, thereby helping them expand their ethical sensitivity.

MAKING MORAL JUDGMENTS: ETHICAL JUSTIFICATION AND IT'S COMPONENT PARTS

Once a student has interpreted the situation for the ethical issues at stake (component one), he or she must also form judgments about the moral worth of the possible actions designed to address the ethical issues (component two). Moral judgment is perhaps the best studied and most accurately assessed component of moral behavior. For teaching purposes, I use James Rest's "neo-Kohlbergian" understanding of moral judgment, with its categorization of three gross stages in the individual's cognition of moral judgment—preconventional, conventional, and postconventional (Rest, 1999). Conventional moral judgment, the dominant stage found in adults, justifies moral actions in terms of the degree to which they maintain the established social order, that is, on the basis of the conventions, or what "is." Postconventional moral judgment justifies moral actions according to the degree to which those judgments fulfill universal ideals that stand in judgment over any and all established social orders, that is, on the basis of what "ought" to be.

Based on research findings and philosophical critiques related to Kohlberg's six-stage, "staircase" model of moral development in the mental operations related to determining what is just, Rest revised Kohlberg's model in four significant ways. First, he replaced Kohlberg's univocal focus on justice with a focus on the organization of cooperation. Kohlberg was solely concerned with what is fair and just. Rest, like many modern philosophers and social theorists, finds this too narrow and overly political. Rather than asking only "What's fair?" Rest asks, "How do we organize our relations and actions in a cooperative fashion?"

Second, Rest revised Kohlberg's "mental operations" model of moral epistemology with a "schema" model of moral conceptualization. Rest noted the consistency between the findings of psychological research into the operation of "schemas" and the regularities observed in Kohlberg's constructivist account of moral epistemology. Schemas structure the content of human experience by determining the selection, encoding, configuring, and retrieval of information as well as the speed by which individuals process information, solve problems, and evaluate solutions (Taylor & Crocker, 1981). Rest proposed that Kohlberg's stages might actually be "schemas," which can be investigated by studying the complexity and normative adequacy of the concepts that people produce. Whereas Kohlberg was interested only in the structure, not in the content, of people's moral thinking, Rest studied both. I follow Rest's lead in focusing on the complexity and adequacy of the concepts that people produce in thinking about and wrestling with the problems of coordinating human action.

Third, Rest rejected Kohlberg's notion that people move along the developmental progression one stage at a time. Rest found evidence that people are not in one stage at a time but in several and that development is not marked by universal shifts in moral meaning making but in the frequency with which people use more complex concepts. Rest replaced Kohlberg's "hard stage," staircase model with a "soft stage," shifting distribution model of moral schemas whereby more complex, higher stage schemas increase in use while less complex, lower stage schemas diminish.

Fourth, and perhaps most importantly for the purposes of this chapter, Rest replaced Kohlberg's Kantian, deontological conception of postconventional moral thinking with a more pragmatic, philosophically agnostic conception of postconventional morality. Whereas Kohlberg identified postconventional morality with universal rights and justice, Rest identifies it with any sharable ideal for organizing cooperation that is "open to debate and tests of logical consistency, experience of the community, and coherence with accepted practice" (Rest, 1999). Kohlberg limited postconventional judgments to deontological arguments, which necessarily excludes all utilitarianism and probably all pragmatism as well. Rest opens postconventional moral judgment to the latter. Thus, Kohlberg admitted only the likes of Kant, Rawls, and other deontologists, while Rest leaves room for the likes of Mill, Hegel, Dewey, Nozick, Walzer, and Rorty. They, too, view conventions as alterable instruments serving moral purposes that can be critiqued and improved on the basis of universal ideals that are open to rational critique, logical analysis, and empirical evidence.

I am principally concerned with raising the level of my students' moral judgment to the postconventional level in the belief that postconventional justifications *of any kind* will be more adequate, morally speaking, to the complexity of the issues those justifications address. Conventional ethical judgments, by their very nature, will not provide the kind of leverage and critique required to resolve moral problems and dilemmas. Developing fundamental solutions to moral problems and dilemmas requires a level of thinking that is free of the contradictions and limitations that generated the moral problems and dilemmas in the first place.

In my concern to raise the level of my students' moral judgments, I assume that I am in agreement with the majority of my colleagues who see fit to teach ethics in relation to business. I also take it that this aspect of teaching business ethics is fairly well understood. Less well understood, however, are the pedagogical interventions that help to raise students' level of moral judgment. I have experienced special challenges in trying to raise the moral judgment of novices and advanced beginners. While all my students struggle with the tension between the specific ethic embedded in their social and legal conventions and the ethical claims of postconventional moral reasoning, novices and advanced beginners struggle the most. They exhibit greater frustration and difficulty in learning to deliver what is expected of them in their specific roles and concomitant social and organizational conventions while simultaneously exercising their own moral judgment about the ethical justification of those conventions and expectations. Questioning the moral validity of the conventions from a postconventional perspective appears to threaten their sense of competency in, or loyalty to, the conventions. Competent and proficient students, by contrast, exhibit greater willingness to question the reigning conventions and are less threatened by calling status quo conventions into ethical question.

After years of trying various methods, I finally settled upon an approach developed by Muriel Bebeau and others which assesses students in terms of the adequacy their moral judgment, rather than the "rightness" or "wrongness" of it (Bebeau, 2002). Like Bebeau, I assess the adequacy of their ability to identify four subelements of moral judgment:

1.   the interested parties and their legitimate needs and interests;

2. the possible courses of action open to the decision maker/protago-
    nist and the likely consequences of those actions;

3. the duties and obligations of the protagonist; and

4. the ethical issues that arise in light of elements 1-3.

The more interested parties, possible courses of action, duties and obligations, and ethical issues that a student is able to identify, the more adequate his or her judgment will be to the complexity of the situation. The
fewer of each that the student is able to articulate, the less adequate his or
her judgment. Evaluating students based on their ability to articulate the
elements, rather than on their ability to justify their decision, appears to
decrease students' defensiveness and their sense of arbitrariness regarding ethical justification.

I find it effective to require students to justify ethically their recommended course of action, but I do not grade that aspect of their answer.
Rather, I comment on the strengths and weaknesses of their justification
in light of their analysis of the case's interested parties, possible action,
duties and obligations, and ethical issues. Different cases lend themselves
to different conceptualizations and applications of ethical justification
and I make extensive interpretive comments that direct students to ethical
theories that illuminate their particular line of justification. This enables
students to see how ethical theory applies to *their* moral intuitions and
arguments. I find that they are far more likely to advance their understanding of ethical theory if they appreciate how specific theories illuminate their own line of argument.

Like other "applied" ethicists, I present the major types of ethical justification—deontology, utilitarianism, virtue theory, et cetera—as "resolution principles" for deciding "right versus right" issues (Kidder, 1995). It
must be admitted, though, that presenting theories of justification as resolution principles is a gross simplification intended to aid novices and
advanced beginners in achieving proficiency in ethical analysis and justification. Each of the schools of ethics that produce specific lines of justification can be interpreted as offering a complete answer to my three
foundational questions. But I find that such a complex, nuanced way of
understanding ethical theories of justification, while it appeals to academically trained experts, has a stultifying effect on novices and advanced
beginners. They appear overwhelmed by, and unable to defend their
moral intuitions against, such formidable theories. So I let my students,
and especially my novices and advanced beginners, articulate their own
version of the interested parties, possible actions, duties and obligations,
and framing of the ethical issues. I am more concerned to help my students advance their own lines of ethical reasoning and make it more adequate to the complex challenges they face than having them recreate what

Kant would argue about the issue. As they form their own justifications I suggest to them complementary lines of reasoning. If Kant does not help them to advance the adequacy of their own judgment, then too bad for Kant. Perhaps John Dewey or Michael Walzer can.

JUSTIFICATION IS OVERRATED: THREE CHEERS FOR ETHICAL MOTIVATION AND IMPLEMENTATION SKILLS

In terms of the four components of ethical behavior, I believe that ethical justification is overrated anyway. If my students develop the ability to make a postconventional argument of any sort, I consider my teaching a success. This is not to say that justification is unimportant, but the vast majority of people's ethical experience takes place under conditions that do not lend themselves to tidy rational justifications. Most of our ethical experience occurs in areas that are quite familiar to us and in which we have attained some degree of competence and perhaps even proficiency, but which have now been rendered unfamiliar to us because of the ethical challenge(s) we face. Significant ethical challenges can quickly render us disoriented in our familiar places. Add to this sense of disorientation the ill-structured characteristics of real-life challenges—time pressures, high stakes, inadequate and/or missing and/or ambiguous or even erroneous information, ill-defined goals, poorly defined procedures, dynamic conditions, and the need to coordinate our decisions with others—and you have conditions that defy linear, rational analysis and justification.

In the face of such real-life challenges, the linear, four-stage model that I teach to novices and advanced beginners is wrong. Of course, all models are wrong, but some are useful. The linear four-stage model is useful because it isolates context-free aspects of moral action, enabling novices and advanced beginners to gain conceptual purchase. It is wrong because it fails to capture the nonlinear way that people respond to ill-structured situations.

The linear assumption that we form moral judgments based on an assessment of the situation, followed by prioritization of the moral and nonmoral issues, followed by implementation assumes too much and distorts our actual mental operations. First, when confronting ethical issues, the goals available for use in interpreting a given situation are usually unclear and/or competing. Second, the incompleteness of information or the conflict between different information and sources of information renders any judgment problematic. Third, dynamic conditions imply that all information and interpretations regarding the situation are necessarily provisional. Fourth, moral motivation does not enter as a third stage consideration but factors into our account of the obstacles, solvability, and anticipated constraints of the situation as we mentally simulate our possible solutions to the situation. Finally, the linear model assumes that implementation skills are mere add-on's to the real meat of ethics, namely justification. Research indicates, however, that our implementation skills determine how we frame and interpret the situations we confront (Klein, 2009; Norros & Klemola, 2005; Varela, 1999). The more skilled we are in intervening in circumstances, the more sophisticated our assessment of the situation becomes. We "see" dimensions and leverage points that less skilled actors do not see or quickly reject because they cannot mentally simulate themselves taking successful action amidst such complexity. More skilled actors will consider a more adequate range of ethically justifiable actions because they possess enough know-how to simulate those actions mentally. What we can do—our skill level—constrains what we can "see" or "mentally simulate," that is, the decision we are willing to justify ethically and then execute.

Furthermore, psychological research on incompetent and less-skilled performers demonstrates that they fail to recognize their own incompetence because they lack "metacognitive" skills for accurately assessing their performance (Hodges, Regehr, & Martin, 2001; Kruger & Dunning, 1999; Schrader, 2003). Paradoxically, the only way to raise the accuracy of their self-awareness regarding their performance is to raise their skill level, that is, to teach them the very skills for implementing in a given domain (Kruger & Dunning, 1999). So, too, with teaching ethics. Novices and advanced beginners don't know what they don't know. They only become aware of what they don't know when someone teaches them the skills for skilled performance in an area, such as the skills of using their emotional reaction as clues to the nature of the situation they are confronting or skills for identifying the needs and interests of different actors. To teach these skills I use the above mentioned simulations, structured role-plays, and consultations on current and past dilemmas, plus "case-in-point" self-study of what is currently happening in the classroom.

Far too often, the literature of ethics ignores the interdependent elements of moral motivation and implementation skills by assuming that neither element plays a role in the formation of ethical judgment and by assuming that once an ethical judgment has been formulated, its implementation is simply a matter of "will." I will not rehearse the philosophical and psychological critiques of the antique metaphor of "will," which rests on an outdated and unsubstantiated faculty psychology (Johnson, 1993). I will point out, however, that in assuming that the real work of ethics lies in conceptualizing ethical justifications and in assigning concern with implementation to the black box concept of "will," traditional moral philosophy leaves off precisely at the point where engagement with the concrete messiness of moral life begins. I will also note that if we take an interdependent view of the four elements, then it becomes clear that the vast majority of our moral experience passes as "skillful coping" without ever rising to the level of articulated justification (Dreyfus & Dreyfus, 1986). The ethical dilemmas that garner the lion's share of attention in the field of ethics, especially applied ethics, turn out to account for a small portion of our ethical experience. The majority of our ethical experience passes "unreflectively" within our value-laden institutions and organizations and our attendant roles and responsibilities because we do not experience ethical difficulty in fulfilling our roles or discharging our duties.

The skillful coping that my students already possess provides the foundation on which I seek to build greater skills. Presenting them with their own dilemmas or with challenging simulations brings them up against the limits of their skills and skillful coping. This is where their real learning will take place. By advancing their skills within their own zones of proximal development, I hope that they will begin to understand what they don't know and to appreciate what they currently can't do or can't do adequately.

I emphasize working with students' current dilemmas or past failures because those situations bring the students up against the limits of their skillful coping and their current way of holding their roles, responsibilities and identities. I am interested in the domain specific "microidentities" that my students have formed and are shaping, because I believe that these role-specific identities, with their specific duties, obligations, and organizational-institutional frameworks, form the real basis from which moral motivation proceeds (Varela, 1999). Contra-Kant, we don't derive our specific duties and obligations from our transcendentally derived identity as rational agents, but from our specific, socially embedded roles and their concomitant responsibilities, expectations, duties, and obligations (MacIntyre, 1984; Varela, 1999).

The debate over whether or not to make management a true profession highlights the importance of identity in motivating moral action (Khurana & Nohria, 2008). The "MBA Oath" constructs a professional identity toward which an MBA degree holder can aspire, and with that aspirational identity, certain behaviors will be motivated (Anderson & Escher, 2010). Socially constructing a professional identity for certified business professionals creates the organizational and institutional frameworks, rules, and expectations that provide the scaffold upon which MBA students and others can construct their micro-identities as business professionals.

If there is a Kantian moment to my teaching of ethics, it enters at precisely this point. That is, I believe we have a moral duty to maintain, protect, and extend the conditions for moral action, including the social, organizational and institutional frameworks that make ethically "good work" possible. To will for ourselves ethically good work but then to act in ways that do not maintain, protect and extend the conditions that make such ethically good work possible is self-contradictory (Gardner, 2007). If I can impress upon my students their "Kantian" duty toward the conditions that make ethical identity and morally good work possible, then I feel I've really done my job.

Stated explicitly, my strategy with regard to the third component of teaching business ethics is to use moral motivation as a lever with which to move the institutionalized mental models of microeconomic theory and conventional business practice. By grounding moral motivation in an unshakeable foundation of ethically-defined personal and professional identity, the student's identity provides a fulcrum upon which to foist the arguments of postconventional ethics. The strange, sometimes "alien" force that postconventional ethics exercises on all conventional arrangements creates transforming leverage. I assume that postconventional ethics critiques ALL concrete ethical arrangements, even the most adequate. If there's a gap between what ethics enjoins upon us and our current state of affairs, then I want my students to grapple with the ways that our laws, their organizations, and their business practices fall short of what ought to be. The only way they will sustain that, in my experience, is to ground their sense of ethical duty in their sense of identity, the values and aspirations and social expectations they choose to live on behalf of.

To assist my students in articulating their sense of moral identity, I administer to them the *Values Management Inventory*, developed by Brian Hall and Benjamin Tonna over a 30-year, cross-cultural research program (Hall, 1994). The inventory identifies the ideals and priorities that a person chooses repeatedly and consistently and which give meaning and purpose to his or her life. The values range across three sets of priorities, beginning with the "foundational" priorities like "food, warmth, and shelter" or "physical affection" that endure throughout the life-span, to the priorities that are the current "focus" of most people's energy and attention, like "responsibility" and "management," to the long-term ideals toward which we aspire, like "global justice" and "global sustainability."

Hall and Tonna discovered that even the most "values conscious" persons could articulate no more than about thirty percent of their actual values. The Inventory teases these priorities out of students and states them explicitly so that they may be fully embraced and used in career and development planning. I use the subset of long-term ideals and aspirations, which Hall and Tonna termed "vision" values, as the basis for an interpretive and appreciative exercise that articulates one's sense of moral identity. Using these long-term ideals, each student constructs the moral identity to which he or she aspires. Being true to this identity and acting in ways that express and apply it is, I think, the strongest and most sustainable basis for moral growth and development. When one has a strong sense of who one is and what one's values are, a powerful "cannot not" develops. That is, students find they "cannot not" do something without violating their sense of who they are and want to become. Like the authors of the research related in *Common Fire: Lives of Commitment in a Complex World* (Daloz, 1996), I find that students with an unshakeable sense of moral identity "cannot not" persevere against great challenges in pursuit of their high ethical ideals.

Of course, no one knows what his or her real moral identity is until it is tested. Moral identity is most tested when moral motivation is most tested, that is, under conditions requiring moral courage. I don't really think I can teach students moral courage, but I can create conditions in the classroom that nurture and call forth the moral courage they already possess. In the classroom, this mostly takes the form of courageous speech—speaking one's deepest values, one's truth and one's honest experience to others, especially to those who don't want to hear it, and especially to those in power.

While the classroom domain is necessarily limited in opportunities for teaching moral courage, I believe that learning to exercise moral courage in the classroom teaches lessons that can be transferred to other domains. For example, in work contexts involving interdependent tasks, ethical vulnerability is created on a daily basis by the breakdown in common ground understanding that occurs during transitions, during handoffs between shifts or team members, and by the conflicting interpretations of situations generated by incompatible frameworks and functions (Klein, 2009; Smith & Berg, 1987). Given the human tendency to suppress negative communications, as testified to by the well-known "MUM effect" (Tesser, Rosen, & Batchelor, 1972), the very stuff of ethics tends not to be spoken at the precise moments when it is needed the most. Insufficient moral courage to speak degrades our ability to build the common ground understandings that are vital to interdependent action (Klein, 2009). Teaching students the skills of courageous speaking and providing them opportunities to exercise courageous speech in the classroom prepares them for the challenges of ethical action outside the classroom (Gentile, 2010).

CONCLUSION: WE TEACH BUSINESS ETHICS BEST BY MODELING IT

I believe that teaching business ethics is foundational to business education. We're always teaching some kind of ethics, even when we think we're not. The ethics implicit in our business disciplines, however, are grossly inadequate. They constrict the parties considered to the bare minimum required by law. They ignore whole ranges of human and nonhuman interest and need. They curtail duties and obligations, and they choke off the sources of ethical learning and growth in individuals, organizations, and societies.

Invoking the duties and obligations entailed by transcendental reason against these inadequacies is futile. The traditional practices of business and business education, with their embedded mental models and embodied duties, swamp the edicts of disembodied reason. Too bad for Kant.

To address the ethical inadequacies of traditional business education and practice we need ethical role modeling by business professors and business managers within their own disciplines and functions, as they struggle with the full range of parties, needs, interests, duties and obligations entailed by business operations. Ethical learning in business, like ethical learning elsewhere, advances slowly and painfully. It cannot be otherwise. Nor should it be. We cannot and will not revise our mental models, intellectual paradigms, and professional practices until we have been emotionally confronted with the pain of their inadequacy.

In teaching business ethics, I try to do my part in role-modeling this painful learning. This largely entails creating holding environments within which such learning can take place. The good news is that anyone who shares his or her struggles in learning these lessons is also modeling ethical learning for others. If the results of our struggling and grappling to learn these painful lessons don't satisfy the canons of transcendental reason, well, then too bad for Kant, because we have real work to do.

REFERENCES

Anderson, M., & Escher, P. (2010). *The MBA oath: Setting a higher standard for business leaders*. New York, NY: Portfolio.

Bebeau, M. (2002). The defining issues test and the four component model: Contributions to professional education. *Journal of Moral Education, 31*, 271-295.

Biesta, G. (2010). Five theses on complexity reduction and its politics. In G. Biesta & D. Osberg (Eds.), *Complexity theory and the politics of education* (pp. 5-13). Rotterdam, The Netherlands: Sense.

Daloz, L. A. (1996). *Common fire: Lives of commitment in a complex world*. Boston, MA: Beacon Press.

Dreyfus, H. L., & Dreyfus, S. E. (1986). *Mind over machine*. New York, NY: Free Press.

Everett, J. (2007). Ethics education and the role of the symbolic market. *Journal of Business Ethics, 76*(3), 253-267.

Friedman, M. (2007). The social responsibility of business is to increase its profits. In W. C. Zimmerli, M. Holzinger, & K. Richter (Eds.), *Corporate ethics and corporate governance* (pp. 173-178): Berlin, Germany: Springer.

Gardner, H. (2007). *Responsibility at work: How leading professionals act (or don't act) responsibly*. San Francisco, CA: Jossey-Bass.

Gentile, M. C. (2010). *Giving voice to values: How to speak your mind when you know what's right*. New Haven, CT: Yale University Press.

Ghoshal, S. (2005). Bad management theories are destroying good management practices. *Academy of Management Learning and Education, 4*(1), 6.

Hall, B. (1994). *Values shift: A guide to personal and organizational transformation*. Rockport, ME: Twin Light.

Hardin, G. (1968). The tragedy of the commons. *Science, 162*(3859), 1243-1248.

Hart, S., & Milstein, M. (2003). Creating sustainable value. *Academy of Management Executive, 17*(2), 11.

Hodges, B., Regehr, G., & Martin, D. (2001). Difficulties in recognizing one's own incompetence: Novice physicians who are unskilled and unaware of it. *Academic Medicine, 76*(10), S87-S89.

Hosmer, L. T. (1987). *The ethics of management*. Homewood, IL: Irwin.

Johnson, M. (1993). *Moral imagination: Implications of cognitive science for ethics*. Chicago, IL: University of Chicago Press.

Kegan, R. (1982). *The evolving self: Problem and process in human development*. Cambridge, MA: Harvard University Press.

Kegan, R. (1994). *In over our heads: The mental demands of modern life*. Cambridge, MA: Harvard University Press.

Khurana, R., & Nohria, N. (2008). It's time to make management a true profession. *Harvard Business Review, 86*(10), 70-77.

Kidder, R. M. (1995). *How good people make tough choices*. New York, NY: Morrow.

Klein, G. (1998). *Sources of power: How people make decisions*. Cambridge, MA: MIT Press.

Klein, G. (2009). *Streetlights and shadows: Searching for the keys to adaptive decision making*. Cambridge, MA: MIT Press.

Kolodner, J. (1993). *Case-based reasoning*. San Mateo, CA: Morgan Kaufman.

Kruger, J., & Dunning, D. (1999). Unskilled and unaware of it: How difficulties in recognizing one's own incompetence lead to inflated self-assessments. *Journal of Personality and Social Psychology, 77*(6), 1121-1134.

Lifton, R. J. (1986). *The Nazi doctors: Medical killing and the psychology of genocide*. New York, NY: Basic Books.

MacIntyre, A. C. (1984). *After virtue: A study in moral theory* (2nd ed.). Notre Dame, IN: University of Notre Dame Press.

Mahoney, J. T. (2005). *Economic foundations of strategy*. Thousand Oaks, CA: Sage.

Mitroff, I. (2004). An open letter to the deans and the faculties of American business schools. *Journal of Business Ethics, 54*(2), 185-189.

Norros, L., & Klemola, U. (2005). Naturalistic analysis of anesthetists' clinical practice. In H. Montgomery, R. Lipshitz, & B. Brehmer (Eds.), *How professionals make decisions*. Mahwah, NJ: Erlbaum.

Ostrom, E. (1990). *Governing the commons: The evolution of institutions for collective action*. Cambridge, England: Cambridge University Press.

Rest, J. R. (1994). *Moral development in the professions: Psychology and applied ethics*. Hillsdale, NJ: Erlbaum.

Rest, J. R. (1999). *Postconventional moral thinking: A neo-Kohlbergian approach*. Mahwah, NJ: Erlbaum.

Schrader, D. (2003). Moral metacognition in adolescence and adulthood. In J. Demick & C. Andreoletti (Eds.), *The Plenum series in adult development and aging* (pp. 301-327). New York, NY: Kluwer Academic/Plenum.

Senge, P. M. (1990). *The fifth discipline: The art and practice of the learning organization* (1st ed.). New York, NY: Doubleday/Currency.

Senge, P. M. (2008). *The necessary revolution: How individuals and organizations are working together to create a sustainable world*. New York, NY: Doubleday.

Smith, K. K., & Berg, D. N. (1987). *Paradoxes of group life: Understanding conflict, paralysis, and movement in group dynamics*. San Francisco, CA: Jossey-Bass.

Solomon, R. C. (1992). *Ethics and excellence: Cooperation and integrity in business*. New York, NY: Oxford University Press.

Swanson, D. (2005). Business education at bay: Addressing a crisis of legitimacy. *Issues in Accounting Education, 20*(3), 247-253.

Taylor, S. E., & Crocker, J. (1981). Schematic bases of social information processing. In E. T. Higgins (Ed.), *Social cognition: The Ontario Symposium* (Vol. 1, pp. 89-134). Mahwah, NJ: Erlbaum.

Tesser, A., Rosen, S., & Batchelor, T. R. (1972). On the reluctance to communicate bad news (the MUM effect): A role play extension. *Journal of Personality, 40*(1), 88-103.

Varela, F. J. (1999). *Ethical know-how: Action, wisdom, and cognition*. Palo Alto, CA: Stanford University Press.

Zimbardo, P. G. (2007). *The Lucifer effect: Understanding how good people turn evil*. New York, NY: Random House.

CHAPTER 2

BUSINESS ETHICS CURRICULUM DEVELOPMENT

Balancing Idealism and Realism

Johannes Brinkmann and Ronald R. Sims

INTRODUCTION

The traditional format and course design for teaching business ethics seems to downplay controversial goals, obstacles and possible conflicts with the rest of the business curriculum. Additionally, it is our suspicion that if business ethics is marketed as a loyal and uncritical servant of the business school community there is a risk of criticism from its supporters—for being too superficial, uncontroversial, and inconsequential. This chapter suggests that

- ideals should be discussed and if necessary defended against the mere use of rhetoric;
- business ethics teaching needs to be done in close cooperation and coordination with colleagues in charge of the other courses in the curriculum;

Experiences in Teaching Business Ethics
pp. 27–51
Copyright © 2011 by Information Age Publishing
All rights of reproduction in any form reserved.

- the convictions and attitude level of students and colleagues needs to be addressed rather than just focusing only at the opinion level, and that; and
- business ethics competence is presented and perceived as inseparable from basic business professional competence (rather than as counter-expertise only).

In the first two sections, the chapter focuses on what we believe should be the targeted learning goals of teaching business ethics (why go where?) and on the working conditions of an initiative to teaching business ethics (go from where?). We think that the third component of the traditional threefold distinction in teaching pedagogy, curriculum design (go how?) should be addressed and discussed as late as possible, that is, *after* an in-depth and consensus-driven constructive discussion among the most important stakeholders about the targeted learning goals and working conditions of the business ethics course (cf. Figure 2.1).

Goals of business ethics teaching are important to address (see, e.g., Brinkmann & Sims, 2001; Business Roundtable for the Institute of Corporate Ethics, 2007; Krehmeyer, 2007). In our view, goals have to do with justification and perspectives—such as why business schools should teach business ethics and why students should learn something about business ethics. Justification and perspectives can serve as criteria for an important distinction between two goal levels, with different functions. *Purposes* or end goals have mainly an outside world perspective and refer to intended, often promised positive functions of a business curriculum for

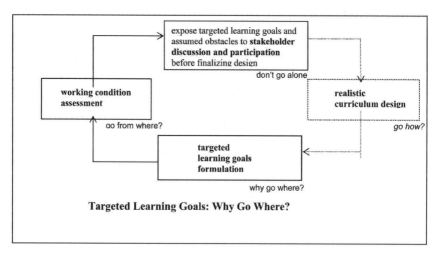

Figure 2.1.   Main steps in stakeholder-sensitive curriculum development.

society and its labour market. Such ideals and purposes of a program are not easily disagreed with or falsified, and are quite often formulated as a rather vague justification of the benefits of business education as such.

Objectives refer to specific goal states, with an emphasis of internal perspectives and justification toward internal stakeholders. Objectives are used to formulate realistically what students can be expected to learn when attending a program or parts of it. Objectives are what are measured and measurable by given exams and curriculum evaluation procedures. Ideally, objectives should be realistic operationalizations of idealistic end goals, and contribute to the keeping of end goal promises made by a business school. In practice, purpose or mission statements typically appear in the public relations (PR) and marketing materials for business school programs, presented in glossy brochures and on homepages, without significant impact on practical school life. Objectives on the other hand, in our experience, live their own lives at the course level (competing with perceived exams or other student-performance agendas as shadow objectives).

The following two quotations give an idea of how we believe our faculty colleagues can rediscover and reacquire their role as idealistic and self-conscious academics, if necessary at the expense of rhetorics and PR staff, and how one could formulate end- or targeted-learning goals that almost ask for or focus primarily on course level or program level operationalization:

> Managers should consider themselves as professionals for societally responsive, strategically effective and operationally efficient allocation of scarce resources in complex organizations with a division of labour. They should not consider themselves as promoters of a given and partial interest orientation. Future-minded and socially responsible management does not require any noneconomic business ethics as a moral counter-part of business rationality, but a moral-philosophically enlightened concept of business rationality. (Ulrich, 1987, p. 81, authors' translation)

> Business ethics as a teaching subject works with a vision of an enlightened, holistic and long-range thinking, empathetic and responsible business professional, who has the civil courage to follow up such thoughts in practice. (Brinkmann, 1998, p. 190)

Such considerations can be formulated as the following proposition (cf. for similar thoughts Brinkmann & Sims, 2001):

Proposition 1: The targeted learning end goal or mission statements of business schools regarding moral responsibility development are "empty rhetorics" which can create distancing rather than loyalty unless such statements have been discussed properly among faculty and students, not the least from an operational perspective.

Before addressing the more specific teaching business ethics targeted learning objectives, we offer an additional proposition that we believe builds a bridge to the targeted learning end-goal formulations quoted above and that makes the background assumptions more explicit and open to further discussion:

> **Proposition 2:** The intention of teaching business ethics should not be to teach students certain attitudes or even moralism, but to further awareness and critical examination of the students' preexisting attitudes. As a result of such self-examination, the students should acquire a more critically reflected, mature and holistic understanding of their current or future professional role, of business activity and of the interdependence between business activity and the natural environment.

In other words, we strongly suggest that the focus should be on the *moral reflection* of attitudes rather than specific culturally desirable moral attitudes. With such an overarching concern, James Rest's four-component model of moral behavior determination seems useful to us as a theory reference and as a point of departure (see Rest & Narváez 1994). Given our underlying premise that students should not be indoctrinated but forced to work with their own attitudes the following seven-objective component model has been useful to us in our efforts to teach business ethics (see Figure 2.2).

All of these components are interdependent in various ways but can be sorted and addressed in a fruitful order. On the next few pages, we elaborate and provide further justification on each objective component, not the least as an invitation to a discussion, component by component, among the various stakeholders (i.e., colleagues and students) involved in an effort to teach business ethics.

Targeted Learning Objective 1: Know Thyself, Your Own Moral Values and Thresholds

As early as possible after entering the business program students should be asked to assess their own values, moral attitudes and moral thresholds, using qualitative or quantitative instruments (cf., for example, http://www.yourmorals.org/loh.php,   http://www.yourmorals.org/explore

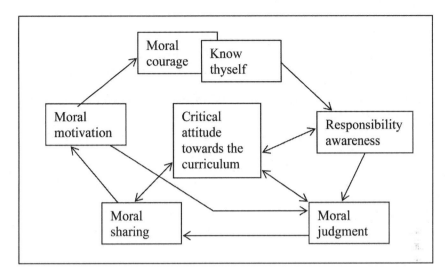

Figure 2.2.   Seven targeted learning moral-goal components.

.php, http://www.yourmorals.org/5f_new2_survey.php, http://www.your-morals.org/schwartz.php, http://www.caseplace.org/d.asp?d=3335). The intention of such an assessment is to ensure that any ethics exposure is on the students' own terms rather than meant as a form of superficial indoc-trination with politically correct values and standpoints. In our experi-ence, such a test can help to create moral self-awareness and, once those types of questions have been asked, almost guarantees increased interest for the moral dimension of business throughout the following courses.

Targeted Learning Objective 2: Learning to See Moral Issues, Conflicts, and Responsibilities

While students tend to see the importance of their values and thresholds in private life situations, this is often less so in business and professional sit-uations which seem clearly dominated by other dimensions: profit, quality, competition and survival in markets. A moral responsibility awareness component is similar to what Rest calls *moral sensitivity*: "the awareness of how our actions affect other people. It involves being aware of different possible lines of action and how each line of action could *affect* (our italics) the parties concerned. It involves imaginatively constructing possible sce-narios, and knowing cause-consequence chains of events in the real world; it involves empathy and role-taking skills" (Rest & Narváez, 1994, p. 23).

The main point is to develop moral imagination as a condition of a sense of moral obligation and personal responsibility (Sims, 2002) and carry out a good enough analysis of consequences, in advance.

Targeted Learning Objective 3: Learning to Identify the Specific Moral Aspects of a Situation

Once one is aware of one's *own* values and of *others* as potential victims and that a given situation seems threatening to oneself, to others, or both, one needs to *judge* explicitly the *fairness* of different alternatives. This again requires a set of concepts and criteria, tools for labelling things, comparing and ranking of alternatives. Here the most traditional part of ethics training is addressed as business students develop skills in the identification and analysis of moral issues: learning a language and methodology for problem identification, not the least of which is being able to formulate one's own moral standing and one's responsibilities toward others. Rest identifies this as the traditional *moral judgment* component on which L. Kohlberg's moral maturity development research has focused. This is judgment regarding "which line of action is more morally justifiable. Deficiency [in this component] comes from overly simplistic ways of justifying choices of moral action" (Rest & Narváez, 1994, p. 24). Or, formulated as a discussion proposition:

> Knowledge of key terms and of the most important schools of thought is an important objective. Such knowledge, however, should not be isolated from the key terms' function as useful critical tools. Learning the words and rhetoric is relatively easy and not very controversial. The correct words without critical enlightenment can be worse, however, than no words at all.

Targeted Learning Objective 4: Learning to Share Moral Understanding

This component is an addition to the Rest catalog. We are sceptical about the highly individualistic ethics conception in the Anglo-Saxon tradition, with the individual fighting an integrity conflict against others. On the contrary, students should be invited to share moral issues with others rather than keeping them to themselves. There are a number of good reasons for such an objective: two individuals usually see more than one does, and others can function as a corrective and help with simulating action chains and with sharing responsibility. In his book about "moral muteness," Bird (1996) has praised such moral sharing as productive moral conversation:

> Our concern is to limit, reduce and overcome moral silence, deafness, and blindness ... by finding ways (that) ... are interactive and take place over time, help individuals address and master their moral reluctance, inarticulateness, inattentiveness, and blurred visions.... Good moral communications are constructive. They help to clarify and do not obscure issues. They elicit and foster ongoing participation, helping people to overcome their shyness and reticence to speak and to attend to the concerns of others. (pp. 204-205)

Targeted Learning Objective 5: Learning How to Handle Moral Issues and Conflicts

At first sight, this objective looks most important and tests in a way if the previous four targeted learning objective components are realized sufficiently. However, we believe one should not start with this objective right away, even if case-teaching approaches and many moral-conflict-handling checklists in the literature (see below) seem to suggest otherwise. Two important subobjectives become clear if one looks at Rest's *moral motivation* component: really being *willing* to apply moral understanding in specific moral conflict situations and not forgetting that the most interesting conflict can be between moral and *other* considerations.

Targeted Learning Objective 6: Acquiring Moral Courage

Rest calls this the *moral character* component, involving "ego strength, perseverance, backbone, toughness, strength of conviction, and courage" (Rest & Narváez, 1994, p. 24). Moral character or courage has to do with the individual self-confirmation effect of proper moral conflict handling and the consistency of feeling, thinking and acting on the individual level. Nielsen (1984) seems to think of such an attitude when he suggests extending the widely accepted political citizen role model to business life, to corporate or institution citizenship as a moral right and duty: cultivating "the courage to think and judge independently as oneself as a basis for acting civically and courageously with other managers ... as to resist the immoral 'ideal type' behaviors" (p. 160). In the psychological literature, development of such courage is referred to as *"armoring,"* whereby individuals go through a process of psychological strengthening to develop a protective armor that will buffer them from the unsavory elements of the outside world. Through armoring we hope that our students develop a certain amount of resiliency to comfortably resist external pressures to act immorally.

Targeted Learning Objective 7: Acquiring a Critical Attitude Toward the Business School Curriculum and Its Disciplines

Given our own experiences as business ethics teachers we wonder if business ethics teaching pays too much attention to practice in the business world and too little attention to theory in the business school world. Business school professors with more freedom carry even more responsibility for their student output, and hence for the future moral climate in business, than businesses and their employees, working under day-to-day bottom-line pressure.

It has been said that business ethics is mainly taught by all the other courses (Etzioni, 1991). If this is so, the critical potential (and moral responsibilities) of business ethics in relation to all the other business school courses deserves the status of an additional objective. As for business ethics in general, the question here is how much (or how radical) criticism one should encourage. Supporting and contributing to internal self-criticism of the different business disciplines is probably more valuable than top-down criticism, which can be counterproductive.

The targeted learning objectives for business ethics teaching presented above can be summarized in the following two propositions:

(4) Furthering of critically reflected understanding should focus on six different though interdependent, moral attitude components: self-knowledge, sensitivity, judgment, sharing, motivation, and courage.

(5) Business students should not wait to apply what they have learned until after completing school, but start with other business courses, with asking the critical questions that the students have learned one can ask.

THE ENVIRONMENT FOR TEACHING BUSINESS ETHICS: WORKING CONDITIONS

In our experience, agreement on the goals of teaching business ethics by key stakeholders and good intentions are important, but do not work all by themselves. Good intentions can be controversial, too. A realistic understanding of the environment for teaching business ethics is at least as important, in particular an understanding and handling of obstacles and conflicts. In our view, business ethics teaching faces three categories of obstacles and conflict potentials (see Figure 2.3) which need to be addressed and discussed:

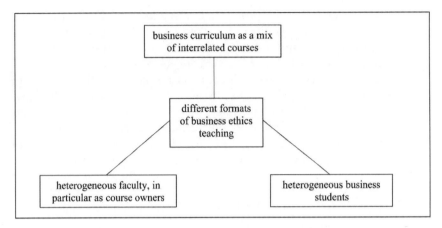

Figure 2.3.   Curriculum-related and stakeholder-related obstacles to business ethics teaching.

- the existing business curriculum as a whole and the courses which comprise it;
- the students' working situation and mind-set; and
- faculty's working situation and mind-set.

Obstacle Type 1: The Existing Business Curriculum and Other Courses

Business ethics is not taught and perceived in a vacuum, but in relation to its business curriculum environment and to other courses. Without proper understanding and handling, such interdependencies easily become obstacles. There are differences between teaching business ethics and core business courses (such as accounting, marketing, finance) that should be taken into account. Such differences are usually experienced vaguely and not made explicit (see the Appendix for an "explicit" draft of potentially relevant antonyms).

Unclear relationships between business ethics teaching and other courses can be even more problematic. If the specific differences between business ethics and core business courses are not addressed, explained and justified as a broadening of perspective or as an extension of the other courses on the curriculum, business ethics can easily be perceived and defined as irrelevant, disturbing, dissonant, and contradictory (e.g., Alam, 1999).

One can understand such problems in a systems perspective (i.e., look at business ethics in terms of its positive or negative functions for the business curriculum as a whole). Clear differences and contradictions of the kind mentioned above are not necessarily negative as such, as long as they are explained and justified vis-á-vis students and faculty, with reference to positive functions, internal or external ones, or both. Without such explanation and justification students and faculty tend to see increased fragmentation only, which is indeed only dysfunctional. Such differences between courses, contradictions, and possible system weaknesses should be addressed explicitly and offered for discussion, or formulated as another proposition:

> **Proposition 6:** An essential question is how business ethics can function as a bridge builder across disciplines, as an integration mechanism for the business curriculum as a whole, by promoting holistic understanding, and where necessary, as a legitimate place of alternative thinking.

This first mentioned obstacle has to do with system weaknesses, that is business ethics as a system element and its frictions as well as potential catalyst functions in relation to a curriculum environment. The next two obstacles to business ethics as a teaching subject have mostly to do with lacking empathy (i.e., lacking understanding of target group mind-sets and lacking target group participation).

Obstacle Type 2: Students' Working Situation and Mind-Set

Business ethics is not the only subject students are taught. This means that business ethics competes with other subjects for short student working time and for short student attention. In our experience, business ethics is easily perceived selectively with mind-sets that are acquired in previous courses. Before such conditions are discussed, two short preliminary remarks are necessary. First, students are not a homogeneous group. Our experience suggests (and our course evaluation statistics, too) that there are clear attitude differences among students toward business ethics and toward the issues raised by it. If our impression is right, business ethics is not popular or unpopular with business students, but rather controversial. Some students tend to like business ethics as a subject, others clearly don't. Popularity differences could be symptoms of differences in underlying moral maturity (in a Kohlberg perspective, see, e.g., Kohlberg, 1985) and of differences in open-mindedness regarding the place of business and business professions in society. A second issue concerns responsibility. If many students feel frustrated and insecure toward business ethics because of course differences and system frictions, one shouldn't blame the students, but rather listen to them.

Students are not responsible for any information overload or for over-scheduling of the curriculum. When courses and terms are overloaded already, putting "more" on the agenda often means "less," taking attention away from what is defined as less relevant. A similar system-related obstacle involves time-pressure of course level exams. Such pressure contributes to a short-sighted, course- and exams-focused mind-set and to "rational" study behavior. More specifically, the relevance of what one is taught and reads in the books is defined narrowly, by immediate relevance of teaching and reading to the respective examination. Such curriculum weaknesses and such mind-sets must be taken into consideration, both when communicating and when considering student participation.

The most obvious student-related obstacles have to do with communication, with communication barriers such as lack of receiver sensitivity, with mismatches of expectations, or with other barriers. While teachers, and in particular ethics teachers, tend to offer complex theory and abstractions, many students look for the opposite: for simple models, for checklists for "practice," for examples, and even for entertainment. Even if the students are wrong and the teachers are right, it is important to offer reasons why such types of expectations are frustrated. As a result, we have found that it is important to check communication effects, too, since students normally don't expose to curriculum contents passively and completely, but selectively. Defensive or "reactance" tendencies (i.e., boomerang effects), are possible, too, if students feel that personal, private values are addressed, and fear that somebody is trying to manipulate something which is none of his or her business.

We offer another two propositions based on this obstacle.

Proposition 7: Business ethics is not the only subject students are taught. This means that business ethics competes with other subjects for limited student working time and attention, and that business ethics is perceived selectively with mind-sets which may be acquired in other courses.

Proposition 8: Listening to students is important, since students quite often are better curriculum judges than most business ethics faculty (e.g., of how well-mixed and well-integrated courses are as parts of a curriculum and how they compare).

Obstacle Type 3: Faculty's Working Situation and Mind-Set

Like students, business school faculty are more or less well-adjusted to a curriculum system with its strengths and weaknesses. One example of such adaptation is compartmentalization, with clear boundaries between courses and much less clear relationships between them. Faculty heterogeneity is even more obvious than student heterogeneity due to academic identification with research specialization rather than with teaching, due to traditional academic individualism. Of course, status and power differences come into play, too. If Hosmer's (1999) observations are true, skepticism toward, and dislike of, business ethics is one of the few common denominators among faculty.

While almost 2 decades old, a well-known report about how the Harvard Business School (HBS) addressed business ethics teaching; faculty received special attention (Piper, Gentile, & Parks, 1993). One chapter (written by M. Gentile) deals with "engaging the power and competence of the faculty" and lists 14 faculty-related "barriers" (reconstructed from a survey among HBS business faculty (pp. 79-94). We suggest operating with fewer barrier categories, or maybe better, barrier perception categories, and to use them then for structuring our observations:

- information deficits;
- curriculum logistics;
- effort without appropriate reward; and
- fears of personal dissonance and of losing control in the classroom.

While the three first obstacle types are rational, the last one has to do with self-confidence in one's role as a teacher. If one wants to, one could relate our categories roughly to the above-mentioned Harvard items:

- information deficits (1, 2, 4, 9, 13);
- curriculum logistics (7, 11, 12);
- effort without appropriate reward (3, 8); and
- fears of personal dissonance and of losing control in the classroom (5, 6, 10, 14).

Information Deficits

Faculty disinterest in business ethics can be a natural way of handling information deficits. It is only fair not to have an opinion about something one knows nothing or very little about. As a point of departure, it seems wise to us not to overestimate how much faculty know about how business ethics as a teaching and research field looks at itself. We also think it is wise to be prepared for misperceptions, simplifications, and perhaps even prejudice. Even if goal formulations of the type suggested above provide some information, it is not fair to invite to a dialogue about ethical issues in business without first providing some easily accessible basic information about the field and its state of the art.

Curriculum Logistics

Business school faculty face a similar information overload and time pressures as their students do. In such a situation a curriculum status quo tends to be perceived conservatively and in a constant sum fashion. Any newcomer or competitor for short space and time threatens the given course and topics establishment, in particular if most actors are content with the given status quo. Given our points to this point we offer the following proposition: Curriculum logistics is the obstacle that is most closely related to a business school's power and prestige structure, where interference with a colleague's course and in particular suggestions to shorten or even drop other courses easily can challenge the faculty establishment.

Our experience suggests that quite often business ethics and similar courses seem to enter when there are vacancies which can be filled, when parts of the curriculum are redesigned, or when a prolongation of a curriculum is discussed and there is a need to fill it with something new. The curriculum logistics obstacle depends, of course, on which business ethics teaching format one considers--dedicated ethics courses or ethics as an integrated part of most other courses. Separate courses, in particular voluntary courses, are probably much less threatening than integration demands, since all new separate courses confirm rather than challenge compartmentalization (more will be said about curriculum logistics later in this chapter).

Effort Without Appropriate Reward

University faculty, and in particular business school faculty, seem to have an economic attitude toward course development and course change. Developing a new course or changing an existing course is a costly. At best it is an investment of energy and time, with expected return as a key variable.

Efforts to motivate and qualify more business faculty to become experts in ethics quickly raise the issue of opportunity costs, of learning new tricks and new approaches. Increased research and publication pressure over the years furthers a tendency toward the publishable (and teachable) and toward the empirical rather than the reflective. Such rational behavior for individual faculty and institutions in the short run is unlikely to foster an atmosphere of willingness to put one's "career" on the line in the long run. We think one could consider a proposition like the following one:

Proposition 9: Those who are willing to put their careers on the line would do well to ensure that there is close coordination among their research, publication, and teaching, since spreading these activities is time consuming and risky.

(And experience suggests that involvement in business ethics often is perceived as a distraction rather than as a chance to make research more problem-oriented and interdisciplinary.)

Fears of Personal Dissonance and of Losing Control in the Classroom

In our experience, teaching business ethics can be emotionally more challenging and more risky for faculty than teaching other subjects. Such challenges and risks relate to the teacher's self-image, to the communication climate in the classroom, and to the teacher's authority as a function of both, particularly when it comes to the discussion of provocative and controversial moral dilemma cases in class (cf., for example, Brinkmann & Sims, 2001). Faculty may be afraid that such provocation and controversy can easily turn into a boomerang where they can be asked awkward questions about what they feel personally and what they would do themselves. We wonder if case discussions that raise fundamental questions regarding the moral legitimacy of capitalism, business, marketing, or the legitimacy of teaching professional sophistication in these fields are above the average threat level, especially when teachers are asked for principal confessions of any contradictions between their private and their professional convictions. Another proposition could then be as follows:

Proposition 10: Nonrational faculty perceptions, in particular self-confidence problems, can represent obstacles that are harder to assess, and hence harder to work with, than "politically correct" rational ones, since this requires more of a climate of mutual trust and openness than is usually found at a business school.

STAKEHOLDERS, COMMUNICATION, AND PARTICIPATION

Thus far we have addressed targeted learning goals and obstacles to their realization. However, the most important single condition for realizing targeted learning goals and overcoming obstacles of the types mentioned seems to be *open communication* with and *active participation* of the stakeholders involved, in particular faculty and students as primary stakeholders. We believe such an assumption is consistent with modern business ethics positions. Open and fair communication can address conflicts, produce consensus and prevent unnecessary conflict. And the parties affected by a decision or a change of a status quo have a moral right to be heard and to participate. We recognize that calls for business ethics teaching often comes "from outside" or "from above" rather than from inside (i.e., from faculty and students, as the key internal stakeholders) (cf. Epstein, 2010; Paton, 2010).

If faculty and students have not had the opportunity to discuss the goals of teaching business ethics or to participate in curriculum design decisions, then there should be no surprise if they exhibit superficial like or dislike for business ethics teaching, passive resistance to it, or repressive tolerance of it. As in any situation where those impacted most by a change are not included in the dialogue related to the change, resistance is inevitable.

In other words, to avoid such resistance and to ensure the active participation of all the key stakeholders, dialogue must first start with the formulation of clear goals and agreement about them. They must be discussed openly and thoroughly by faculty and interested students alike. And schools must be prepared to revise these goals as a consequence of such discussion. Our suggestion for such a catalogue of goals has been outlined above already. The design of such communication and participation co-determines their effect, and perhaps their success. In order to prevent domination by the most vocal or opinionated leaders, we suggest to start with an anonymous survey of goal acceptance and of views about various design alternatives (e.g., early versus late, mandatory versus voluntary, separate course versus integration into other courses, etc.). Well-monitored and power-free focus group discussion, with or without case references, should be the main focus, since this simulates real-life conflict handling and consensus-building. Or in proposition format:

Proposition 11: A curriculum discussion can benefit from a survey of concerns, worries, questions, perceptions and misunderstandings. With or without such a start-up survey it is important to address openly as many of the obstacles mentioned above as possible (and other ones as well if raised by the respondents). The aim should be to reach at least a minimum consensus about all the issues. As a result of such "action research" it is much easier to identify best points of departure.

The HBS survey reference to misperceptions of business ethics teaching (Piper et al., 1993) suggests that business ethics and other key terms cannot be used without clarification. Additionally, one cannot understate the fact that if faculty feel they are asked to leave a secure professional platform, they must be provided with safety nets such as shared responsibility and team teaching. Like Piper et al. (1993) our experience suggests that understanding and addressing faculty implications is the most crucial task in increasing business ethics teaching efforts. Our own firsthand experience suggests that there are interdepartmental rivalries and internal markets in business schools (especially in an atmosphere of resource constraints, "publish quickly, or perish" reward structures), that faculty may lack self-confidence in being experts in ethics, and that there is an unwillingness to engage in broad dialogues about business ethics teaching. The traditional response would be that top-down organizational commitment is a necessary condition for overcoming such barriers. Heavy funding might be a sufficient condition. But, in reality, in our experience, faculty support is essential to business ethics teaching efforts, and especially in any efforts to integrate ethics across the curriculum.

The story could end here and often does end here. In fact, not letting the story end here corresponds with the very core of business ethics as an idealistic discipline. If there is a gap between realities and ideals, realities don't necessarily prove that better alternative realities are wrong or impossible. The challenge to teaching business ethics is to identify barriers to change and realistic ways around such barriers. We wonder if one could and should modify the traditional argument about "there are no things that money can't buy," business ethics enthusiasm at a business school included. An alternative phrasing of the point could be *"there are some things money shouldn't buy"*—that is, if business ethics enthusiasm at a business school is bought by various material rewards, one never knows if there is any meaningful and trustworthy academic involvement behind it. In short, from our standpoint, there seems to be no other alternative than ongoing, open, and fair communication among faculty and students in the discourse-ethics tradition. We do hope, idealistically, that such dialogue and interaction build or at least further an open communication climate, which then might further more successful business ethics teaching in business school contexts. Additionally, we hope that our idealism is not equivalent to naiveté. Maybe it would be indeed naïve to expect that all colleagues and all students, or a majority of colleagues and students can be convinced that business ethics teaching deserves a reserved place in a business school curriculum. To convince a critical mass of idealistic, nonconformist academics and students is probably sufficient but in our view worth the ongoing effort.

A CURRICULUM LOGISTICS PERSPECTIVE

As we have briefly claimed earlier, in a curriculum logistics perspective toward business ethics is almost defined by its filler status, as a subject which typically enters the business school curriculum when there is a sudden opening and disappears equally suddenly whenever there is a shortage of curriculum space. Business ethics is often the posting used to balance the budget. Such a fate easily creates an add-on prejudice toward business ethics courses and toward their content. The school offers and uses the business ethics course(s) when it is convenient, and skips it when convenient. With or without such a connotation, curriculum logistics also influences how business ethics is perceived by students and faculty.

For example, at one of the authors' business school an undergraduate course titled "business and society" is only offered: (1) when students complain about the lack of sufficient electives being offered, (2) when faculty recognize that while the course is listed in the course catalogue, it has not been offered in 2 or 3 years, (3) when other stakeholders decry the schools failure to help develop "ethical" students in response to a recent questionable act by a student, and (4) when an important stakeholder (i.e., an alumnus with money to give) shows an interest in what the school is doing to help develop more "ethical" students and future employees. At the other author's school, a PR and business ethics course was developed as a mandatory undergraduate course, with PR for the new program as a welcomed side effect. When the curriculum changed in 2010, the competition among fewer courses for the same total credit space in the curriculum increased, and the mandatory course was skipped in favor of a less specific elective.

In such situations we have found that it might be wiser to develop and offer smaller modules of business ethics than quarter- or semester-long courses. In other words, offering modules which fit the students' and future employers' needs might be better marketing for business ethics than offering full-format courses too early. This can be perceived as being too long and many students may feel they have learned enough after the first half of the course.

The question of *who* should design, offer and teach-- in other words the business ethics teacher background—can be considered as a logistics issue, too. Should business ethics be taught by "ordinary" business school faculty with a background in management, marketing, finance, etc. or should it be taught by ethicists or even business ethics experts, with a position inside or outside the business school? One neutral and clear answer could be that people with advanced degrees in ethics should do it (i.e., philosophers and perhaps people in religious studies). The curricular inference is that we need more courses in ethics and ethicists in schools of business. However, we believe this approach is insufficient for two reasons, one methodological and the other institutional. The latter reason is less controversial. If all the ethics teaching in business schools is to be done by ethicists, only a limited amount will be done. There aren't enough ethicists and, in particular, there aren't enough with the credibility to work in business schools. And it is not clear either if the ethics approaches cultivated in departments of philosophy are sufficient, even on the level of normative theory. Philosophers need to be partners in the conversation, to be sure, but it is less likely that they will be solvers of problems. It appears that in trying to decide who should teach business ethics one has necessarily to grapple between the multiple conceptions and reasoning of ethics offered by faculty within philosophy (and perhaps theology) and the wide range of business practices within the disciplines of business school faculty, who often have no formal training in ethics. Some authors also question whether business professors have the qualifications required to teach business ethics and argue that academics who teach business ethics have to first understand the complex ethical situations in which they find themselves if business ethics is to be taught in a meaningful way (cf. Chesley & Anderson, 2003).

The key issue remains: the identification of faculty who can bring a proper balance between philosophy and business practice, particularly with regard to moral principles and material practices, into business ethics teaching efforts. The frustration of deciding who should teach business ethics, in our experience, is often compounded by the fact that when one turns to philosophers to teach business ethics, one encounters a form of moral relativism. And, when one turns to business faculty with no training in ethics, one discerns that they are most concerned with a tendency to focus to heavily on the bottom line or the impact of ethical decisions, for example, on business profits. Given the diverse disciplines and perspectives of philosophy and business faculty it is important to recognize that the decision on *who* should teach business ethics is not a choice between philosophy *or* business professors but rather an appreciation of what each can contribute to the teaching of business ethics. Thus, the best choice is an interdisciplinary approach to teaching business ethics that relies on faculty who can effectively contribute to the teaching and learning of business ethics, regardless of their discipline.

While our discussion to this point has highlighted a number of propositions regarding important conditions and considerations for teaching business ethics the next section focuses on another three propositions, related to strategic choices for business ethics curriculum design.

THREE STRATEGIC CHOICES FOR TEACHING BUSINESS ETHICS: EARLY VERSUS LATER, INTEGRATED VERSUS STAND-ALONE, MANDATORY VERSUS ELECTIVE

One way of managing or addressing curriculum logistics issues is to look for an *optimum mix* of integrated and separate, mandatory and elective business ethics teaching. When looking for such a mix one needs to be sensitive to the mind-set differences between undergraduate and graduate students and that such differences must be taken into consideration when formulating and discussing the goals or targeted learning objectives of any business ethics teaching unit, or in other words, one needs to "start where the students are."

The primary issue here is just *when* students should be exposed to or take ethics courses. This view is in line with an important aspect of The Hastings Center report's (1980) special emphasis on teaching ethics at different levels of education and Sims and Sims' (1991) suggestion that undergraduate and graduate students should be exposed to different kinds of business ethics teaching.

Based on our own and our colleagues' experience to date, graduate and undergraduate students are indeed different (by social and mental maturity, work experience, etc.) and deserve a curriculum tailored for their specific situation. Teaching business ethics should start and focus on where the students are or on the kinds of jobs they will have and the decisions they will have to make, since the actual work experience of undergraduates and graduates will be different once they complete their education. As we see it, starting where the students are suggests integrating business ethics teaching into a sufficient number of other undergraduate business courses and postponing separate business ethics teaching to the graduate level, as an elective or mandatory topic. Before briefly discussing these two suggestions, the next few paragraphs provide a brief summary of what we believe business ethics teaching could and should focus on for undergraduates and graduates, separately and as a whole.

Undergraduate Students. In most instances, undergraduate students enter a business school with little exposure to moral or ethical issues in business. In other words, they have less maturity and work experience compared to their graduate counterparts. With an eye to the background of the undergraduate student, faculty should include in the undergraduate curriculum a variety of experiences that assist in the students' moral development (such as increasing the students' self-knowledge and helping them to assess their own moral values, and thresholds, as mentioned briefly above). The purpose is to try to create moral self-awareness and to create increased interest for the moral dimension of business throughout ensuing courses.

Graduate Students. The emphasis on departing from self-knowledge exercises for undergraduates does not exclude such a focus when teaching business ethics to graduate students. However, the graduate business curriculum typically focuses on the kinds of responsibility problems the students will encounter as professionals and managers. This means the graduate students should learn to more fully understand the reasons that support their ethical principles and how to put those principles into practice in real work world situations. Graduate students should have at least one well-organized elective or mandatory business ethics course. Such a course would allow students to grasp the seriousness and complexity of business ethics and acquire the tools for dealing with ethical problems. In short, graduate students must be taught that learning about ethics is important in gaining competence in functional areas and in understanding the relationships between their day-to-day work and the broader values of their organization and the needs of society.

Undergraduate and Graduate Students Alike. An important focus for both undergraduate and graduate business ethics teaching efforts should be the seven interdependent target learning objective components introduced earlier in this chapter (see Figure 2.2): self-knowledge, sensitivity, judgment, sharing, motivation, moral courage, and acquiring a critical attitude toward neighboring business disciplines.

As noted earlier, the *moral sensitivity* objective is focused on students' learning to see moral issues, conflicts and responsibilities. This involves being aware of different possible lines of action and how each line of action could *affect* the parties concerned. The main point is to develop moral imagination as a condition of a sense of moral obligation and personal responsibility. The *judgment* objective concerns how students learn to identify the specific moral aspects of a situation. The judgment aspect emphasizes the point that once one is aware of one's *own* values and of *others* as potential victims and that a given situation seems threatening to oneself, to others, or both, one needs to judge explicitly the fairness of different alternatives. Here students develop skills in the identification and analysis of moral issues. It is also important for both undergraduate and graduate business students to learn to *share moral understanding*. This component suggests that students should be invited to share moral issues with others rather than keeping them to themselves. Such sharing provides the opportunity for students to discuss their moral issues with others. It also helps with simulating action chains and with sharing responsibility. The *moral motivation* component tests if the previous four components (self-knowledge, sensitivity, judgment, and sharing) are sufficiently realized. This component helps students learn how to handle moral issues and conflicts while recognizing their inevitable competition with other values that will surface throughout their work lives. Acquiring moral character or *courage* has to do with the individual self-confirmation effect or proper moral conflict handling and the consistency of feeling, thinking, and acting on the individual level. Both undergraduate and graduate students must learn how to develop a certain amount of resiliency to comfortably resist external pressures to act immorally. The *critical attitude* objective repeats an assumption underlying this whole chapter: that business ethical understanding needs to be integrated with what the same students are taught by the business school colleagues, why not with some hope of business ethics as a potential interdisciplinary bridge-builder across a fragmented business curriculum?[1]

Inspired by this discussion we'd like to formulate two specific suggestions. A first suggestion is to proceed from integrated business ethics teaching as part of other undergraduate business courses to more or less separate business ethics courses on the graduate level. Our second suggestion is to make business ethics essentials mandatory on the undergraduate level (by integrating ethics teaching with mandatory business courses) and then on the graduate level to reserve a deepened state-of-the-art presentation for an elective business ethics course (such an approach can hopefully create a critical mass of motivated students as role models, for ensuring identity and continuity of this field as a necessary part of the curriculum).

PRACTICAL RECOMMENDATIONS

As a combined repetition of some main points made previously and as a practical end to the chapter, we offer the following recommendations to help the reader think about how to design business ethics teaching efforts:

1. Fair and open communication, as well as stakeholder participation, is not only recommended *by* business ethics teaching, but also *for* business ethics teaching, assuming that deeds convince more than words.

2. Avoid the tendency to view the issues of separate versus integrated or mandatory versus elective as alternatives. Rather, view them as mutually reinforcing.

3. Business ethics recommends fair consensus-building around common interests by power-free and open communication. It would be naive, however, to deny the existence of conflicting interests and power-differences. Rather than preaching false consensus and uncritical acceptance of power, business ethics should look

critically at illegitimate use of power in the business school world as well as in the real business world.

4.   Developing communication and participation possibilities for stakeholders as early as possible through appropriate listening-mechanisms is important (e.g., by inviting essay writing and group discussion about moral views and standpoints which individuals "bring with them").

5.   Diversity of moral views and standpoints, documented by such data-collection as mentioned or not, should be viewed as an important resource for simulation of real world moral and cultural diversity.

6.   For the sake of developing the best possible communication climate in the sense of open and constructive pluralism, business ethics competence should be presented as open and interdisciplinary rather than as exclusive and dominated by one or by a few disciplines, such as mainstream business thinking and/or academic moral philosophy.

7.   It is important to be sensitive toward various types of miscommunication risks (such as boomerang effects) and to unexploited communication possibilities (such as two-step-communication in which students and/or faculty function as go-betweens in communication with students and faculty).

8.   Course design should not come *before* an open discussion of goals and obstacles with faculty and students. It should come after to ensure a fair chance to suggest adjustments and revisions before it is too late in the process.

9.   Business ethics teaching efforts should be evaluated continuously and thoroughly, going significantly beyond superficial customer satisfaction measures, and strive for institutionalization of continuous learning and revision by way of outcome measures.

10.   Unnecessary conflicts should be avoided as much as possible. However, one must be prepared for conflicts regarding essential goal elements. Business ethics should be cooperative in the business world and business school world alike, but not at the expense of its integrity. If business ethics does not lead to an attitude of constructive self-criticism, it should perhaps be dropped rather than offered as moralistic rhetoric in which some parties are comforted by the words, while others are happy since they do not feel threatened. Negative examples and obvious lack of ethics can often have a better educational effect than preaching to the wrong target groups, at the wrong time, and in the wrong place.

A FINAL REMARK

Eventually, business ethics curriculum development is about the *wise allocation of resources* and a question of spin-off effects, such as building bridges across the various courses and disciplines. Without some minimum commitment by guaranteeing the continuity of a full-time business ethics position there is indeed a danger of a "hello-and-goodbye" status such as described above. Ideally, there should be even more than one tenured business ethics person—a minimum critical mass of several interested faculty with teaching and research interests in business ethics, publishing in the interfaces between more or less traditional business disciplines and ethics, individually or even better jointly, in the business ethics journals, or even better, in the traditional academic business journals. Only such a situation ensures in the end the authority needed toward the various stakeholders of the "business ethics business."

NOTE

1. Compare Sims and Brinkmann (2003, pp. 71-72), where we claim that "an interdisciplinary approach to business ethics teaching has the potential to build bridges across different courses and parent disciplines by demonstrating the relationship between the subject areas studied (accounting, marketing, economics, organizational theory, etc.), counterbalancing 'managerialist' with 'critical-interdisciplinary' perspectives (Macfarlane, 1998), opening both faculty and students to new points of view, new questions, and new discoveries."

APPENDIX: ASSUMED PROFILE DIFFERENCES BETWEEN CORE BUSINESS COURSES AND BUSINESS ETHICS

Core Business Courses	*Business Ethics*
• Money	• Other values
• Standard of living	• Quality of life
• Self-interest	• Common interest, caring
• Directly measurable	• Indirectly measurable, if at all
• Clear answers	• Complex questions
• Problem solving	• Problem definition
• Lecturing	• Dialogue
• Antiacademic	• Academic
• Typical testing by multiple choice	• Typical testing by essay and/or case
• Ahistoric, present and near future	• Historic, past and distant future

• Analytic	• Holistic
• Knowledge	• Understanding
• Modern	• Premodern, postmodern
• Objective	• (Inter)subjective
• Pro establishment bias	• Antiestablishment bias
• Positive functions of business	• Negative side effects of business
• Public	• Private

REFERENCES

Alam, K. F. (1999). Ethics and accounting education. *Teaching Business Ethics, 2*(3), 261-272.

Bird, F. (1996). *The muted conscience.* Westport CT: Quorum books.

Brinkmann, J. (1998). Teaching business and environmental ethics. In C. J. Shultz II & J. Schroeder (Eds.), *Redoubling efforts: Proceedings of the 23rd Macromarketing Conference* (pp. 188-206). West Greenwich, RI: University of Rhode Island.

Brinkmann, J., & Sims, R. R. (2001). Stakeholder-sensitive business ethics teaching. *Teaching Business Ethics, 5*(2), 171-193.

Business Roundtable Institute for Corporate Ethics. (2007). *Shaping tomorrow's business leaders. Principles and practices for a model business ethics program.* Retrieved from http://www.corporate-ethics.org/pdf/mbep.pdf

Epstein, J. (2010). Economic crisis leads business schools to meld ethics into MBA. Retrieved from http://www.usatoday.com/news/education/2010-05-05-ihe-mba-business_N.htm

Etzioni, A. (1991). Reflections on teaching business ethics. *Business Ethics Quarterly 1,* 355-365.

The Hastings Center. (1980). *The teaching of business ethics in higher education.* Hastings-on-the Hudson: NY: The Institute of Society, Ethics, and Life Sciences.

Hosmer, T. L (1999). Somebody out there doesn't like us: A study of the position and respect of business ethics at schools of business administration. *Journal of Business Ethics, 22*(2), 91-106.

Kohlberg, L. (1985). A current statement on some theoretical issues. In S. Mogil & C. Mogil (Eds.), *Lawrence Kohlberg, consensus and controversy* (pp. 485-546). London, England: Falmer.

Krehmeyer, D. (2007). *Teaching business ethics: A critical need.* Retrieved from http://www.businessweek.com/bschools/content/oct2007/bs20071025_096141.htm

Nielsen, R. P. (1984). Toward an action philosophy for managers based on Arendt and Tillich. *Journal of Business Ethics, 3*(2), 153-161.

Paton, N. (2010). *Business schools put ethics high on MBA agenda.* Retrieved from http://www.guardian.co.uk/money/2010/jan/23/business-schools-ethics-mba

Piper, T. R., Gentile, M. C., & Parks S. D. (1993). *Can ethics be taught?* Boston, MA: Harvard Business School,.

Rest, J., & Narvaez, D. (Eds.). (1994). *Moral development in the professions.* Hillsdale, NJ: Erlbaum.

Sims, R. R., & Brinkmann, J. (2003). Business ethics curriculum design: Suggestions and illustrations. *Teaching Business Ethics, 7*(1), 69-86.

Sims, R. R. (2002). *Teaching business ethics for effective learning*. Westport, CT: Quorum Books.

Sims, R. R., & Sims, S. J. (1991). Increasing applied business ethics courses in business school curricula. *Journal of Business Ethics, 10*(3), 211-219.

Ulrich, P. (1987). *Business ethics and its relationship to business economic reason* (Working Paper #42). Münster, Germany: Academic Society for Marketing and Management.

CHAPTER 3

BUSINESS ETHICS TEACHING

Working to Develop
an Effective Learning Climate

Ronald R. Sims

INTRODUCTION

No matter how many years I have been teaching I never forget that a crucial component of teaching business ethics for effective learning is developing the necessary learning environment. And that often means remembering that the learning environment is more about how a classroom or other environment *feels* that what it looks like. I have found that content, context, conduct, and character are key dimensions of designing a business ethics course, each dimension having its own pedagogical consideration. In my efforts to develop, attend to, and manage the learning environment in my business ethics courses I find myself answering the following questions: What is the appropriate context or learning environment I should try to foster? What is the process or conduct or model to use in developing, attending to, and managing the learning environment? What is the character of my role as the business ethics teacher given the classroom learning environment? What are

Experiences in Teaching Business Ethics
pp. 53–82
Copyright © 2011 by Information Age Publishing

53

some of the process issues that I must attend to and manage throughout the business ethics course that support a learning climate learning environment that promotes respect, student involvement, clear expectations, and rigor?

This chapter provides my answers to these questions as I reflect on how I continue to try to develop a learning environment that facilitates learning in my business ethics courses. More specifically, the chapter discusses the importance of the "psychological contract" to my efforts to develop an effective learning environment in my business ethics courses. A basic premise of this chapter is that in my role as a business ethics teacher I must work to create the kind of learning environment most responsive to my own and to my students' needs. The model I use for managing my own and student expectations, and contributions during my business ethics course is also presented. In my experience, the model creates learning environments that facilitate shared responsibility for the learning process between me as the business ethics teacher and my students

HOW DO I DEVELOP THE LEARNING ENVIRONMENT IN MY BUSINESS ETHICS COURSE?

In my role as a business ethics teacher I am responsible for managing the content, process, and learning environment within the various courses I teach on ethics. I view content as the material to be covered and the general sequence in which it will be presented, while process encompasses the approaches by which that content is delivered. And, environment is the physical and psychological surroundings for the business ethics course.

I spend the first hours of a business ethics course trying to develop a sense of community and deciding how to use experience, and the interactions of students for maximum learning. For me the business ethics course has to become a *learning community*—a community in which students support one another, are open with one another during our discussions about their feelings and opinions related various ethical issues, situations, and so on, and are willing to confront or compare different opinions, responses, insights, and experiences. In my view, learning to learn is important enough (and difficult enough) for students that I must commit to spending quality time trying to systematically building such an environment. A key aspect of this sort of learning environment in my business ethics course involves students learning how to utilize their experiences and those of others effectively.

Important Aspects of the Learning Environment in My Business Ethics Course

A critical aspect of any of my teaching business ethics efforts is considering the learning environment I want to create. Hiemstra (1991) defined a learning environment as "all of the physical surroundings, psychological or emotional conditions, and social or cultural influences affecting the growth and development of an adult engaged in an educational environment" (p. 8). Different writers have focused on different aspects of the environment that promote and encourage learning. Some have stressed the importance of the physical setting. For example, Vosko (1991) described the impact of seating arrangements, sight lines, and equipment on learning. Other writers have emphasized the importance of psychological or interpersonal variables related to learning environments. I have also suggested that teaching business ethics efforts should "take place in a setting conducive to safe, honest interpersonal exchanges, to uninhibited self-exploration, and to hopefulness that the desired change can be made" (Sims, 2002). Knox (1986) highlighted the need for a balance between support and challenge and defined a challenging environment as one that "is problem-centered, is neither boring nor threatening, promotes worthwhile educational achievement, and helps participants (students) understand the problem situation, as well as the problem, and strategies for formulating effective solutions" (p. 132). Knowles (1980) suggested that an educative environment should include "respect for personality, participation in decision making, freedom of expression and availability of information; and mutuality of responsibility in defining goals, planning and conducting activities, and evaluating" (p. 67).

The learning environment model I most often use in my business ethics course that I will discuss in this chapter differs in some key respects from the stereotype of a traditional business course and is based on the following. First, it is based on a psychological contract of reciprocity. Reciprocity is a basic building block of human interaction which emphasizes that relationships based on a mutual and equal balance of giving and getting thrive and grow: those based on unequal exchange very quickly decay. This process of reciprocity is particularly important for creating an effective learning environment when teaching business ethics because many initial assumptions about learning run counter to it. Learning is most often considered a process of getting rather than giving.

I view the process of getting rather than giving as most evident in conceptions of my role as the teacher and students' roles. Traditionally, faculty members give and students get. Yet, in my experience for successful learning to take place, both giving and getting by me and the students is critical. In getting there is the opportunity to incorporate new ideas and perspectives. In giving there is the opportunity to integrate and apply these new perspectives, and to practice their use.

A second characteristic of the learning environment model I use in my business ethics course is that it is experience based. The motivation for learning comes not from my dispensation of rewards but from problems and opportunities arising from the student's own life and classroom experiences. Third, the learning environment in my course emphasizes personal application. Since the students' learning needs arise from their own experience, then for me the main goal of learning about ethics is for students to be able to apply new knowledge, skills, and abilities to the solution of the kinds of business situations they will encounter in the real world.

Fourth, the learning environment is individualized and self-directed. Just as every student's experience is different, so are each student's learning goals and learning style. A major concern of mine in the management of the learning environment in my business ethics course is to effectively organize resources in such a way that they are maximally responsive to what each student wants to learn and how they learn it. Essential to achievement of this kind of learning environment in my course is the students' willingness to take responsibility for the achievement of their learning objectives. I believe that one of the most important of the students' responsibilities is evaluating how well they are getting the learning resources they need to achieve their goals and alerting the learning community (me and other students) to problems when they arise, since they are in the best position to make this judgment.

Finally, in my course it is important for me to enhance the learning environment by integrating learning and living. So, for me there are two goals in the learning process. One is for students to learn the specifics of the business ethics subject matter. The other is to for students to learn their own strengths and weaknesses as a learner (i.e., learning how to learn from experience). When the process has worked well, students finish the course or their ethics learning experience not only with new intellectual insights, but also with an increased understanding of themselves (i.e., learning style). This understanding of learning strengths and weaknesses helps students in the application of what has been learned to real-world situations and provides a framework for continuing learning. In this instance, learning is no longer a special activity reserved for the classroom; it has become an integral and explicit part of the work world my students will encounter upon graduation.

The remainder of this chapter describes my experience in contracting with students to build the learning environment and to share responsibility for the learning process in my business ethics course(s). A main goal of mine is to use the model described in the next section as a catalyst for conversations among me as the business ethics teacher and students directed toward building and maintaining a highly effective learning community.

Learning Environment and Psychological Contracts

In my effort to build an effective learning environment during my business ethics courses it has always been important for me to start with an understanding of the nature of the psychological contract and how such a contract influences student functioning in the course. A psychological contract is implicitly formed between the student and the course or class of which he or she is a member. It also deals with my own and the students' expectations of the course and the contributions for us both to meet those expectations. However, before going any further I will provide a clearer definition of the psychological contract in the context of the course I teach in business ethics.

When students decide to participate in my business ethics course, they enter into a psychological contract with me as the instructor, their fellow students and the business school. A psychological contract is a set of unwritten reciprocal expectations between the student and me or the course. It is the foundation of the link between me and the student because learning is based upon an implicit exchange of beliefs and expectations about the actions of the student vis-á-vis me as the business ethics teacher/course and the course/me vis-á-vis the student. As such, the psychological contract involves expectations about learning conditions, requirements of my business ethics course, and the level of effort (participation) to be expended by the student in the course.

Unlike a legal contract, a psychological contract in my business ethics course defines a dynamic, changing relationship that may continually change and be renegotiated. Often the students and I may have different levels of expectation clarity, since some of the items may have been explicitly discussed and others, only inferred. Important aspects of the contract are not always formally agreed upon.

Expectations are sometimes unstated, implicit premises about the relationship. My contributions, such as a sense of challenge in the business ethics course, and student contributions, such as active participation, are expected and in some instances are not consciously weighed. Yet the contract is a reality that has many implications for the effectiveness of the business ethics course and students' satisfaction. If my business ethics course is filled with students who feel "cheated" and expect far more than they get then the course is headed for trouble. The student who feels my course does not meet his or her expectations in my experience becomes a stumbling block to a productive learning environment. On the other hand, if my business ethics course demands total compliance to peripheral norms such as manner of dress or dedication to one particular ethical theory that is in favor with me then this will stifle student creativity, sharing and participation.

Establishing Reciprocal Expectations and Contributions

The dynamic quality of the psychological contract developed in my business ethics course means that students' and my expectations and contributions influence one another. Students entering into the psychological contract in my course are expected to contribute their productive and participative capacity directed toward achieving the course's purpose. High expectations on my part have to be outlined in the course syllabi and discussed in the first few classes if I intend to achieve the objective of increased student contributions (i.e., class participation in the form of listening, self-reflection and sharing), and great contributions will likewise raise expectations. For me the questions become, "How can I teach the students so that I maximize their individual contributions?" and "How can I create a learning environment that meets students' expectations and our norms?" For the student the question is, "How can this business ethics course increase my learning, knowledge or performance, personal growth, and ethical development?"

Entering my business ethics course for the first time is very much like the first day on a new job. In my experience, the typical orientation for students in a traditional business ethics course is one-sided. Most communication flows from the instructor to the student: "These are our policies, procedures, and expectations as outlined in the syllabus."

One effect of this one-sided process is to cause students to feel that the professor is much more powerful than they are as individuals. So instead of trying to formulate and articulate their own expectations, students often say what they think the professor wants to hear. Another effect is the tendency to over-socialize students. Students' feelings of powerlessness often lead them to be more passive than they might ordinarily be in the situation, and in my experience this can contribute to many of the fears students may already bring to a business ethics course.

It is important that I do not read passivity as a sign that the students want and need more direction and control. This situation can create a feedback cycle that I find in the long run operates to the detriment of the relationship between the students and me and the learning environment I am trying to build in the course. It is important that I maintain a balanced psychological contract which is necessary for a harmonious relationship between the students and me during the course. Since the psychological contract is entered into as soon as the students enter my course, whether or not the students' expectations about the contract are met is crucial to the tenor of the relationship established with me as the instructor (i.e., course). For example, if students take my business ethics course with the expectation that their psychological contract included some input in evaluating my performance only to find out that my view differed, then the student is likely to suffer considerable dissatisfaction with the course, based primarily on the perception that their psychological contract has been violated by me.

The violation of the psychological contract by me can signal to the students that we no longer share (or never shared) a common set of values or goals or norms for expected behavior. Once this happens, in my experience, I know I can expect a breakdown of communication between me and the students, a failure in mutual understanding, increasing levels of frustration (and subsequent emotional responses) on both of our parts, and a learning environment less conducive to learning. This is something that I do my best to avoid *ever* happening!

In preparing for and planning my business ethics course I constantly have to be sensitive to the reality that students do not find the learning environment in the course dull, boring, and unexciting. I have failed to create the appropriate learning environment if students sit passively in class, uninvolved in their own learning, and work half-heartedly to meet the course's expectations. Their own expectations for learning, involvement, and stimulation will go unsatisfied, in large measure because I may never have given them the opportunity to make such expectations explicit. I have to work hard to make sure that this is never the case. When the students and I can initially share our expectations and goals and can establish an environment where a shared responsibility is maintained, then the result has been a greater chance of meeting everyone's objectives or learning and teaching needs.

Learning: A Dynamic Process

It has been important for me to remember that the psychological contract is not set forever in the initial business ethics class meeting. As mentioned at the outset, I believe the initial class meeting represents a starting point for me to begin to establish a dynamic learning process that will necessitate continued discussion and updating of mutual expectations throughout the life of the course. The remainder of this chapter will introduce two models I use in my business ethics course for thinking about a dynamic learning process that I have found helps create an "early warning system" for me to identify problems and reinforce a set of norms for the course (i.e. learning community) that will encourage students to evaluate their own learning progress and to sound alarms for me when learning objectives are not being met. I think the psychological contract is perhaps the central determinant in whether my business ethics course is effective, generating student commitment, loyalty, and enthusiasm for the course and its goals. I believe this depends to a large measure on two conditions: (1) the degree to which the students' expectations of what the business ethics course will provide them and what they must give to the course match what my expectations for the course and what they will give and get; and (2) assuming there is agreement between me and the students on expectations, what is actually exchanged? An example of such an exchange includes active participation and commitment by students during the course in order to enhance their learning, personal growth, and development. Figure 3.1 illustrates the importance of the match between expectations and contributions in my business ethics course. The more students establish psychological contracts that are made up of matches in expectations, the greater will be their satisfaction with my business ethics course.

Often students are not clear on what they want or need, or what they are capable of contributing initially during my business ethics course (I have recognized over the years that when this happens it is often the

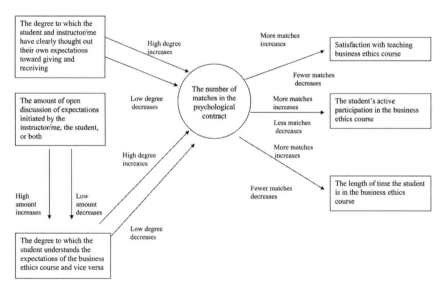

Figure 3.1.   The importance of the match between teaching business ethics contributions and inducements in the psychological contract.

result of my failure to show sufficient interest in students' expectations). Fortunately, with experience and reflection I try to be as clear as possible both in the course syllabus and during my first few classes as to my expectations of the students. So, I make an extra effort to cover in the syllabus and talk to students about as many areas as possible. Mismatches can occur by accident, but they should not occur because of neglect on my part.

What is needed then is for me to create as many opportunities as possible for students to carefully consider all areas of expectations for the course in order to overcome the problem of clarity. This occurs because I make it a point to have students consider the importance of thinking about and discussing our mutual expectations. My effectiveness in teaching a business ethics course is enhanced when I work toward increasing the number of matches in the psychological contract depicted in Figure 3.1.

A MODEL FOR MANAGING PSYCHOLOGICAL CONTRACTS

Sherwood and Glidewell (1971) have developed a simple but powerful model, the pinch model, which describes the dynamic quality of psychological contracts and suggests ways of maintaining the potentially dysfunctional consequences of shifting expectations. I use a modified version of the model (depicted in Figure 3.2) in teaching my business ethics course.

The model provides me with a framework for the continuous management of the psychological contract in the day-to-day work or classroom setting in my business ethics course. The model, which has often been referred to as the "pinch model of contract negotiation," is cyclical and includes four phases which I can easily apply toward the development of more matches in the psychological contract in my course. I have adapted the four phases to develop an effective learning environment in my business ethics course:

1. Phase I involves sharing learning information and negotiating expectations by me and students during open discussions.
2. When properly conducted, Phase I leads to mutual commitment to defined roles by both me and students.
3. With commitment and role definition by both me and the students, actual implementation (i.e., teaching) of the course results in a positive learning environment, stability and productivity (i.e., student learning).

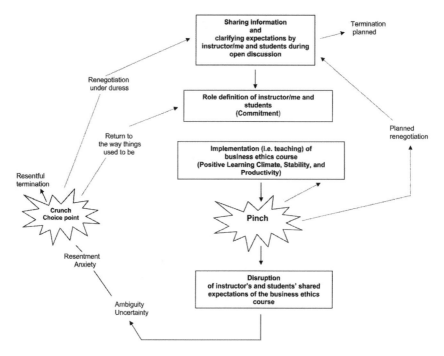

Figure 3.2.   Model for managing psychological contracts in my business ethics course.

4.   Often the emergent and individualized nature of the learning process in the course will inevitably lead to a new state of disruption.

The first stage of the learning relationship is characterized by open discussion between me and the students through sharing of information and a negotiation of expectations. A simple way to understand the first stage is to consider the following: Suppose that students voluntarily taking my business ethics elective course were informed by me at the first class meeting that there would only be two graded written assignments. The students expect two written assignments. However, at the end of the third class I inform the students that I have decided that a third graded written assignment will be required. If this difference in expectations cannot be resolved at this point, I and the students may part ways (i.e., "I can't trust what Prof. Sims says."). In this instance students have found out immediately that they may have an irresolvable mismatch. Or suppose the students were expecting that my course would rely primarily on my lecturing only to find out on the first day of the class that an experiential learning approach would be the predominant pedagogical approach used in the course. This presents an immediate mismatch that may be further compounded by the fact that active participation by the students in class discussions and a service learning component will be key components of successful performance in the course.

Assuming that both the students and I hear enough of what we expect to hear from the other, we will end up working toward making a joint commitment and heading off any real mismatch. If commitment and an understanding of roles and ground rules occurs, the students and I can both expect to experience a positive learning environment and move into a period of stability and productivity as we get down to work during actual implementation (teaching and learning) of the course.

Even with the best of intentions, assuming full sharing of initial expectations (which is often unlikely), I realize that changes are likely to occur over time. These changes can and do take a variety of forms but the consequence is the same—there is a disruption of shared expectations. Since the "rules" that were agreed to initially have been upset, I or my students (or both) experience heightened uncertainty, which invariably results in heightened anxiety. Human nature being what it is, the students and I then have to invest energy in reducing this anxiety. Typically, what should happen at this point is an effort to return to the way things used to be. This usually requires my attempting to clarify the misunderstanding, resolve the conflict, and renew the commitment. To the extent that both the students and I remain unsatisfied in this cycle, the result is invariably some form of termination—psychological (apathy: "I'll be darned if I'm going to do any more than I'm required to do for the remainder of this course") or physical (i.e., students no longer actively participate in discussions or actually withdraw from the course).

At the point of anxiety, I find that it is much more productive if I cycle back to the starting point and test whether or not any new information is now available. Given the dynamic, changing nature of most relationships (and especially the relationships between students and professors), it is very likely that a new psychological contract is appropriate and realistic. If I discover that new, changed expectations cannot be successfully negotiated, termination is still a possibility, but in my experience this is an extreme and I do my best to avoid this at all costs. The critical difference, however, in this condition is that the termination is an agreed-upon joint decision versus a unilateral decision based upon untested assumptions.

I must realize that such a disruption, depending on its seriousness, will inevitably lead to some degree of uncertainty, anxiety, and discomfort. The discomfort can in turn lead to a number of possible outcomes depending on how it is handled. As noted earlier, it can lead to termination, withdrawal or avoidance by students of the course altogether. It can lead to a kind of conservative return to the way things were at the price of avoiding new learning opportunities (i.e., being open to listening and sharing with others) and resources (i.e., myself and fellow classmates) or it can lead to a renegotiation by a resharing of the new information and expectations that have been generated as a result of the disruption.

Over the years, I have also realized that there is also a natural tendency to ignore a host of early warning signs ("pinches") which signal a potentially disruptive situation. "I don't have time to test this issue with the instructor or student." "If I raise this issue with Prof. Sims, he will think I'm just complaining so I'll ignore it." There is another approach to achieving a positive learning environment and stability in the psychological contract without all the unpleasant side effects of disruptions. This approach is called planned renegotiation and is based on the development of group norms for the course that allows the students and me to announce signs ("pinches") that we feel signal an imminent disruption. These signs—when noted during, say, at the beginning of my business ethics course (the stage of positive learning environment, stability, and productivity)—can provide data that I have been able to use for preventative renegotiation of expectations, which may avoid costly disruption of an effective learning process. Some of the examples of "pinches" that I have found signal the need for renegotiation in my business ethics course are:

- A student feels bored or tuned out of a discussion.
- I sense that preparation assignments haven't been completed.
- Classes don't start on time or go past the designated end time.
- Students are not actively participating in experiential learning exercises, sharing personal experiences or speaking up in discussions.
- A student feels pressured to share an ethically-related experience before he or she is ready.

Dealing with the pinches head on allows both me and the students to conduct the renegotiation process in a planned manner without the heat of emotion that can accompany a disruption. (It's like an automatic safety valve on a boiler.) When students and I let each other know when we feel these subtle pinches, it is then possible for us to make changes and minor adjustments without pressure, anxiety and a crisis atmosphere.

HOW I CLARIFY THE PSYCHOLOGICAL CONTRACT?

Creating a safe and trusting environment where students are willing to share their experiences is essential for the depth of personal learning that can occur when one grapples with ethical issues is in my view critical to the success of my business ethics course. The next few sections offers an example of how I try to clarify the psychological contract and create a course and classroom learning environment conducive to sharing beginning with the first class in several of my business ethics courses.

Developing the Course and Classroom Learning Environment Beginning With the First Class

Once I have decided I want to create a learning environment conducive to self-reflection, listening, and sharing, it is important for me to start the first class with in-class and independent experiences to support my activities. In my own business ethics courses, I plan activities to coincide directly with the kind of course and classroom learning environment I hope to create. For example, one way I begin the first class is with a familiar exercise of introducing classmates, which I incorporate into an ethics theme. I ask students to think of a situation in which they were confronted with an ethical dilemma and give them about 5 minutes to jot down some notes about their experience and their feelings. I then ask them to pair with someone they do not know. (I also pair up with one of the students.) Each pair's task is to introduce themselves to one another and to describe their experiences and feelings related to the ethical dilemma they identified. When they have each told their stories, we convene as a large group and each person introduces his or her partner and describes the partner's ethical dilemma. This is followed by the person being introduced responding to questions about the experience that group members ask.

This exercise sets the stage for many aspects of the learning environment I am trying to create. It engages students in active participation, self-disclosure, and especially, reciprocity, or sharing responsibility for talking about experiences. It provides an opportunity for students to begin to understand their own experiences with ethics (i.e., ethical dilemmas in this situation) and to learn about the experiences and feelings of others. It sets the tone in the class for openness, trust, and interest in one another. And it creates the beginning of feelings of community I want to create within the class.

As I continue in the course, I design several types of opportunities for students to be actively involved in the class sessions. They discuss issues and experiences in dyads, trios, small groups, and as a large group. I usually mix students each time so that they interact with, learn from, experience themselves with, and (we hope) learn to trust a variety of people. Occasionally I group students by like characteristics—for example, by sex, by major, or by occupation—especially since when self-understanding and specific group learning are important.

When I select topics for discussion in the course or for a particular class, I usually integrate or build on some issues raised in the reading assignments with experiences from students' personal and working lives. For example, after reading about cross-cultural ethics, I ask them to discuss, in groups representing various countries or cultures, questions concerning ethical conduct for individual decision makers in multinational corporations. An example of such a question is: "When ethical perspectives, values, and behaviors conflict, whose ethics are right, and how does one resolve the differences?" Students are expected to discuss their responses to the question from both the perspective of the host-country and their own home-country. This compare-and-contrast design supports openness and trust among the students. I then have each group provide a summary of their discussion and feelings to the other groups. This enhances disclosure and risk-taking. It also develops an understanding of the experiences of another group. I also discuss the implications of cross-cultural ethics for the workplace in general and changes that they might need to make in current and future jobs.

An alternative to the first class exercise presented above that I have used at least twice in my own business ethics courses (and will be using again next semester) is offered by Fort and Zollers (1999). Like others (see, i.e., Brinkmann & Sims, 2001), Fort and Zollers acknowledge that there are many stakeholders in the education "business," including accrediting organizations, colleagues, deans, alumni, and future employers (Fort & Zollers, 1996). Because students are affected by academic action and have some insights about how they can best learn it is important to tap into that insight. Fort and Zollers suggests using a "total quality management" (TQM) survey that can show what things are most important to students as they begin the class. The following is an adaptation of the introduction to and the actual survey that I use in my business ethics course (readers interested in the full text should see Fort & Zollers, 1999).

As discussed earlier, I need to establish my expectations/requirements or targeted learning outcomes for my business ethics course periodically to see if they are being met throughout the course as well as at the conclusion of the course. And of course students are one of the stakeholder groups whose requirements and expectations I must meet. The other groups (i.e., school administrators, accrediting agencies, and so on) requirements are partially reflected in my business ethics course materials and topic coverage described in the syllabus. What remains to be communicated are my requirements/expectations for the learning process in my business ethics course. A modified version of Fort and Zollers' first class exercise continues to stimulate my thoughts and ideas, and I follow their basic framework in which I strive to capture my course expectations.

1. Expectations of the professor;
2. Expectations of your fellow students;
3. Expectations of the material;
4. Expectations of yourself; and
5. Expectations—others.

I distribute the survey to the students on the first day of class. The instrument allows students to bring their concerns into the class. The survey asks students to list their expectations for me as the professor (such as being energetic, responsive to students' learning needs, being available, and being prompt about returning assigned work), for the course material (such as being relevant, a resource for later thinking, and manageable in length), for each other (mutual respect, openness, attentive, prepared, and willingness to challenge perspectives), and a final miscellaneous category (such as meeting the ethics teaching expectations for the school!).

I then tabulate the results and, at the next class meeting, inform the students of the most central concerns they have raised in the surveys. The students and I learn what expectations are most important to the class as a whole. These then become the expectations for the course. Like Fort and Zollers I have found that in the few times I have used the TQM survey to date the technique has three immediate benefits:

First, the exercise provides very helpful information to me about what is important to students. If there are particular things that are helpful to students, I am then able to make adjustments to make sure the class learns in the most effective way. Getting this information early is especially important given my commitment to an experiential learning approach to teaching business ethics as I am able to get an early indication of students' receptiveness to this pedagogical approach and the degree to which I will need to supplement the approach with other approaches.

Second, occasionally a student expectation cannot be met. Discussing this right away with students is much appreciated by them and can resolve misunderstandings about the course immediately. For example, it is not unusual for students to come to class believing that they will by the end of the course be able to consult a list of simple dos and don'ts to handle ethical dilemmas. I find that it is important to quickly dispel this belief and reinforce my belief that ethical dilemmas are far more complicated than that. I also use such opportunities to explain that we will be using codes of ethics mainly as broad (and suggestive) normative guidelines for behavior, not as definitive specifications for ethical decision making. Related to this is the expectation that I will be foisting upon them my moral biases and expecting them to adopt my ethical views. Like the ethical dos and don'ts such misunderstandings must be handled early in the course.

Third, the survey sends an early message about the importance of student involvement to the success of the class. I believe that message is emphasized by the respect I show for the students' ideas, as evidenced by using the instrument.

Fort and Zollers (1999) suggest that a follow-up technique is to appoint a group of four or five randomly selected students to conduct an oral in-class assessment of how well the expectations are being met. I have found it useful to appoint other groups of students to take on this responsibility one third and two thirds of the way through the course. This way I am able to get more students involved in the class and course assessment. This group assessment activity also promotes trust in the classroom and sends a valuable message to the students about my respect for and commitment to them.

I encourage you the reader to take the time to read Fort and Zollers's article which offers other valuable insights on (1) "nominating" and "electing" class virtues, and telling personal stories of moral action and (2) how classes can be organized to operate by leading business ethics theories (i.e., social contract, rights, stakeholder, and virtue) that can lead to a "community" seeking and discovering moral truth that can help build a climate of trust in the classroom.

Another option I find useful in developing the psychological contract in my business ethics course is an experiential exercise, "Instructor/Student Interview," adapted from Kolb (1974). It is offered here in the form I actually use.

Instructor/Student Interview: Developing the Psychological Contract

Total time suggested: 1 hour

A. Purpose
The goal of the exercise is to make explicit and share some of the major expectations and obligations between students and instructors. It provides an opportunity for the instructor to find out what the class expects and for the students to learn what the instructor expects.

B. Procedures

Part A: Instructor's Interview of Students
- Step 1: The class forms into groups of four to five persons.
- Step 2: Each group elects one person as representative.

- Step 3: Each group prepares its representative for the interview, and should be sure that they understand the group's position. (See the Suggested Question Guide for Instructor's Interview of Students.)

Time suggested for Steps 1 to 3: 15 minutes

- Step 4: The representatives, one from each group, meet with the instructor. The instructor interviews them about their expectations while the rest of the class observes.

Time suggested for Step 4: 20 minutes

Suggested Question Guide
for Instructor's Interview of Students

1. What are your expectations/objectives for this course?

   a. To learn ethical or moral theories?
   b. To reach some desired level of knowledge?
   c. To learn new skills?
   d. To gain new behaviors?
   e. To get a good grade?
   f. To get required credit hours?

2. How can the instructor best help you to achieve your goals?

   a. By giving lectures?
   b. By assigning and discussing readings?
   c. By giving exams?
   d. By leading seminar discussions?
   e. By relating personal experiences?
   f. By letting you work on your own?
   g. By being a stern task master?
   h. By being warm and supportive?
   i. By providing feedback?

3. How can other class members help you achieve your goals?

   a. By sharing prior experiences?
   b. By participating in group discussions?
   c. By coming to class prepared?
   d. By sharing educational background?
   e. By doing nothing?
   f. By being enthusiastic and supportive?

      g. By being critical (providing feedback)?
      h. By being flattering?
      i. By giving honest appraisals?

4. How should class members be evaluated?

      a. By quizzes, exams, and tests?
      b. By written assignments (essays, journals, personal application assignment (PAAs))?
      c. By instructor?
      d. By peers?
      e. By quantity and quality of work?

5. How should the course/class be motivated and how would you in reality act toward this motivation?

      a. By self-motivation?
      b. By peer pressure?
      c. By instructor pressure?
      d. By class interest?
      e. By grade pressure?

6. What is the best thing that could happen in this class?

Part B: What Do I Want From This Course?

A. Purpose
1. To focus on key goals for this course.
2. To share expectations of what you want from this course.
3. To form a psychological contract for the class.

B. Procedures

- Step 1: Individually complete Column 1 of the Psychological Contract Worksheet.
- Step 2: In small groups, exchange views, achieve consensus in completing Column II of the Worksheet, and develop group responses to the questions.
- Step 3: Each group discusses any questions it would like its representative to ask the instructor. The representative should be sure to understand the group's questions and concerns. (See the Suggested Question Guide for Students' Interview of Instructor.)

Time suggested for Steps 1 to 3: 15 minutes

• Step 4: The representatives, one from each group, interview the instructor to clarify the instructor's expectations of the class.

Time suggested for Step 4: 20 minutes

I have found that it is helpful to incorporate into Step 4 the following: The representatives and the instructor should write on the blackboard a consensus of course expectations/objectives. This will not only reaffirm and support expectations/objectives listed in the syllabus (by allowing the class to come up with the expectations/objectives), but will allow the students and instructor to delete or add other expectations/objectives that they feel may be important to the learning process in the business ethics course.

The Psychological Contract Worksheet

Issues	Column I Individual Responses	Column II Group Responses
1. What were your expectations for this course when you enrolled in it?		
2. What do you expect to get out of this course?		
3. What will be the most enjoyable part of this course?		
4. What skills must you work on?		

Suggested Question Guide for Student's Interview Of Instructor

You may ask the instructor any questions you feel are relevant to effective learning. Some areas you may want to discuss are:

1. How do people learn?
2. What are expectations about attendance?
3. What is the philosophy of evaluation? How are students evaluated?
4. What is the instructor's role in the class?
5. What stereotypes about students are held?
6. Is there anything else that you feel is important?

Part C: Identifying and Establishing Norms

- Step 1: Meeting in the class session, discuss the following:
  1. Identify the pivotal and peripheral norms that are being established.
  2. Which of these norms are functional or dysfunctional to the class?
  3. Which of these norms would you like to change?
  4. Do you have any additional behaviors you would like to see become norms?
  5. How much trust is being developed among students, and between students and instructor?

- Step 2: For the norms you would like to change, make some specific plans for the changes.

Time suggested for Steps 1 and 2: 15 minutes

Creation of a classroom environment that encourages students' sharing of experiences is important both for developing trust but also for setting the groundwork for dialogue, good moral conversation, conversational learning, and debriefing the business ethics education experiences. The "Instructor/Student Interview" exercise is also an effective vehicle for debriefing various learning activities in the business ethics course.

It is important that I understand there are times when students' and my own expectations are congruous. To communicate expectations, I spend time discussing with students the targeted learning objectives, purpose or expectations of the business ethics course, learning needs, and the strategies to be used to develop students' knowledge, skills, abilities, and attitudes. This means that I go beyond simply including my expectations in the syllabus. Typical questions that I ask students to help identify expectations throughout the business ethics course are:

1. What two or three things are most important to you in this course or class?
2. Do you feel that your learning needs are being fully addressed in this course? Why or why not?
3. If you had complete freedom to reconstruct this course, what changes would you make? Why?
4. How would you describe the positive and negative aspects of this or previous business ethics classes or experiential learning exercises in the course?

5. How well does/has the business school's course(s) meet/met your personal needs?
6. What do you think this course expects of you at this point?
7. What have you learned are the objectives or expectations of this class or course?

While not all encompassing, these questions can help me define changing expectations and the current fit between the students' and my own expectations. I find it helpful to consider the question "How well does the course meet your personal needs?" If the answer is primarily negative, modification of the course, improved management of, or some change in teaching/learning methods used may be necessary. However, a positive answer may indicate that I and the students should move on with the learning effort.

MORE ON MY ROLE IN ATTENDING TO AND MANAGING THE LEARNING PROCESS

Faculty and students have specific roles that they play in business ethics courses. As evident in the discussion in this chapter to this point, in my view, in the beginning of an ethics course (class, module, or experiential learning exercise) I must take on an active role in discussing the norms that will characterize the learning environment. That is why I place such an emphasis in my courses on mutual respect, openness, trust, and the values of listening and sharing one's own experiences, and learning from the experiences of others. As part of building a positive learning environment in my course, my primary responsibility is also to design learning situations and experiences, encourage self-understanding, facilitate understanding of others' perspectives and experiences, heighten appreciation for the impact of ethics in one's personal life, and foster critical thinking about organizations and business ethics.

The way that works best for me to do this is by facilitating students' learning by engaging them in active or experiential learning experiences in which their participation is central to the learning processes. I focus on discussing and reflecting on real-world issues, readings, and films; sharing personal experiences of mine and the students; and participating in experiential learning exercises. Here my role is to design classroom activities, present relevant background information, engage students in thinking and active participation, and then support their learning. And, as stressed earlier I have to actively participate with the students in the process as a learner myself.

I do my best to serve as a role model for the behaviors I want students to demonstrate in class. When I share my personal values and ethical experiences I: (a) demonstrate the safeness of relating a personal experience, (b) which allows students to see my humaneness, and (c) this often sparks ideas for students to reflect on their own values and experiences.

I model caring for and respecting students. Modeling my own vulnerabilities, openness, self-disclosure, and risk-taking helps make the learning environment safer for students to take their own risks. But my modeling these behaviors does raise questions about the extent of my openness and personal risk-taking. I am cautious as to not alienate students whose values and attitudes differ from my own. Again, I need to be sensitive to the fact that as the professor I will be viewed as the authority figure but I cannot let this perception negatively impact students' openness. I have to be able to remain detached enough to support the students as needed and to remain neutral if any disagreements should emerge. Managing the degree of openness is always an ongoing challenge for me in my business ethics course.

I also must fulfill my role as an evaluator. I never forget that I am responsible for assigning students' grades for their work and for the course. In many business schools evaluation is often equated with measuring performance on examinations. Indeed, if the professor has presented a highly structured unit on statistics or accounting, a pencil and paper test may well be an appropriate choice to assess how well the learning objectives have been met. If, however, the learning objective is one like I have in my course for students to develop the ability to make well-informed ethical judgments, evaluation is more complex than simply measuring the ability to master a body of factual knowledge.

My role as an evaluator or assessor influences my behavior. I find that it is important for me to assure students that I will not grade then on their ethics experiences or their "correct" views, values, and attitudes. Instead, I evaluate students on their class participation, their impact on the learning community, their willingness to examine and share values, their openness to new ideas and thinking, their willingness to examine the impact of their behavior, values and attitudes on others, and their application and integration of the class experiences and reading material. In other words, I assess students on the quality and impact of their participation and writing, rather than the nature of their ideas or opinions.

I continually monitor the boundaries between being a leader and a participant in my course. My role as leader lends expertise, respect, and credibility to the work I do in my business ethics course. When I set the stage and step aside to let students explore their own learning, I am participating actively with students in some sense as peers without the concern of my approval or disapproval. When I participate in the learning, students see me as more like them—open and growing. Students learn to be more open in my presence, and they experience my modeling of desired learning behaviors, such as self-reflection and self-disclosure. In the end, my active participation in my business ethics course adds to the learning experiences of students.

The primary role of students in my business ethics course, for example, is to be what can be termed a self-directed learner. A self-directed learner does not operate as a passive receiver of information, but takes responsibility for his or her own learning and the achievement of learning outcomes. The traditional professor-student divide becomes increasingly blurred in my course as the student learner proactively participates in the business ethics learning process.

As noted earlier, my role is one of a facilitator and resource to be tapped, as required by the student. Ultimately the student becomes capable of not only identifying what resources and skills are needed to achieve the course objectives, but also of applying these resources and skills to real world situations. When taking on such a role in my course, for the students the learning is less one of something being done to them and becomes more of an experience in which they educate themselves about business ethics.

The achievement of self-direction requires the development of a cooperative learning environment, which I hope students perceive as being democratic, flexible, challenging, and most importantly, nonthreatening in the course. This requires that I break down barriers to learning and self-direction that may be present. These include barriers created by the student during the course (wrong choice of learning approach, poor motivation, lack of confidence), those barriers that the course itself may indirectly create (lack of flexibility, lack of direction and guidance, poor course structure), and barriers that the student brings to the course (poor learning skills, previous bad learning experiences).

Another critical role for the students in my course is to become "learning self-aware," that is, to have an appreciation and understanding of how they learn, their own learning capabilities, and the outcomes they wish to achieve in my business ethics course. I expect that such an awareness exhibits itself not only during my course, but more importantly becomes part of the students' pursuit of life long learning.

In partnership I do my best to facilitate business ethics learning and I believe students should actively contribute to the learning. Thus, I and my students must view the learning not as a passive process in which knowledge is absorbed, but as an active process in which learning is "constructed" by the student.

Finally, my job is to use the students' experiences, abilities, motives and expectations or objectives to help them make more sense of the business ethics material and to integrate the learning into their thinking and behavior. Interactive and small-group activities are carefully monitored by me and I am vigorously engaged throughout the course, which in my experience promotes strong, impactful, and relevant learning.

ISSUES THAT OVERLAP WITH DEVELOPING A POSITIVE LEARNING ENVIRONMENT IN MY BUSINESS ETHICS COURSE

There are a number of other issues that overlap with my efforts to develop a positive learning environment in my business ethics course. These are issues that I also pay attention to in my business ethics course and are briefly highlighted in the remainder of this chapter. The issues include: teaching business ethics strategies, controversial or "hot button" topics, student critiques of course content, conflict in the classroom, and building rapport.

Teaching Business Ethics Strategies

Students bring an array of learning styles to a business ethics course. So, if I rely on a small repertoire of pedagogical strategies, I may provide effective instruction for only a small subset of those in my course. It is important that I am honest with myself on my preferred teaching or ped-agogical strategy (which happens to be an experiential learning approach). I need to consider alternative techniques that will help all the students learn more effectively. If I typically have a reliance on experien-tial learning exercises I remind myself that I need to consider giving mini-lectures, using cases, and so on to balance out the teaching strategies I end up using in my course.

"Hot Button" or Controversial Topics

Teaching business ethics means that I have to be prepared to deal with "hot button" or controversial topics which always arise in any of the fol-lowing unintended outcomes: (a) verbal altercations between individual students or groups of students, (b) silence from students who fear conflict or feel intimidated, (c) the assertion and perpetuation of false stereotypes or problematic assumptions or views, or (d) the expression of offensive speech or charges. In my experience, there are no easy answers for deal-ing with these situations when they occur and especially given that the topic of ethics or business ethics is very often a highly charged subject in itself. I have found that where appropriate it is best for me to work toward the prevention of these occurrences by investing time in the planning process.

When working with a particular controversial topic (i.e., racism, sexism, cultural differences, etc.), I find it best for me to try to anticipate possible responses and how I might address differing yet passionate views on that topic. I also have to plan strategies that provide structure for these discussions and that foster the students' ability to express their own ideas well while also increasing their ability to listen to and learn from others. In the interest of free speech I encouraged students to honestly share their views during our discussions. This means that I need to be prepared, however, to correct inaccuracies, extreme viewpoints, stereotypes, and challenge students' assumptions when comments are shared. At times, it is a difficult task to reconcile the tension between challenging say, offensive speech which occurs during heated debates on an ethical topic, and not suppressing free speech or students' desire to be actively engaged in in-class dialogue or conversations. I have to consider my response to various levels of emotion in the classroom and use this awareness to inform my course planning.

Establishing agreed upon guidelines or norms early in the course via the psychological contract continues to be an important aspect of productive discussions in my course. When norms or guidelines are established early, there is still the need for me to periodically remind students of the rules throughout the semester or during particular in-class exercises, especially if their behavior suggests that they are ignoring them. If I fail to establish such rules or expectations at the beginning of my course, it is doubly hard to establish them when a problem becomes apparent later in the course.

I have also found that it is quite helpful, at the beginning of the course and as part of establishing a positive learning climate to focus on group processes. Activities and assignments during the first weeks of the course center on getting to know each student and for students to get to know one another and me. Establishing rules for classroom dialogues, building a trusting and open climate, modeling appropriate behavior during dialogues and conversations, and giving students the opportunity to practice these behaviors with topics that are not explosive or fearful are in my experience important for positive dialogue and conversational learning in my business ethics course. When students and I engage in these behaviors early on, when a problem does arise, I am in a better position to address the problem by discussing the norms and expected appropriate behaviors on an as needed basis.

Providing Opportunities for Student Critiques
of the Business Ethics Course Content

As discussed earlier, creating a safe and trusting learning environment is conducive to effectively teaching business ethics in my view. And part of that learning environment includes a focus on the following:

- *Creating a classroom climate that encourages and expects questions about and critiques of the content (and process) of my business ethics course.* Such a learning environment helps to create a norm of critical thinking that I find facilitates the learning process for all students during the course. In my experience, as students share their critiques with the total group or class, other students benefit by being exposed to different interpretations, perspectives, and concerns regarding the material, activities, and experiential learning exercises I use in the course. This learning environment also provides an opportunity for students to add to the course content by recommending specific ethics-related topics, subjects and issues related to my overall targeted learning outcomes for the course.

- *Making decisions about when to devote unanticipated time to discussions to deal with issues raised by students that pertain to content or process.* These issues, which may deal with an ethics-related topic or cultural perspective on an ethics issue, for example, are an equally important part of my business ethics course. I find that it is best to be honest about my lack of knowledge on a particular ethics issue or topic, acknowledge students' points, and make an effort to secure information about the students' points to share with the total group or class in a future session. It is also important for me to emphasize that everyone can be a teacher and that I, like the students, can learn from them. I have also found that it is important to ask students to send me e-mail messages, talk with me during office hours, or drop notes in my mailbox as concerns about course content arise. I find that it is especially important for me to make every effort to address these issues or explain to students why they will not be addressed.

- *Being open to students' reactions to the course material, even when I feel uncomfortable with the manner in which they are expressed.* It also best for me to be prepared for students to publicly challenge viewpoints about particular ethics topics or issues that appear in the course readings or other learning activities. Some students react strongly upon hearing what they perceive to be different views or beliefs or values expressed both by me and their fellow students. I have found myself teaching a business ethics course that has the reputation (from the students' perspective) of being full of controversy and conflict or highly charged content.

- Creating a positive learning experience for students can be challenging. In this situation, it is most important for me to be open to the perspectives students share. Giving serious consideration to students' views that are in the "minority" also encourages them to respond honestly about issues and to think more broadly about issues. This does not, however, mean that I have to agree with the students' views or feel that their views are above critique.

- *Giving serious consideration to students' requests for alternative materials (or learning activities) when the course materials used are perceived as overly biased (i.e., American viewpoint of ethics is right or preferable versus one from another part of the world or culture) or include ethical theories that don't equally portray competing views).* Changes in my course material are sometimes justified. If I receive criticisms about materials or activities, I make it clear to students that the criticism should be accompanied by specific recommendations of alternative materials or activities.

Classroom Conflict

Conflict in the classroom is inevitable when one considers the highly-charged or controversial nature of the subject of ethics or business ethics. In an effort to effectively manage such a classroom it is important that I work to build an inclusive learning environment in which students and I work together to create and sustain a positive learning environment in which everyone feels safe, supported, and encouraged to express their views and concerns. In this environment, I do my best to view the content from a variety of perspectives and varied experiences of a range of individuals and—where appropriate—groups. I present my course content with the goal of reducing students' experiences of marginalization and, wherever possible, help them understand that their experiences, values, and perspectives influence how they learn and grow. The following are some specific things I focus on to manage or address conflict in my business ethics course:

- *Respond to conflict in a manner that helps students become aware of the "learning moment" the conflict provides.* I try to facilitate heated discussions or debates in a manner that does not result in hostility among students and a sustained sense of bad feeling during the course. I am able to avoid these outcomes by encouraging students to tie their feelings and conflicts to the course material and by looking for underlying meanings and principles that might get buried in the process of conflict during the course. In my experience, students appreciate it when tensions between individuals and groups are recognized and effectively addressed in my course.

- *Recognize student feelings and concerns about conflict.* Students enter my course with different levels of experience and comfort with conflict. It is important that I normalize the experience of conflict in my course, particularly given the reality that business ethics often focuses on controversial topics or issues. I am able to accomplish this through explicit discussion of student experiences with conflict and the use of structured discussion exercises.

- *Maintain the role of facilitator.* One of the challenges of teaching business ethics is maintaining my role as the facilitator under a variety of conditions. For example, I too can get caught up in expressing my own perspective in heated discussions or can become overly silent in discussions that go beyond my own knowledge base or experience or comfort level. While these responses are understandable, such role abdication on my part as the business ethics professor can create chaos in the course or force students to fill in the facilitator role I abdicated in the course. In order to avoid this outcome, I reflect on my own responses to conflict and take corrective action as appropriate.

Building Rapport in the Course

In concluding this section, it is my belief that perhaps nothing is more important to good dynamics in any business ethics course than rapport between the professor and students. Some behaviors that help me promote the establishment of good rapport include:

- willingness to share personal experiences;
- willingness to admit uncertainties;
- openness to new ideas;
- ability to suspend judgment of others;
- ability to listen carefully to others' statements; and
- tolerance of opposite points of view.

As you the reader should recognize, building rapport is the same as creating a positive learning environment. This is a critical component to effectively teaching business ethics.

CONCLUSION

The psychological contract is an implicit, yet important agreement between students, business ethics teachers and a business school. It should specify what students and I expect to give and receive from each other in a business ethics course. The process goes to the heart of motivation, productivity, learning satisfaction, involvement, and the creation and management of the learning environment. There are a number of general points that result from me as the business ethics teacher taking the time to develop the learning climate in a business ethics course. And, I believe these are important things you the reader should take away from this chapter.

First, the development of a psychological contract early in the learning process *is* very important, and as such is worth carefully managing. Second, what I don't know *can* hurt me. A clear understanding of my own and students' expectations in a business ethics course will help form better contracts. Third, the key to contract formulation is achieving a match or a fit, *not* getting more, or the best, or whatever. Fourth, if students and I have one or more very central basic mismatches, that may be counterproductive us both in my business ethics course. Finally, with the development of matches in the psychological contract students begin the process of self-directed learning and setting personal directions for learning throughout my course.

Teaching a business ethics course, with clearly defined targeted learning objectives, should come close to meeting the expectations of students. Likewise, as a business ethics teacher I should have the knowledge, skills, and abilities to help create sound psychological contracts that will develop a positive learning environment in my business ethics course. In the final analysis, the payoff for me as a business ethics teacher depends on my awareness of the importance of psychological contracts, and on my creativity in finding solutions for better management of the learning environment and a number of issues that can impact the teaching learning process. In conclusion, I continue to be challenged and rewarded in my effort to create a positive learning environment in my business ethics course—an environment where students, the business school and I are all rewarded.

REFERENCES

Brinkmann, J., & Sims, R.R. (2001). Stakeholder-sensitive business ethics teaching. *Teaching Business Ethics*, 5, 171-193

Fort, T. L., & Zoellers, F. E. (1996). Total quality management in the classroom. *Journal of Legal Studies Education, 14*, 1.

Fort, T. L., & Zoellers, F. E. (1999). Teaching business ethics: Theory and practice. *Teaching Business Ethics, 2*, 273-290.

Hiemstra, R. (1991). Aspects of effective learning environments. In R. Hiemstra (Ed.), *New directions for adult and continuing education: No. 50. Creating environments for effective adult learning* (pp. 41-50). San Francisco, CA: Jossey-Bass.

Knowles, M. S. (1980). *The modern practice of adult education: From pedagogy to andragogy* (Rev. ed.). New York, NY: Cambridge University Press.

Knox, A. B. (1986). *Helping adults learn*. San Francisco, CA: Jossey-Bass.

Kolb, D. A. (1974). *Organizational psychology*. Englewood Cliffs, NJ: Prentice-Hall.

Sherwood, J., & Glidewell, J. (1971). *Planned renegotiation: A norm*. OD Intervention. Paper No. 338, Herman C. Krannert Graduate School of Industrial Administration, Purdue University, Lafayette, Indiana.

Vosko, R. S. (1991). Where we learn shapes our learning. In R. Hiemstra (Ed.), *New directions for adult and continuing education: No. 50. Creating environments for effective adult learning* (pp. 23-32). San Francisco: Jossey-Bass.

CHAPTER 4

PUTTING CAREER MORALITY ON THE AGENDA OF BUSINESS STUDENTS

How One Could Use a Play and Survey Results for Triggering Moral Reflection

Johannes Brinkmann

INTRODUCTION

This chapter discusses the design of a teaching unit which addresses the students' (heterogeneous) career visions, ambitions, and strategies in an ethical reflection perspective. Such a teaching unit can be used with undergraduate, graduate, and continued education students as target groups. It could be used as a stand-alone session (for example in a guest lecture), or as a module presented at the beginning or end of a generic business or professional ethics course, or perhaps even as part of an ethics program presented through plays and novels. It might also be used in an introductory research methodology class.

Experiences in Teaching Business Ethics
pp. 83–96

The chapter consists of three somewhat independent parts, with career strategy and morality as a common denominator. First a theater piece is presented, about what one might call career strategy. Then parts of an older pilot survey are summarized, where business students and marketing professionals were asked questions about such a topic. Finally, some suggestions for how one could invite serious reflection about such important topics among business students is discussed.[1] Because of the independency of its parts, the chapter's contents can be rearranged rather freely—one could for example begin with some of the assignments and teaching suggestions in the third part, rather than start with the play as emotional entertainment and stimulus for discussion.

FIRST ILLUSTRATION: A COMEDY ABOUT CAREER STRATEGY AND CAREER MORALITY

The comedy *The Parasite or the Art to Make One's Fortune* is a piece by the German playwright Friedrich Schiller (1759-1805), written in 1803 as a translation and remake of Frenchman L. B. Picard's piece *Médiocre et rampant ou le moyen de parvenir.* When the well-respected theater in Bochum set up the play during spring 2001, the theater homepage claimed: "With this comedy about the court intrigue-maker Selicour, tragedy specialist Schiller has left the Germans a comedy which is not shown frequently but which is not inferior compared to his classical German dramas—when it comes to sophistication, star roles and well-developed design" (author's translation). The core of the piece can be summarized in a few sentences. "Parasite" and wheedler Selicour is responsible for the job loss of his subordinate La Roche, who for this reason becomes his enemy. Selicou also exploits another subordinate, competent and modest Firmin, and receives recognition by the new minister Narbonne; in reality this recognition is deserved by Firmin. When the minster tests the competence of Selicour (by letting him write a memo under time pressure) Selicour himself becomes the victim of an intrigue which is staged by La Roche.

The piece tells a funny, entertaining and timeless story about career paths which lead uphill and then stop suddenly. In our context, the story is less interesting than the most important roles, as ideal types of different career strategies.

Opportunism as a Career Strategy

Selicour uses various means for furthering his career. He wheedles whenever necessary and changes his opinions whenever such a change appears to be advantageous. "That is what I meant to say ..." is his stan-dard expression, which does not communicate honest agreement but rather purposeful rhetoric. Selicour is also good at changing truths to half-truths and accepts lies when necessary: "Was I wrong in saying, that it was not always advisable to tell the truth?" (Schiller, 1856, p. 81). In this way he also ends up in a positive fashion and conceals anything profes-sional or personal. He also likes to reap the benefits of others' perfor-mance. And he is good at manipulating information, letting important people know of important things (or not), and at the right time. Selicour is good at seeing the weaknesses of others and understands that such knowledge gives him power over others. Referring to his boss his com-ment is: "Thus you are also a man—you have weaknesses—and I am your ruler" (p. 73). He also defends his position by nurturing informal contacts with the right people in his social network and tries to instrumentalize them as allies for himself.

Integrity as a Career Strategy

Firmin is the clear opposite of Selicour and serves as a contrast type. He is highly case and task focused. It is most important to him that a given task is carried out properly and conscientiously (now and then he is pedantic). His work incentive is good results rather than personal success. Referring to Selicour he remarks, "Let him do his work himself, or get it done by another—let it only be done" (Schiller, 1856, p. 5). He likes to cooperate and says that "we must mutually oblige one another" (p. 5). His ideals of reciprocity almost naively overlook the fact that not everybody has the same type of motivation as he has himself. To the same extent as he focuses on professional accomplishments he stays backstage as a per-son. Thus he avoids exposure and any forms of potential competition. "I will not push away anybody from his place, and I gladly remain where I am, in the dark" (p. 5, author translation).

Staging Intrigues as a Career Strategy

Opportunism and integrity as opposite career types can coexist rather well, as long as the parasite finds partners who can be manipulated and exploited. Career success however is often a question of winning in the competition for scarce positions. This is the same in Schiller's play as in real work life. In Schiller's comedy tension is created not through a coun-terrole with integrity, as a personification of high work morale and good organizational citizenship, but rather through a career competitor who creates all kinds of intrigues. Due to Selicour, La Roche has lost his employment and plans his revenge. With reference to Selicour he declares: "And we must beat him with his own weapons" (Schiller, 1856, p. 70). LaRoche criticizes Selicour and his behavior, but his criticism is moralistic rather than ethical. He talks behind the back of his opponent about his behaviors and searches for traps for hurting him. In this project he employs the same means as Selicour, but for advancing his own interests. La Roche is good at twisting the truth too, using lots of rhetoric and claims the status as a victim of circumstances. "For myself I would on no account play an intrigue" (p. 11). At the same time he admits that such an intrigue would give him some "heavenly pleasure" (p. 11), and later in the play he concludes: "How much faster one gets on with knavery, than with honesty" (p. 73).

The Boss as the Moral Institution

The role of the minister and the expected leadership behavior is portrayed as the moral higher road. While Firmin represents a case and task focus, the minister Narbonne has higher-level objectives and duty as a principle: "Where duty speaks, I consider nothing. And whatever the consequence may be, I never shall repent having done my duty" (Schiller, 1856, p. 81).[2] Narbonne assumes also that the respective subordinate has a duty of finding suitable work tasks which correspond to one's competence, also a duty of positioning: "The man of talent ... seeks himself the eye of his principal, and endeavours to obtain the post which he is conscious of deserving" (p. 50). His staff is not only evaluated by accomplishments, but also by their behaviors: "We are answerable for the good which we do not perform, as well as for the evil which we allow" (p. 51). When it comes to the conflict among the career competitors the minister stays neutral and fair, as to be expected from a wise leader. He demands for example that Selicour is to be heard when La Roche complains about him. But leaders can make mistakes too. Minister Narbonne is impressed by Selicour for quite some time (and this is required for keeping the tension in the piece). Narbonne trusts Selicour and appreciates him until he notices that he is betrayed (through a "friend's service" by Selicour). Narbonne personifies the wise leader, who not the least is quick at learning and adjusting viewpoints when necessary. Not surprisingly, he is the one to summarize the whole play in a few sentences: "This time merit has obtained victory—it is not always so! The web of falsehood ensnares the best ones, the honest one cannot prevail, creeping mediocrity is getting on better than winged talent, show governs the world, and justice exists only on the stage" (p. 84).

Moral Idealism and Moral Skepticism

The moral message of the Schiller piece is easy to understand and quite predictable. There is no doubt about deservingness and justice. Modest and competent Firmin is successful. He is taken out of the shadow and justice is reestablished ("on the stage"). In real work life alternative outcomes can be imagined. At the Bochum theater the moral of the story was presented in two additional variations. The common denominator of the add-on outcomes is that Firmin is not rewarded for good work, but punished because he has not sought the attention of the boss. In the first add-on outcome La Roche is promoted and selected for the attractive ambassador position, as a true copy of Selicour (during the minister's recruitment interview La Roche gives identical, sanctimonious answers known to the spectators from Selicour earlier in the piece). In the second add-on outcome La Roche is promoted and the piece could continue forever. LaRoche's promotion is just an intermezzo, an intermediary victory in the competition. Selicour reenters once more and announces revenge, with "heavenly enjoyment" (quoting Schiller) and also otherwise in the same wordings as LaRoche earlier in the piece. The add-on outcomes where justice does not even win on the stage are more skeptical when it comes to describing reality. A more subtle evaluation of the different career strategies is invited. The director's approach to ending the play replaces Schiller's index finger morality with a more up to date Brecht-type invitation to reflect about career strategy and career morality.

The Parasite tells that integrity is a virtue and that true deservingness is rewarded (not always, however). One learns more if a moral evaluation of career paths is postponed somewhat, by inviting one first to try a precise description and to understand the context properly. With a suitable mix of realistic and holistic understanding (moral aspects included) the comedy can serve as an entertaining point of departure for a more critical and reflective look at career strategies. Selicour acts as if he had read and learned Jens Bjørneboe's *Ten Commandments for a Young Man With High Aspirations of Making his Way in This World*.[3] But distancing oneself from Selicour (and from Bjørneboe's advice), and then superficially siding with the old-fashioned Firmin ideals would be too simple as a conclusion. Most individuals are probably a mix of some degree of Selicour and some degree of Firmin, depending on the circumstances. The role played by La Roche raises the most interesting questions about the most efficient and wisest self-defense against the Selicours in this world. As we know from the Prisoner's Dilemma experiments, the moral climate in the world of work and business is sustained and ruined jointly, in interdependent behaviors. Most people tend to behave decently, at least as long as the others behave decently, too, but then to fight back in the same currency once one feels treated unfairly. The suspicion is that opportunism and intrigues are at least as contagious as integrity.

SECOND ILLUSTRATION: SURVEYS AND A FEW SELECTED RESULTS

A few findings in my own studies from a number of years ago suggest that many business students might be potentially ruthless careerists (but of course not all of them).[4] If one uses different views of career strategy and career morality as a criterion, one finds that the surveyed business students consist of two subgroups of about equal size, the tough ones versus the more cautious ones. Two statements referred to expected conditions for career success, in other words to the ramifications for more or less moral behavior. The more pessimistic one's view of the business world, the more important become ability and willingness to employ less moral means. The two following statements asked more directly if one as an individual expected to behave ruthlessly when required and then even one step further if one had any moral doubts when it comes to defending one's career. The four last statements addressed the importance of a career and conditions for making a career more generally. With some reservations when it comes to different connotations of words such as "ruthlessness" in different languages and cultures, the answers can lead one to believe that (see Table 4.1):

- female students are less pessimistic and more compromising in their career orientation; and
- thirty-five percent of the male Norwegian students and about half of the U.S. students are mentally prepared for a career that requires some ruthlessness (among the female Norwegian students the proportion is clearly lower).

Most interesting about such response distributions is the fact that a lecture audience at a business school normally consists of sufficient size subgroups with clear differences when it comes to career attitudes and career morality. Teaching should take this into account, not least as a point of departure for productive discussions, for example asking for any comments about clear gender differences.

In another simple pilot study (carried out in 1991)[5] questions were asked about minor dishonesty in one's own work situation, in order to reconstruct different moral norms. Two important conclusions were that norms of helping colleagues in trouble had relatively stronger support than, for example, exploiting workplaces resources, taking sick days without being sick, and claiming slightly inflated expense refunds. Many of

Table 4.1.   Career Attitudes, Career Conditions, and Career Morality (Percent of Norwegian Business Students, Data Collected 1993/1994)

	Norwegian		U.S. Students	
	Male	Female	Male	Female
Students who agree that ruthlessness is often more successful than acting ethically	41	33	36	23
Students who agree that "if you want to reach higher aims you can't always avoid unjust means"	64	46	38	32
Students who are prepared to behave ruthlessly for getting to the top of a chosen career, if necessary	35	15	57	48
Students who would be prepared to do something unethical to defend their career success	69	45	47	23
Students who are prepared to sacrifice family and private life for staying successful in their careers	37	28	6	6
Students who agree that being successful in life is most important	32	20	51	37
Students to whom it is important or very important to work hard because there is nothing for free	89	83	84	78
Students who are pessimistic or skeptical about the moral business climate in their home country	23	41	35	27
n (100%)	157	162	157	129

the statements checked with Likert scales could have served as operationalizations of behaviors presented in the theater piece above, such as:

- blame innocent colleagues for one's own mistakes;
- accept acknowledgment for work done by others;
- talk negatively about others behind their backs; and
- conceal one's own mistakes.

Consistently with other research, most respondents expect that colleagues and superiors have somewhat lower moral standards than they do themselves (an interesting question is if this indicates moral self-deception or at least a lack of moral self-criticism).

USING THE ILLUSTRATIONS FOR TRIGGERING REFLECTION

Put simply, business ethics teaching has two interdependent purposes: teaching skills in *moral conflict management* and encouraging holistic *reflection* about nonsuperficial, realistic ideals for business life and business careers.

Reflection has to do with taking a break, taking a step or two backwards for observing better and thinking things over. Often there is a trigger and catalyst, an event, or as in this case a theater piece or set of survey results. Reflection can start with a neutral presentation of facts and with some kind of analysis. But the point is *patience*, not to stop here and give up with one's thinking, but to continue with asking why-questions again and again. Reflection is also often associated with *critical* thinking, with *meditation* or with *holistic* thinking and with handling of complexity (cf. Brinkmann, 2002, p. 83, referring to Hub, 1994; Probst & Gomez, 1989).[6] Moral storytelling in plays and novels, written by the experts, is often praised as for triggering moral reflection and moral imagination (see e.g., Brinkmann, 2009a; Ghesquiere & Ims, 2010; Singer & Singer, 2005). Relevant instruments for asking questions about values, attitudes or hypothetical moral conflict situations and well-presented empirical results can also function as triggers of reflection, almost in a literal sense, by holding up a mirror and then asking target groups if they like what they see or not and why (Brinkmann, 2009b).

In line with this chapter's title promise and with the illustrations in the previous sections, the general objective of encouraging reflection is here narrowed to reflection about a limited topic, career goals, strategies and moralities. In other words, the focus is on raising and answering rather personal questions about oneself as a moral person, about personal career ambitions and ideals, a focus which at the same time is wider than single cases, for example, single, conflict-management decisions.

When it comes to drafting a number of teaching suggestions it makes sense to proceed from goals and objectives, to contexts and then to more specifics tricks of the trade. The next section provides a brief look at the goals and objectives for moral reflection.

Goals and Objectives

The less one believes in the success of such invitations to moral reflection and the less idealistically one assumes that such reflection will deepen and survive on its own, the more one will look for a clear enough pedagogical design, not least for learning objectives which then can be translated into precise follow-up questions (see Brinkmann & Sims, 2001, about how to convince students to work with their own attitudes and competencies, referring to a model inspired by James Rest, with seven interdependent objectives). Table 4.2 departs from such learning objectives and shows at the same time how one could build a bridge between learning objectives and questions one could ask and discuss concerning the presented play. Another reference could be the "promised" learning outcomes typology in an elective course at the author's business school, where such a unit primarily

Table 4.2. Possible Debriefing Questions One Could Ask After Exposure to the Parasite Play, Related to Learning Objectives

Know thyself, your own moral values and thresholds	• What are the participants' most important life goals and career goals, perhaps using the Schiller play characters as a reference
Learning to see moral issues, conflicts and responsibilities	• Which conflicts in the play are moral conflicts and why? Which other moral problems and issues are seen by the participants?
Learning to identify the specific moral aspects of a situation	• What are the specific moral aspects of the conflicts and issues referred to above? To what extent can more or less well-known normative ethical theories be useful when asking and answering such questions?
Learning to share moral understanding	• Which conflict perception differences and perhaps which potential conflicts exist, for example among the participants?
Learning how to handle moral issues and conflicts	• To what extent can more or less well-known normative ethical theories be useful when formulating suggestions for how to resolve such identified conflicts?
Acquiring moral courage	• What can one learn from the play and the different typical roles about the importance of moral courage, and of following up moral convictions by action?
Acquiring a critical attitude towards the business school curriculum and its disciplines	• How do business students respond to such humanistic course contents, compared to core specialties in the business school curriculum? • Can such alternative contents inspire that traditional business school subjects are asked critical questions?

would fit with the "reflection" outcomes (rather than the acquired knowledge and skills outcomes):

> Ethics means reflection about complexity, dilemmas, questions of right and wrong, in this case in business and professional contexts. After completing the course, students should have acquired a reflective attitude when it comes to their own morality, i.e. have developed personal ethics and a sense of social responsibility as a business school graduate and have acquired an ability and a willingness to follow up words with deeds, never forgetting that business ethics is about the wise and responsible balancing of business and nonbusiness considerations. (http://web.bi.no/info/kurs2010.nsf/vWebKurs-lookupeng/ele+3710)

Context-Sensitivity

The context, where a teaching unit about career morality is offered (or if one prefers, the working conditions), plays a role, of course—such as *where* on a given curriculum level it is offered (undergraduate or graduate, and there again at the beginning or at the end), or if such a teaching unit is offered as a *stand-alone* guest lecture (e.g., at the very beginning or at the very end of an undergraduate program), or in the opening *stage* or closing stage of a more or less *generic* introduction to a business ethics, perhaps also as a subunit in an imagined course about *literature* and leadership ethics, where such a taste of Schiller could be combined with a taste of Goethe, Ibsen, Brecht or Shakespeare, or perhaps as a subunit of a methodology class, for a discussion after collecting and summarizing personal, sensitive and important data about the participants' life and career goals.

Target group sensitivity is at least as important as curriculum sensitivity: meeting the students where they are—right "now" and with a "past," as products of subcultural socialization, but also with more (or normally less) clear "future" perspectives. One can hardly imagine a topic which could be better at meeting the students "where they are" and "where they want to go" than career morality, which explicitly puts such grand questions on the agenda and invites discussion. Not the least for this reason the author has used such a unit at the first or second meeting during a typical undergraduate or master student course in business ethics, for communicating explicitly that the course is meant to listen to and to depart from the students preexisting attitudes and values, rather than preaching to them. With or without some kind of empirical ethical self-assessment, one can also address explicitly the moral heterogeneity of the course participants, as a sample of likely future challenges, having to coexist and discuss with one another and to convince one another by good arguments.

Ideas for Teaching

Once one is conscious about goals and objectives as well as contextual constraints and opportunities (alone or perhaps after discussing them with the students), informed choices and priorities for such a teaching unit become easier.

A first possibility is to ask the students for *preparation*, with or without specified assignments, one assignment at a time, or even with combined assignments:

- Prepare by reading the Schiller play before the class meeting, perhaps write a note about what you like the best and why, or pick favorite scenes and characters, with a short justification why, or read the play for answering specified questions, such as "Could one reconstruct different career strategies in the play and which ones?" or "Which role do you identify the most with and which one the least and why?", or "To what extent does your strategy choice depend on the circumstances and on what your competitors do or your opponents?", or "Do you know of similar plays, literature or movies which one could use as illustrations, in addition to or instead of this one?"

- Prepare for class by writing a half-page essay about your *business career aspirations* and your desirable/acceptable work-life balance, i.e. which sacrifices and means you are prepared for, or about career role models and why.

- Prepare for class by using either self- chosen or teacher-provided self-assessment instruments,[7] and then paint a short moral self-portrait (on half a page or so), for confidential or anonymous sharing in a small group or in class.

Some of such preparation activities can be used *during class*, too, for example, as individual questions or tasks which then are summarized and discussed in small groups, with or without reporting to the plenary. Other alternatives the author has worked with in such a teaching unit are:

- Agreeing on or preselecting one or a few scenes from the Schiller play and then using them for role-plays in class.

- Offering without previous notice a few short scenes from the movie *Wall Street* as an alternative, "for students who prefer old U.S movies and less demanding abstractions," with or without suggestions to compare *Wall Street* and *The Parasite*.

- For the *Wall Street* movie more or less the same debriefing questions work pretty well as in the home assignment above, such as "Could one reconstruct different career strategies in the movie and which ones?" or "Which role do you identify the most with and which one the least and why?" or "To what extent does your strategy choice depend on the circumstances and on what the others do?" or "Discuss the concept of 'moral luck' with reference to the movie."

- Use a handout paper-and-pencil version of the questionnaire (referred to above in the second section) and ask the students to answer them, before perhaps showing the findings in the mentioned previous studies, as a warm-up before a classroom discussion about moral heterogeneity.

- Use a handout paper version of the Rokeach 18-values instrument or a 10-item Likert-scale instrument used and presented by

Carruth and Carruth (1991), as an alternative warm-up before a classroom discussion about moral heterogeneity.

- The following assignment in class works really well, not least as a translation of career morality issues into a very practical situation: *applying for a job* one really would like to get, or a role play of a job interview where career attitudes and career morality turn up as a topic, with questions such as:

  o Is a job applicant obliged to list all employment or every work experience on a resume?
  o Is a resume something like a certificate of authenticity or is it more like a sales brochure?
  o How much self-marketing is appropriate/ justifiable?
  o How do you think other applicants/ your competitors will act?
  o Are you prepared to sacrifice some of your true self for your career?
  o Your boss asks you to draft a letter of reference for yourself.
  o A job application asks you to present your relevant skills, life goals and ideals in a one page essay.
  o Where do you see your career and your work-life balance 10 years from now?

A third possibility is to reuse the topic "career morality" and "know thyself" during *exams*, for example (in addition to adjusted versions of tasks mentioned above already):

- Write a (confidential) essay about you yourself a moral person, before and after participating in an ethics class, with a focus on future career choices.
- Find, present, and discuss a play, literature, or movie fragment of your own choice which can be related to critical career choices.
- Write a job application where are invited to write about what you have learned about business ethics at your business school.

CONCLUSION

As a conclusion, a few theses can be formulated, some as a repetition, others in order to make implicit thoughts more explicit. A *first* and main thesis of this chapter is that the students' career visions and thoughts about their future work-life balance (or the lack thereof) should be addressed as one of the main topics when teaching business ethics. A *second* and derived thesis claims that the students' future work life career as a topic (because of its personal nature and its broadness) is better at triggering deeper *reflection* than many other introductory topics. Most likely, reflection is not only a question of the topic, but also of the means, which are addressed in the two following theses. A *third* thesis could be: literature in general and plays in particular are normally good at presenting and portraying clear role types, typically in clear conflict, often in clear moral conflict. The better the moral of the story fits with the topic one wants to address, the better the learning experience. When it comes to career morality, Schiller's ideal role types of opportunism and intrigue versus integrity and leadership couldn't fit better together. A *fourth* thesis is: good survey questions are good at triggering respondent reflection, and even after questionnaires are filled in and returned. After the answers are collected (ideally among the class participants themselves), they can be held up as a mirror, for inviting reflection in a literal sense, if one likes and would like to comment on the picture one sees. In the case of the present chapter, questions related to career strategy and morality and to work-life balance types were used as an illustration of such a possibility. A *fifth* thesis claims that this chapter and the pieces of which it consists can be used in different ways—the play only, the questionnaire questions and answers only, or in combination. A few teaching ideas are outlined more in detail, but it is of course the teacher, the target groups and the context that determine what will work the best.

NOTES

1. This essay in English and the Norwegian versions before it are the author's half of a cooperative project published as a paper in German together with Gisela Steenbuck, University of Dortmund, Germany. In her portion the specific pedagogical challenges of the piece are addressed (see Brinkmann & Steenbuck, 2002).

2. Compare also the German proverb *Der eine fragt, was kommt danach, der andre fragt ist's recht? Und darin unterscheidet sich die Herrschaft von dem Knecht.*

3. *Ti bud for en ung mann som vil frem i verden*, J. Bjørneboe 1963, in the book *Politi og anarki*, essays, pax: Oslo 1983, pp. 9-10.

4. These questions were originally used in a survey among AISEC-students (Jamard, 1990) and in a study about moral attitudes among German business leaders (Kaufmann, Kerber, & Zulehner, 1986).

5. This study of 364 members of Norwegian marketing associations and among 59 Norwegian marketing students replicated an American questionnaire study (see Ferrell & Weaver, 1978).

6. In another work by the same author (Brinkmann, 2002) one finds references to a range of almost-synonyms for moral reflection, such as moral sensitivity, moral judgment, moral reasoning, moral imagination (and definitions of them). In a next step a qualitative study is summarized about differences in moral reflection willingness and ability.
7. For testing one's moral sensitivity see for example: http://www.yourmorals.org/loh.php or http://www.yourmorals.org/5f_new2_survey.php (for an overview over tools, see http://www.yourmorals.org/explore.php. For clarifying one's own values, see, for example, http://www.yourmorals.org/schwartz.php.

REFERENCES

Brinkmann, J. (2002). Moral reflection differences among Norwegian business students: A presentation and discussion of findings. *Teaching Business Ethics, 6,* 83-99.

Brinkmann, J. (2009a). Using Ibsen in business ethics. *Journal of Business Ethics, 84,* 11-24

Brinkmann, J. (2009b). Putting ethics on the agenda for real estate agents. *Journal of Business Ethics, 88,* 65-82.

Brinkmann, J. & Sims, R. (2001). Stakeholder-sensitive business ethics teaching. *Teaching Business Ethics, 5,* 171-193.

Brinkmann, J., & Steenbuck, G. (2002). Wirtschaftsethik lehren mit moralischem Theater [Using moral theater for teaching business ethics]. *Zeitschrift für Wirtschafts- und Unternehmensethik, 3,* 58-76.

Carruth, P. J., & Carruth, A. K. (1991). Education in ethics: The role of higher education. *Journal of Education for Business, 66*(3), 168.

Ferrell, O. C., & Weaver, K. M. (1978, July). Ethical beliefs of marketing managers. *Journal of Marketing,* 69-73.

Ghesquiere, R., & Ims, K. J. (2010). *Heroes and anti-heroes. European literature and the ethics of leadership.* Antwerp, Belgium: Garant.

Hub, H. (1994). *Ganzheitliches denken im management* [Holistic management thinking]. Frankfurt, Germany: Gabler.

Jamard, M. H. (1990). Der manager von morgen: Typ schaf, pferd oder wolf? [The manager of tomorrow: of the sheep, horse or wolf type?]. *Profil, 47/90,* 2-6.

Kaufmann, F., Kerber, W., & Zulehner, P. M. (1986). *Ethos und religion bei führungskräften* [Ethics and religion among managers]. München, Germany: Kindt

Probst, G., & Gomez, P. (1989). *Vernetztes denken* [Thinking in interdependencies]. Frankfurt, Germany: Gabler.

Schiller, F. (1858). *The parasite or the art to make one's fortune.* New York, NY: Christern. Retrieved from http://books.google.no/books

Singer, P., & Singer, R. (2005). *The moral of the story: An anthology of ethics through literature.* Oxford, England: Blackwell.

CHAPTER 5

TEACHING BUSINESS ETHICS VIA DIALOGUE AND CONVERSATION

Ronald R. Sims

The more genuine conversation is, the less its conduct lies within the will of either partner. Thus, a genuine conversation is never the one that we wanted to conduct ... more correct to say that we fall into conversation, or even that we become involved in it ... a conversation has a spirit of its own, and the language in which it is conducted bears its own truth within it—i.e., that it allows something to "emerge" which hence forth exists. (Gadamer, 1994, p. 383)

INTRODUCTION

When I was an undergraduate student 40 years ago, I had the following experience in my first ethics course: my professor would start to lead a classroom "discussion," but I had a sinking suspicion that it was just a sham. All he wanted from the class was for us to fill in the blanks of what I (and many of my fellow students) perceived as his biased, prepro-grammed views on the "best" theories or approaches to making, say, an

Experiences in Teaching Business Ethics
pp. 97–122

97

ethical decision or handling a potential situation. He would fish around from student to student until he got the answer he was looking for. So we students had to make a choice between sincerely expressing our own thoughts on the subject, at considerable risk to our grade, or simply give the professor what he wanted to hear. The "smarter" students chose to play it safe (i.e., I didn't fall into that category). Their reward was the professor's effusive praise for supplying the "right" answer. The *right* answers—according to him!

As I often reflect on my first ethics course experience it brings home to me how these pseudo-discussions were really colossal missed opportunities for learning. This realization became even clearer in 1986 while in the process of preparing to teach my first business ethics course. I was reminded by what I had personally learned years ago on what was wrong with these fill-in-the-blank discussions, and I worked hard to design a business ethics course that included dynamic classroom discussions.

This chapter discusses the importance of dialogue, good moral conversation, and more particularly conversational learning to teaching business ethics courses for effective learning. The chapter first describes my own experience at coming to the conclusion that introducing dialogue and conversations within the classroom when teaching ethics is critical to effective teaching and learning. Next, attention turns to a brief discussion of dialogue and good moral conversation before focusing on conversational learning and its use in my business ethics course. Special attention is then given to how I see my role as the teacher in using conversational learning in my course. Before concluding the chapter I offer some further reflection on some insights into using conversational learning and dialogue in my business ethics course that should be of interest to the reader.

MY REFLECTION AND SOME BACKGROUND

As I have learned more about learning and teaching over a 30-year career I have accepted that I am a dialogue fanatic! I believe that the true, open exchange of views is fundamental to a successful or effective business ethics course. Students need a forum to express their thoughts, but they also need to be trained to become respectful listeners of diverse opinions. I believe that one of the best places to learn this principle is in business school. It is my strong belief that good classroom discussions lay the groundwork for democratic participation throughout life, giving students a sense of power within a classroom community, and conveying to them the importance of their future role as participants in society in general, and in their organizational lives in particular.

A thoughtful classroom discussion, in my experience, helps students develop critical thinking, reflection and a comfort with openly sharing and listening to diverse views on business ethics and ethical situations. Talking in a business ethics course helps students learn to organize their thoughts and present them coherently. Students also learn to be active listeners, holding other peoples' ideas up to critical analysis. They come to see that there are always alternative ways of looking at a difficult problem or situation. And later on in life students reap the rewards in the real world from thinking creatively and ethically on their feet. So, in my view, classroom discussions in my business ethics courses to date have yielded very powerful individual and social benefits.

Over the years, I believe I have gotten better at both enhancing student learning and effectively teaching business ethics, and this is partly because of my increased use of classroom discussion that relies on dialogue and conversations. Business ethics education in my view requires attitude and behavioral change—an unprecedented and daring undertaking for the classroom. I have realized that teaching and learning about ethics evoke high anxiety and often fear in the most seasoned individuals—teachers, students, and administrators alike. As a subject matter, ethics education has few equals in terms of uncertainty of outcome. Awareness of the strong tone of beliefs and emotion generated when ethical issues are discussed leads to expressions of dismay at a trend that focuses on course content in my business ethics courses without attending to issues of process. It is very difficult for students to talk about ethics, values, beliefs, morals, virtue, integrity, and so forth *still*, after all these years in my business ethics courses. The introduction to these and other ethically-related issues often generates powerful emotional responses in my students ranging from self-doubt and shame to frustration and confusion to even elation at times. My failure to address these emotional responses in open dialogue and conversations will often result in student resistance to listening, sharing and learning.

Feeling safe in the classroom takes on an added significance in business ethics education. In my experience, students must feel supported and believe that they can make choices about the process of learning as they venture into what for many is unchartered territory. New experience is the foundation of learning; however, a sense of security must be attained before learners can begin to consider the unfamiliar (Fry & Kolb, 1979). Trust is critical and enhanced by guidelines and group norms that encourage participation, risk taking, self-disclosure, mutual support, and dialogue (Schor, 1993).

Some Further Background

Twenty years ago I wanted to design a business ethics course for students that covered a range of ethics-related topics pertaining directly and concretely to their lives—something that would help them understand they had the power to make good ethical choices in their lives. I was inspired by a guest speaker in a colleagues' business ethics course. The course was called "Business Ethics in a Time of Greed," and was about values and personal behavior in conflict. The guest speaker was a skillful moderator and facilitator who presented hypothetical situations to the students as part of a role play in which they were to represent a range of competing interests. The guest speaker began with a relatively simple situation and asked the students in their role as panelists how they, in their various professional positions, would handle it. As the situations the guest speaker presented to the students became progressively more complex, the students became increasingly divided. Giving different priorities to different values produced wildly different choices. It was a highly interactive and engaging format both during the actual replay and in the following debrief. In looking back on the situations I can say that it was almost impossible for me to watch the conversations without wanting to participate.

I decided that I wanted to create dynamic classroom discussion, dialogue or conversations for my students in my business ethics course. So, given my experience in my first ethics course and the experience with the guest speaker mentioned in the previous paragraph I have tried to design into my business ethics course highly interactive and engaging learning experiences for my students. With each new course I find myself asking whether or not the students will respond to it with the same enthusiasm I did to the guest speaker or my own reaction to my first ethics course those many years ago? Speaking realistically, the guest speaker and role play flamed my passion, and I think that was because the students cared about the ideas being examined which was in stark contrast to my first experience in the ethics course. But could I create an experience like the former versus the latter in my own course in the years to come?

BUSINESS ETHICS EDUCATION: THE ROLE OF DIALOGUE AND GOOD MORAL CONVERSATION

Building upon the discussion so far in this chapter there should be no doubt that I view business ethics education without dialogue as programmed for failure. Therefore, providing a forum for dialogue is one of the most proactive gestures I think I can do to enhance teaching my business ethics course. For me, this means that business ethics is a source of learning and good dialogue and conversation is a means of students' acquiring learning in a business ethics course. Ideal speech, ideal listening, discourse in relationships, and the promotion of the different voices on ethics, are necessary components of dialogue and a good conversation among students who are learning about business ethics.

Dialogue

The merit of a dialogue is its practicality. Dialogue, however, must subscribe to what is termed "the new decorum," which requires students to listen to others and engage in a moderate tone of conversation. Dialogue plays a role in identity formation. Self-awareness is facilitated by self-disclosure and interaction with others (Jourard, 1971). When in the process of dialogue, each party recognizes the identity of the other both then will become able to understand better their individual identities. Through dialogue we create a broader horizon that serves as the backdrop against which we operate in the world. This broader horizon results from the "fusion of horizons"—situating one possibility, our usual standard, alongside other possibilities, new and unfamiliar standards (Taylor, 1992).

Experiential learning theory insists that genuine learning only occurs when students are engaged in "praxis"—political action informed by reflection (Friere, 1973). A fundamental aspect of praxis is the process of "naming the world." Naming the world is achieved through dialogue among equals, a dual process of inquiry and learning. In my view, a progressive business ethics course rejects the banking concept of teaching, where students are passive receptacles for deposits of fixed content from teachers. The idea is to instill "critical consciousness" in students where the meaning of abstract ethical concepts is explored through dialogue among peers. Dialogue is key to human emancipation of the oppressed (Friere, 1973).

In my experience, dialogue is good conversation. It must adhere to rules of the new decorum. Dialogue serves many purposes in my business ethics course. It facilitates self-awareness and awareness of others. It is a source of learning. It is liberating, and lends to the creation of safety for teaching about business ethics.

Experiential learning theory (Kolb, 1984) supports knowledge in my business ethics course through the provision of a holistic model and process of learning, a structure and tool for assessing learning preferences, a framework for creating effective learning environments, and dialogue as a vehicle for creating psychological safety in the classroom. Psychological safety opens the door for good moral conversation among the students in my course.

Striving for Good Moral Conversation

I have found Nash's (1996) approach to ethics discussion very helpful to me in better understanding the importance of establishing a classroom learning climate in which students talk freely and understand the importance of taking risks, listening and sharing their experiences and views with others during the course. According to Nash, a conversation is

> literally a manner of living whereby people keep company with each other, and talk together; in good faith, in order to exchange sometimes agreeable, sometimes opposing, ideas. A conversation is not an argument, although it can get heated. A conversation is at its best when the participants are not impatient to conclude their business, but wish instead to spend their time together in order to deepen and enrich their understanding of an idea, or, in our case, the ideas in a text, or of a possible solution to a difficult ethical case (p. 24).

A conversation that is moral, from the Latin *moralis* (custom), is one whose conventions emphasize the fundamental worth and dignity of each participant in the exchange, and this includes the authors of texts (Nash, 1996), other reading materials, and experiential exercises (Sims, 2002). To date, it has been my experience that using Nash's view of moral conversation is a useful way to get a student to talk openly about ethical issues, views, beliefs, values or other concerns. This means that I must treat the student with utmost respect. It is important in my role as someone who is committed to facilitating learning that I treat students with the highest regard in the sense that they all have a share of moral truth. That is, that no one of us, though, has a corner on the market of ethical or other insight. No single one of us inhabits the moral high ground a priori. Nash (1996) suggests that we are all moral *viators* (travelers with a purpose) on a journey to find meaning in the work we do (and in our personal life beyond work), and because our journey is our own, it possesses intrinsic worth and is to be respected.

An important purpose in engaging in moral conversation in my courses is to test, expand, enrich, and deepen student's understanding of business ethics so that each student can better implement general ethical theories, principles, rules, virtues, structures, moral ideals, and background beliefs to problems encountered in the world of work. With the ideal of the moral conversation in mind, Nash (1996) suggests that hopefully students (and the instructor) can be genuinely respectful of each other's efforts to work through difficult readings, scenarios and exercises, to find common classroom language to express our individual interpretations of the readings, scenarios and exercises, and to take conversational risks in constructing a more cogent moral discourse.

In brief then, good moral conversation in my business ethics course starts with (adapted from Nash, 1996, p. 25):

1. An honest effort by students to come to class prepared (i.e., having read and come to some understanding of the material, completed prework on experiential-learning exercises, etc.).

2. An acute awareness that we all have moral biases and blind spots.

3. An open-mindedness by the student to the possibility of learning something from the assigned readings, experiential learning exercises and one's peers in conversation.

4. A willingness to improve current moral language.

5. A conscious effort to refrain from advancing one's own current moral language as if it were best.

6. An inclination to listen intently in order to grasp the meaning of other people's languages for expressing their moral truths.

7. An agreement that clarifying, questioning, challenging, exemplifying, and applying ideas are activities to be done in a self- and other-respecting way.

8. A realization that we will frequently get off course in our conversations because a spirit of charity, intellectual curiosity, and even playfulness will characterize many of our discussions, and because, as David Bromwich (1992) says: "The good conversation is not truth, or right, or anything else that may come out at the end of it, but the activity itself in its constant relation to life" (pp. 131-132).

9. An appreciation of the reality that it will take time for us to get to know each other, and a realization that eventually we will find ways to engage in robust, candid, and challenging dialogue and conversation about ethics without being so "nice" we bore each other to death, or without being so hostile that we cripple each other emotionally and intellectually.

It is one thing to speak of the importance of dialogue and good moral conversation in a business ethics course and another to bring it to fruition. In my experience, one way of doing this is to move to a focus on conversational learning in a business ethics course.

CONVERSATIONAL LEARNING IN A BUSINESS ETHICS COURSE

Addressing potential and existing ethical problems, challenges or decisions in today's world of work requires the recognition that conversations
among vastly differing stakeholders are imperative. According to Alan
Webber (1993), formerly a managing editor/editorial director of the *Harvard Business Review* and a founding editor of *Fast Company,*

> the most important work in the new economy is creating conversations....
> But all depends on the quality of the conversations.... Conversations—not
> rank, title, or the trappings of power—determine who is literally and figura-
> tively in the loop and who is not. (p. 28)

The new economy is dependent upon the ease, frequency, and quality of
conversations within and among organizations and communities. It is also
dependent, in my view, on the successful teaching of business ethics and
the creation of a classroom climate conducive to dialogue, good moral
conversation and effective ethics learning.

Building upon the work of many people, including Alan Webber (1993)
and David Whyte (1996), a poet who consults with many of the most successful global organizations, I think it is important that we call for a new
kind of conversation in the business ethics classroom—*conversational learning*. Because the quality of conversations is so critical, the nature, intentions, and contexts surrounding conversations need to improve, leading
to my role as the business ethics teacher vis-à-vis the increasing demands
or pressures to teach business ethics and prepare students for the ethical
challenges presented by changes in the new economy.

Given the fears, challenges and opportunities that come with any effort
to teach business ethics, how is conversational learning relevant? How can
a conversational learning approach contribute to the business ethics
teacher's capacity to possibly reframe student's perceptions of, for example business ethics in general and ways of responding to ethical situations
differently in particular? What does conversational learning involve in a
business ethics course? To address these questions, initially I offer a brief
conceptual description of conversational learning.

What is Conversational Learning?

The concept of learning used in this chapter is one that is grounded in
experience and is described by David Kolb (1984) as "a process whereby
knowledge is created through the transformation of experience" (p. 41).
Conversational learning eludes precise definition. Yet, some parameters

to guide you, the reader, may be helpful. Much of the spirit of my meaning of conversational learning rests in this message from Howard Stein (1994),

> To listen is to unearth rather than to bury. It is to feel rather than to be compelled to act. It gives us all greater liberty and responsibility in our actions.... The heart of listening deeply ... is attentiveness to others' voices ... the capacity for surprise in the face of any and all planning. Serendipity is readiness and playfulness in the face of surprise ... incorporation of the astonishing into the ordinary, the refusal to hide behind a shield of routine. It is a willingness to be moved, changed ... letting go of control. (p. 111)

To support the kind of listening that Stein is describing in my business ethics course, it is essential that I create receptive spaces for conversations to take place in the classroom. When these safe receptive spaces exist in the classroom, in my experience, students can learn to self-reflect and listen deeply to their own inner voice and to the voices of others—to listen in the spirit of learning, of being surprised, of being willing to slow down and reflect and share, and of being open to learning about business ethics.

To prepare students for the ethical challenges they will encounter in their work careers, these kinds of conversations are essential to facilitate learning in my business ethics course where students may reframe how they conceive of themselves and respond to ethical issues they might encounter in their own personal or work lives. I have found that conversational learning requires many substantial shifts in thinking for most students including:

- listening to others with the intention of learning with them;
- reflecting intentionally to gain more understanding of the complexities of organizational life using Schon's (1983) model of the reflective practitioner'
- moving away from assuming there is one way of thinking (either/or) toward assuming that there are multiple legitimate and viable perspectives and possibilities of any ethical situation or experience;
- moving away from assuming there is a right answer or a right approach toward placing more value on trying to learn from the multiple perspectives of as many other people as reasonably possible about business ethics and ethical decision making;
- avoiding reactive behavior by becoming highly proactive in anticipating business ethics situations and finding ways to learn from different perspectives.

A conversational learning approach has been especially advantageous in my business ethics course that often involve:

- recognition of student differences as essential for the continuous learning required, and
- collaborative learning among students with differing ethical, world-views, skills, areas of expertise, vocabularies, and so on.

My experience to date in teaching business ethics has convinced me that there are many unexamined assumptions that could limit the capacity for the kind of learning needed among our students. Some of these might include: their varying preferences and expectations about how ethical decisions should be made; appropriate styles for speaking and presenting themselves; who—or if anyone in the classroom—could be trusted enough to take risks and share one's thoughts, feelings, and/or opinions on complex and sensitive ethical or moral issues; whether the total class should get down to the business of tackling complex ethical theories and issues immediately or should some time be spent getting to know each other first; who had power and who did not have power as well as percep-tions about sources of power—for example, positional, personal, author-ity, influence, et cetera. For example, some of the students have no difficulty jumping in and sharing their views or participating in experien-tially oriented exercises, et cetera. On the other hand, other students are initially reluctant to speak.

USING A CONVERSATIONAL LEARNING APPROACH IN A BUSINESS ETHICS COURSE: WHAT IS MY ROLE?

Now let's consider the implications for the teacher in creating this new kind of conversation among students of business ethics. How would the business ethics teacher's work look different? What competencies and skills would be necessary? The intent in this section is to list some espe-cially relevant implications.

While in no way conclusive, some of the implications for my role as a teacher in my business ethics course include things that typically apply in all teaching engagements, but have a special slant in my view when a pri-mary intention is to create a new kind of conversation that promotes stu-dents' learning in the course. These include:

- understanding and managing self (i.e., "Doing my own personal work [i.e., reflection] first");

- planning and preparing the soil (i.e., the context, the classroom learning space, the students and myself) to build as much psychological safety as possible) in the business ethics course;
- attending with special care to the *beginnings* of my business ethics course;
- broadening and sharing views and experiential histories (ethical or moral stories) among the students (and with me) who participate in the business ethics course;
- emphasizing self-reflection as an essential part of learning and working to improve the quality of reflection in the business ethics course;
- emphasizing the relational, social dimensions of learning in the classroom, thus, transforming the notion of conversations and relationship building as essential to the learning, rather than a divergence from learning in the business ethics course;
- building competence and confidence among students for asking questions that delve below the surface, grapple constructively with ethical or moral issues and conflicts, stay engaged with differing perspectives even when their instincts are to avoid or react, and be able to recognize when and how to allow differences to emerge and be explored and when and how to set appropriate boundaries; and
- Proactively creating new patterns and routines with students that will anticipate personal learning (and change) opportunities and will enable and support continuous conversational learning.

Many of these approaches function like overlapping layers of a textured fabric in my business ethics course that serve to make it more durable, since the use of one often reinforces or strengthens the intentions of several others. Therefore, many of the descriptions below are grouped by similar content and also highlight some of these overlapping uses in my business ethics course. For example, I have used many of the illustrations of ways to broaden and share views and experiential histories in the beginning of a business ethics course to prepare the context and prime students to learn together collaboratively.

Understanding and Managing Self. "Doing one's own personal work first" is one of the guiding principles for me in teaching my business ethics course. In other words, knowing my strengths and shortcomings, being honest with myself, continuously striving to increase my ethical (and other) self-awareness, seeking and listening to feedback from responsible peers and colleagues, knowing my own personal "hot buttons" and how to anticipate and deal with them responsibly, being able to work from a centered place of a commitment to guiding students to find their own paths forward rather than falling into the pattern of imposing my way upon them is all part of "doing my own work first." Yet, I also realize that to be able to create a climate conducive to learning, to model conversational learning, to guide students toward developing their own competence in conversational learning, and to authentically prepare them for the possible tumultuous short-term educational consequences and resistances to this approach requires that I am on a lifelong journey of doing my "own personal work." This approach is not "business as usual" because it calls for *listening to learn* and *ongoing changes* not just in students, but also within me as the business ethics teacher.

Without having a fairly well developed ethical self-awareness and acceptance of who I am, I find it is difficult for me to listen deeply to others in ways that are open to being surprised and hearing new possibilities. Without the calming effect of an authentic acceptance of multiple perspectives, it is difficult for me to help students create safe learning environments that seek alternative and perhaps competing ethical and other perspectives. Without openness to learning from the differences in others, it is also difficult for me to get students to embark upon conversations that raise differing perspectives and to remain engaged with them when the inevitable tension surfaces. Without an understanding on my part that remaining engaged constructively with differing perspectives is an essential part of a classroom climate conducive to learning about business ethics, it is difficult to stand shoulder to shoulder with students and interact with them in developing their skills of constructive engagement in conflict in general and even more so in conflict on ethical, moral or related "hot button" issues.

Planning, Preparing, and Beginnings. Planning for and preparing the soil is a metaphor that may be the quintessential image that encompasses the message of my responsibility as a teacher in a business ethics course. Whether in initial interactions with the whole group of students in my business ethics course, with individual students, teams of students assigned to work together during the course, or with external associates (i.e., colleagues, school of business administrators, potential employers, etc.), my planning and preparing of the soil—the context, the classroom learning space, the students—in my experience, is the single most indispensable part of the process.

Without a receptive space to hold and sustain conversational interactions and relationship building, the question asking and risk taking associated with learning in my business ethics course will be curtailed. Without a strong sense of psychological safety (Edmondson, 1999; Schein, 1999), it continues to be my experience that risk taking, sharing and differences will not surface directly in ways that catalyze learning in my business ethics course. Instead I have found that the results typically will covertly lead to destructive behavior like:

- avoidance;
- reactions;
- alienation; and
- passive-aggressive behavior.

All of these drain energy and resources from the targeted learning outcomes and the primary missions and tasks at hand in my business ethics course.

While trust and safety are easy to destroy by a judgmental comment, a broken promise, or a lie, my efforts to rebuild that trust and sense of safety can take endless energy and time. On the other hand, by attending in the beginning of the course to carefully and consistently creating a shared sense of trust and psychological safety it ends up taking far less time and effort on my part in the long run. Furthermore, when I acknowledge and take responsibility for less constructive behavior and talk about it in the class it can make the inevitable human foibles much less destructive and offer potent teachable moments. Thus, from my first contact with students in my business ethics course to each additional new beginning of the course, there are powerful opportunities for me to model and help the students recognize the potential of being able to venture into conversations and relational interactions that can create what Gadamer (1994) refers to as new ways of knowing and understanding, which would never have been possible without trust, safety, and those connections.

As discussed in previous writings (see Sims, 2002; Sims & Brinkmann, 2003; Sims & Felton, 2006) on my efforts to create a certain kind of classroom climate in my business ethics course, I begin during the first or second meeting with the students to try to establish a relationship of trust and respect by being very candid about my values and approach as a teacher (i.e., my bias or comfort with an experiential learning approach to teaching).

I also make it a point to let students know that I am there to learn from them and that I am committed to building a relationship with each of them based on mutual trust and respect. I assure them that whenever any of them ask to speak to me in confidence, I will respect their wish for confidentiality. I also stress the point that I hope to be perceived as an independent neutral in the volatile or conflictual situations that often arise between the students.

At the first class meeting, the important part of the syllabus is covered and I make every effort to prepare the context and to begin the learning process in ways that would most likely support collaborative conversational learning. I introduce myself and have students introduce themselves by sharing a bit about their hopes and expectations for our time together during the course. I pay close attention to the words that are said and the possibilities that are raised as well as those that were not expressed. I make careful mental notes to revisit themes that I want to reinforce and comments that I think might need to be unobtrusively reframed later.

I also talk very briefly about my hopes and expectations with the intention of beginning to help the group students develop some jointly shared superordinate goals that would call forth the most generous and community-minded intentions, using what I refer to in the next section as a brief (not more than 10 minutes maximum) lecturette given in a conversational manner without notes and using frequent examples that students can relate to easily.

Also as part of the first two class meetings, I ask students to imagine the ideal kinds of conversations that the group might have together and to jot down some of the characteristics of what those conversations might sound like. I suggest that we do some brainstorming (offering their ideas without evaluation or discussion until all ideas are on the blackboard or flip chart paper) to generate together possible norms for us to use in all of our subsequent conversations. I also come prepared with ideas that I feel are important and add suggestions for possible norms. After ideas are captured in writing, we talk collectively about the items on the list and gradually work toward gaining a common consensus—an understanding that while each item might not be shared by everyone with the same enthusiasm, each item remaining on the list is one that students can "live with" as a shared norm. This consensus is usually reached fairly quickly. A large poster of the list is printed and posted in all subsequent meetings of the class, and copies are given to each student at the class meeting. The list of norms is often revisited and slightly modified in light of student reflection after the first class meeting. The list, developed by this particular group of students, serves as the guide for appropriate ways of communicating during the course.

Broadening Student Views and Willingness to Share. One way that I use to broaden student views is by asking them to listen carefully to each other's stories of their experiences (i.e., ethical, moral, etc.) and I find this helps to expand the range of authentic possibilities. The use of stories in my course, unlike the abstract declaration of ideas, helps to engage the students in the possibilities of varied ways of growing up and developing in ways that may generate more empathetic and careful consideration and attention. In my experience, for some students, hearing abstract ideas, separated from personal experience, makes it difficult for them to imagine how these ideas would be manifested in actual behavior. Also, especially when abstract ideas are presented to the students, unless I am especially attuned to my choice of words, tone of voice, verbal and nonverbal attitude, and so on, the students may feel they are being preached to, which generates a reaction against the content and interferes with possible new learning and reflections. I find this distinction between ideas and stories is exquisitely illustrated in the following quote from Alice Walker's novel, *By the Light of My Father's Smile*. The quote is from a conversation between two of the characters in the book, one of whom is a Mundo, from an indigenous population in Latin America:

> No one among the Mundo believes there is anyone on earth who truly knows anything about why we are here, Senor. To even have an idea about it would require a very big brain. A computer. That is why, instead of ideas, the Mundo have stories.
> You are saying ... that stories have more room in them than ideas?
> That is correct, Senor. It is as if ideas are made of blocks. Rigid and hard. And stories
> are made of a gauze that is elastic. You can almost see through it, so what is beyond is tantalizing. You can't quite make it out; and because the imagination is always moving forward, you yourself are constantly stretching. Stories are the way spirit is exercised.
> But surely your people have ideas, I said.
> Of course we do. But we know there is a limit to them. After that, story!
> (1998, pp. 193-194)

Thus, the story can stir the listeners' imagination, tantalize them to stay engaged, and offer an elastic gauzelike frame within which each listener's own worldview can be seen and perhaps expanded. Obviously, the format and the timing for sharing stories in an effort to teach business ethics needs to be contextually appropriate and relevant, but I do my best not to make the assumption that the students just want specific information, a rational approach, the most "efficient" use of time, and so on. This emphasis, however, usually precludes time for storytelling when storytelling can serve multiple purposes simultaneously and become a high point early in my course. The teaching and organizational learning and change literature (Brown & Duguid, 2000, 1991; Schor, Sims, & Dennehy, 1996; Wenger, 1998) is filled with confirmation of the substantial wealth of learning potential that can emerge in the wise use of sharing stories and narratives.

A few other ways I use to broaden student views include brief, easy to understand prereadings to prepare them for group conversations about the readings; brief, easy-to-understand lecturettes by me or by a highly regarded person who has credibility (guest lecturer) either from within the school of business or from outside; and spontaneous strategic inclusion of the ideas and examples of varied philosophical or business ethics views in group conversations, especially when I make connections to examples to illustrate how differing views are filters through which the world is seen and understood.

In one business ethics course, after dividing students into groups during the first class, I had them develop a list of concerns/fears they had in taking the course. One student from each group did a thematic analysis of the data and then shared during the next class common and unique themes that emerged in the previous class group meetings. A commonly shared theme that ran throughout the group data was the lack of trust students had of each other and thus a willingness to share. Another common theme was the skepticism that they had about the possibility of "really" learning anything about business ethics in my course.

One way that I try to get students to increase their willingness to share is by having them complete the following exercise, "Responding to an Ethical Dilemma," where the challenge is for students to increase their awareness of how they themselves behaved when confronted with a particular ethical dilemma. Students are asked to consider a past ethical dilemma which they were confronted with that seriously caused them to reflect on the situation. Students then respond in writing to the following questions:

1. When did you first become aware that you had an ethical dilemma? Part of the learning from this question is for the students to assess their awareness of an ethical dilemma situation.

2. What was the ethical dilemma? The answer to this should include a description of the ethical dilemma.

3. What were your first thoughts (e.g., surprise, confusion, anxiety)? The student's response to this will give a good indicator of the student's attitude to the ethical dilemma.

4. What made you decide that you had to do something? The motive given by the students for their decision(s) given the ethical dilemma will give some indication of their priorities and what they believed was the "right thing to do," or what they felt they *had* to do.

5. What actions did you take? The effectiveness of the actions of the student in this situation may be a reflection of a lack of self-understanding or decision-making skill in dealing with the ethical dilemma.

6. What was the impact in the (a) short and (b) long term? When students understand the consequences of their actions, it gives them

more insight into the reality of the situation and themselves over time. Students need to be able to contemplate the short and long term impact of their decisions or actions.

7. If you could "rewind the tape," would you do something different? If so, what would you do differently? And why? The answer to this question may show what the student learned from the situation, or describe merely a reaction the end result(s) or process. This is a good question for students to work through if they want to gain insight into what lessons they have taken away from an ethical dilemma that seriously affected them.

I first pair students up so they can share their responses to the questions with each other by listening to what the other person is saying and then sharing the information when I next assign the students to a larger group. Next, I have each group share one or two of the members' responses with the total class. We then talk about what it was like for the students to share their responses to the questions with each other to include stating what they would do different in the future. Using this brief exercise early on in my course allows the students to reflect on a situation and then share it with others. This sharing, in my experience, ensures that each student has another opportunity to engage and share with others, and hopefully throughout the course. It appears from student feedback to date that they value having as many opportunities as possible to reflect on various situations and share and hear from their fellow students; this enhances the quality of their learning experience in the course.

Reflecting on Difference and Learning. Generally, it has been my experience that when students reflect upon their differences on ethics-related issues with other people, the potential for their learning from the differences is increased. The likelihood for their learning is further increased when the quality of reflection improves. One of the first people to write about organizational learning was Donald Schon (1983), who also has written extensively about practitioners who reflect on their experiences and "stay in conversation" with organizational situations. These reflective practitioners are like, in my view, the effective business ethics teacher who is able to observe and listen intently to recognize how a unique situation is similar and different from previous ones. They are able to reflect upon intended and unintended changes to let each new situation in the business ethics course "talk back" to them and serve as a possible source of learning. Like Schon, I recognize that it is in the differences among students and in the unexpected and unintended changes that the greatest potential for learning can often be found. And yet, it is also in these very circumstances that breakdowns can occur that not only impede business ethics learning but also often lead to misunderstandings, distractions, and lost energy and productivity in my business ethics courses.

In my experience, business school students typically have limited skills for and little experience with constructive engagement with differences and the surfacing of conflict. The more limited these skills and experiences are, the more likely students are to avoid letting differences come to the surface and be talked about, the more likely students are to avoid others whom they perceive as different, and the more likely students are to become alienated from some other students and parts of the classroom that they perceive as different. For example, we all are aware of those courses in which the students are a diverse mix of business and nonbusiness majors, who, like our colleagues (i.e., faculty) often do not talk to one another, may not be open to hearing one another's views, or have misperceptions about one another (i.e., nonbusiness majors often view business majors as "money hungry" and only concerned about the bottom line, while business majors often view liberal arts students as mainly concerned with social issues). This leads to a lack of coordination, at the least, and a lack of potential collaborative energy that if I manage right can become an invaluable learning resource in my business ethics course.

It has been my experience that students from differing and "opposing camps" on various moral or ethical issues, cases, and so forth seldom listen calmly to others who have opposing points of view on these issues early in the course. Preparing students to trust that there will be civil conversation, that everyone will be treated with respect, that each person will have a chance to be heard, and that my business ethics course will not be a futile waste of their time is among the challenges that require the kind of preparation by me described above.

Much of my preparation comes from trying to listen carefully to the unique experiences and perspective of each student or group and trying to address their concerns. For example, in reference to student's fears about sharing and risk taking, I find it helpful to assure them that the course or experience would be different, putting my own reputation on the line and activating my own adrenalin at the same time—an effective stimulus in my experience for many of my colleagues who teach business ethics, but one that creates the kind of stress we know too well.

I strongly believe that the initial class meetings (the beginnings) are always critical for helping students in my business ethics course learn new ways of engaging so that they can *listen to learn* from their individual perspectives or differences. The jointly-created norms of conversation provide the framework for a new *kind* of conversation. I find it very useful to gently intervene when norms are not being observed (for example, asking the students if they feel we are following our own agreed-upon norms and in some cases naming aggressive behavior when a more gentle approach is not effective). As mentioned earlier, I think it is very important to create a safe, receptive space for conversation by letting students know up front that I will intervene whenever necessary to assure that each student is treated with respect. I ask questions and bring up topics to encourage students to share their views, take risks, and respect one another's differences. I also try to model a new kind of conversational interaction in my own behavior. I find that this kind of work requires me to call on my training and experience in conflict resolution, facilitation, and group dynamics; to have sensitivity to the experiences of each student in the course or class, and to be open to various moral and ethical views and the need to allow differences to surface to challenge the status quo. For example, in my experience, those of us who may espouse certain ethical theories or teaching approaches need to grapple extensively with our own biases and the views that we typically have taken for granted if we are going to have any credibility and viability in teaching business ethics and creating a new kind of conversation among diverse students.

One way I try to incorporate the opportunity of reflecting on and learning from differences is through an exercise called "image of the ideal ethical person." In this exercise students have to identify an individual that had appeared in a book, movie or in their own personal life who fits the image of the ideal ethical person. In identifying that person each student is required to develop arguments (i.e., no more than three paragraphs) to support why the individual fit the image of the ideal ethical person. Students share their supporting write-ups electronically with others in the course prior to class. Each student must read at least one other student's posting with the goal of arguing why the person would not fit his or her own image of the ideal ethical person. The in-class discussions are lively as students discuss their different views on the supposed ideal ethical person. The dialogue and conversation offers insight into how and why students came to their various conclusions, reflection about changing and responding to other's different images of the ideal ethical person.

One of my goals in assigning this is to lay the foundation for using critical thinking skills and to prompt discussion of reasons why one's perception about a given person or the ethical person is often different from the perspective of others in the course. I also use the same exercise by having a group of students identify and come to consensus on their ideal ethical person and then groups discuss their different perspectives in class. One twist on this exercise is to have a student (or a group of students) identify an individual who reflects high ethical values or ideals, and who the student recognizes as a role model, with my goal being to mutually inspire class members through their own stories of ethical people whose role modeling provided them with strength and courage. In either version, it is important to have students support or defend their reasons as to why a particular individual in their view reflects the ideal ethical person while also recognizing that they can reflect on, appreciate and learn from differences.

One question that stimulates the most discussion and ensuing conversation is: As a student reading and listening to the reasons or rationale for the image of the ideal ethical person, did you find that each student had compelling reasons for choosing the individual he or she chose? Why or why not?

Amidst the discussion and debriefing of the exercise students express appreciation for hearing others' images of the ideal ethical person. There have been comments that thinking about how others view an ethical person provides helpful insights on others' perceptions, ideals, and values. Students have said the exercise offered the chance to explore ideas about ethics in general and differences in how people make decisions on what is or is not ethical behavior, that it was enjoyable to prepare and share, and that it encouraged thinking about the importance of appreciating different perspectives as they relate to ethics and ethical behavior.

Relational and Proactive. When business ethics learning is happening in or out of my classroom, it is taking place at and across multiple levels (i.e., at the individual level, the group level, the course level and the business school). As a business ethics teacher, it is critically important that I am able to be proactive, rather than reactive, at each level to the dynamics of ethical and moral situations, challenges, opportunities, dilemmas, and so forth and this demands a relational orientation to the learning process. While an emphasis on relationships and social interactions is embedded in the business education of most students, in my view, the pervasiveness of relational dynamics is intensified in today's increasingly global world of work (a world that exposes employees to increasingly diverse ethical or moral views) where "conversation" and collaboration are the essence of the work.

In my business ethics course, I try to make sure that the preparation and beginning elements are interwoven with the ever changing work environment that confronts our students. Recognizing and being able to track the relational dynamics that are occurring on all levels simultaneously is in my view one of the biggest challenges, requiring me to structure my own frequent reflection upon the business ethics course to learn from the talk back or debriefing of each unique situation. Spending structured and unstructured time in the first few meetings to help students begin to build new relationship is critical to any success I may have in achieving the targeted learning outcomes I have for my business ethics course.

For example, in one second class meeting, I did a visioning exercise. Each student wrote words on index cards that described his or her ideal image for the ethical organization. These cards were then posted on the walls of the classroom. Students were then asked to walk silently around the room reading all the cards. This was followed by time for group reflection, during which the conversation brought out what students noticed as they silently read the cards. Overwhelmingly, the main impression was the similarity of the images of what they wanted for an ethical organization–a transformation from seeing themselves as having very different views into a growing recognition that they shared more common ground than they had imagined. I have found this to frequently be the case, given the number of business and nonbusiness majors that are in my course.

The instilliation of practical discourse or what has been referred to in this chapter as conversational learning is critical, in my view, to effectively teaching business ethics and developing integrity in my business students. As a business ethics teacher I strongly believe that I must strive to give voice to students in my classroom. Further, as one author suggests, and I wholeheartedly agree, "The disposition to hear and be concerned for others is something that must be learned and cultivated, preferably throughout one's entire education, but certainly it needs to be encouraged and reinforced in the business curriculum" (Carroll, 1998).

As a business ethics teacher, I believe I have a responsibility to create a classroom learning environment that values the ideas others have to offer. This means providing students with the information they need to make informed decisions and to assess various ethical theories or philosophical approaches. It also demands open-mindedness and an intense respect for what others may view as the truth, even when it may be counter to our own view. The very act of participating in conversational learning suggests that in some instances there can be genuine consensus and that this can be distinguished from a consensus that is false. I work hard to make sure that my classroom environment is free from constraint and that every student has an equal opportunity to be heard. This means each student has the same chance to command, to oppose, to permit, or forbid, and to express his or her attitudes, feelings, and intentions.

The equality of status between the teacher and students is a pivotal, albeit controversial issue in the business ethics course. The idea of "conversation among equals" that is at the crux of conversational learning cannot go unexamined if the conversational classroom space in a business ethics course is to continue to flourish. It is safe to say that the unique and diverse composition of today's students plays a significant role in creating and making the conversational learning space in my business ethics course possible. Students' rich lives and experiences further contribute to the richness and complexity of the learning process in my business ethics course. It is interesting to notice, however, how students perceived themselves as learners upon entering one my business ethics classroom settings.

Regardless of their prior status as accomplished and autonomous individuals, lingering somewhere inside their minds is the idea Freire (1992) described as "internalized oppression," a process whereby students as learners relinquish the valuable experience and knowledge they already possess in the name of the expert knowledge of the teacher. By surrendering their power to the teacher, students relegate themselves to the position of passive recipients of information and knowledge. Perhaps a typical classroom scene commonly shared by most traditional educational institutions is the one in which, in a classroom of thirty students, only one person, the teacher, does most of the talking while the rest are left in silence. Remember the chapter opening description on my experience in my first ethics course. In the conversational, classroom learning space I strive to create in my business ethics course however, the status of the teacher as the sole authority had to be reconsidered as I deliberately shifted my position as a power figure to that of an equal participant in the course. Although I provided the syllabus and reading assignments early in the semester, and set a learning agenda based upon the course's targeted learning outcomes, I did not automatically give specific direction in the class discussions throughout the semester. The stance I maintained over the course of the semester was that of an equal participant who encouraged students to have their voices in stark contrast to the traditional lecture format, where the business ethics teacher dominates most of the airtime in the classroom.

SOME FURTHER REFLECTION

At this point I hope it is clear to you the reader that I believe dialogue and conversational learning should be built into the curriculum itself and developed as a skill in our students at the preprofessional level. Business ethics courses should be geared consciously and sincerely to take into account what others have to say. I find that this is essential to the integration of ethics into business education and my own efforts to teach business ethics for effective learning.

The concept of conversational learning grew out of David Kolb's (1984) aspiration to explore a new approach to teaching and learning based on the theory and practice of experiential learning. Unlike a traditional method of learning that places primary emphasis on abstract and conceptual dimensions of knowledge, dialogue and conversational learning equally values the learner's (student's) emotional, sensual, and physical engagement in the learning process in a business ethics course.

In a 1998 interview in a European journal, David Kolb voiced his conversational learning philosophy (upon which I base my own teaching in business ethics courses) as follows:

> One of the key concepts behind the conversational model of learning is the idea of a learning process where teachers and students come together as equal learners. When learning is viewed as a dialogue and conversation among equals, the teacher is no longer viewed as the sole provider of the expert knowledge. The status of the expert is equally shared among learners who actively take responsibility in offering expert knowledge when needed ...
>
> Paulo Freire writes that you can't deny the fact that teachers know more in some regard. I think that it means that knowledge is a dynamic process which changes all the time. While I may know a lot about management, the others may happen to know a lot about engineering or some kind of expert knowledge. Dialogue among equals doesn't mean that in any single conversation there isn't a point in which one person is an expert and the other person is not. (Kolb, 1998, p. 51)

Inevitably, students always face a period of adjustment in my business ethics courses in order to become familiar with this new concept and configuration. The lingering "internalized oppression" does resurface from time to time in the course, as students look to me and ask for my voice and direction at crucial points during various conversations.

Particularly during the early part of a course, the shift in perspective from a lecture format to the conversational mode was met with hesitation. By and large, I think that as the business ethics professor I have been viewed as the primary purveyor of knowledge, which shouldn't be surprising given the students' experience in other courses across campus and in the school of business.

It is important to emphasize, however, that the awakening process of students moving beyond viewing me as the primary purveyor of knowledge in the course did not happen overnight. Students chose to approach conversational learning from multiple perspectives and personal interest in my business ethics courses. For some students conversation triggered in them a desire to act in the service of a cause they deeply cared about:

> Many times I leave class wondering how we can translate these great conversations into some ethical action that will make a change for the better in some way, whether it's the school of business, work world, the natural world, my world as a student, or my world as a member of this course or college.

Yet for different students conversation is experienced as the manifestation of the gift cycle of the learning process as the selfless exchange of giving and receiving among students promotes cohesion or unity, understanding, and authenticity in the classroom:

> Yet, what better way to truly depict the exchange of sharing between two human beings; sharing, which ignites the mind, enlivens the spirit and awakens, rejuvenates, and touches the soul. You tell me something. I tell you something. Together we enrich our existence, our lives and our "being" in that moment and time. The conversation starts, grows and unfolds. The conversation takes on a life of its own. It spreads its wealth all around the classroom.

Other times students resorted to the exploration of the theoretical and conceptual side of conversation as they inquired into the connection of the theory and practice of conversational learning:

> Conversational learning: Learning occurs in many ways for many situations and for many people. I wish that I felt confident with when and how conversational learning is a good idea. Short of that, I am confident that it is a powerful learning mode. Now seeing myself as a lifelong learner, I can probably find more opportunities than I ever expected to learn about business ethics and other things through conversation with others. In so doing, I am inherently valuing what others have to offer me short of books, their own views and experiences and knowledge. What actually is a conversation anyway?

CONCLUSION

By building the capacity for a new kind of conversation, the possibilities of enhancing students' learning of business ethics and their ability to carry this skill from the classroom to the business world is limitless. In my experience, to be most effective as business ethics teachers we must help our students develop a new kind of conversation in the classroom. I continue to come to the conclusion that it is important for me to be on a personal lifelong journey of increasing ethical self-awareness, to collaboratively reframe my perceptions of teaching and learning business ethics and develop increased skills in facilitating conflict resolution, and to collaboratively create with my students receptive conversational spaces imbued with psychological safety in my classroom.

With the increasing complexity of business ethics and knowledge intensive work in a pluralistic world, the nature, intentions, and contexts that surround conversations need to be given considerable attention—leading to an important role for the business ethics teacher vis-à-vis building continuous learning opportunities in the classroom. Classrooms that encourage dialogue, good moral conversation, and conversational learning contribute to whatever effectiveness I have in my business ethics courses.

Spirited classroom discussions are valuable for encouraging critical thinking and learning about business ethics. They promote articulate speech and respectful, active listening. They also can be a lot of fun, even for students who are not usually at ease speaking in a group. When students participate in a real discussion, in which they formulate their thoughts on a topic like business ethics, express their personal judgments, and are respected for their opinions by the other students and myself, then real learning takes place. In these kinds of discussions I have found that students have a more memorable learning experience. Moreover, in-class discussions serve as a learning lab for open-dialogue and conversation that I believe really pays off later in life when, as more mature adults, the students participate in the society at large. Therefore, the entire process is good for the students and for the society as a whole.

In retrospect I now know how fortunate I was to have had that first experience in the ethics course as an undergraduate student many moons ago. The experience was a hugely important learning opportunity for me. It gave me the chance to try to get it right early in my teaching career. As I sit down now planning and preparing the beginnings for a new business ethics course next semester, I am able to closely analyze the dynamics of classroom discussion and observe how students have responded to different lines of questioning, dialogue and conversation in my previous courses. And, I already know what I have to do.

REFERENCES

Bromwich, D. (1992). *Politics by other means: Higher education and group thinking.* New Haven, CT: Yale University Press.

Brown, J. S., & Duguid, P. (2000). *The social life of organization.* Boston, MA: Harvard Business School Press.

Carroll, R. F. (1998). The integrity factor-critical to accounting education. *Teaching Business Ethics, 2*(2), 137-163.

Edmondson, A. (1999). Psychological safety and learning behavior in work teams. *Administrative Science Quarterly, 44*(2), 350-383.

Freire, P. (1992). *Pedagogy of the oppressed.* New York, NY: Continuum.

Friere, P. (1973). *Education for critical consciousness.* New York, NY: Continuum.

Fry, R., & Kolb, D. A. (1979). Experiential learning theory and learning experiences in liberal arts education. *New Directions for Experiential Learning, 6,* 79-92.

Gadamer, H. G. (1994). *Truth and method.* New York, NY: Crossroad.

Jourard, S. M. (1971). *The transparent self.* New York, NY: Van Nostrand Reinhold.

Kolb, D. A. (1984). *Experiential learning: Experience as the source of learning and development*. Englewood Cliffs, NJ: Prentice-Hall.

Kolb, D. A. (1998). Experiential learning: From discourse model to conversation. *Lifelong Learning in Europe, 3*, 148-153.

Nash, R. J. (1996). *"Real world" ethics: Frameworks for educators and human service professionals*. New York, NY: Teachers College Press.

Schein, E. H. (1999). *Organizational culture and leadership*. San Francisco, CA: Jossey-Bass.

Schon, D. A. (1983). *The reflective practitioner: How professionals think in action*. London, England: Temple Smith.

Schor, S. M. (1993). Understanding and appreciating diversity: The experiences of a diversity educator. In R. R. Sims & R. F. Dennehy (Eds.), *Diversity and differences in organizations: An agenda for answers and questions* (pp. 73-92). Westport, CT: Quorum Books.

Sims, R. R. (2002). *Teaching business ethics for effective learning*. Westport, CT: Quorum Books.

Sims, R. R., & Brinkmann, J. (2003). Business ethics curriculum design: Suggestions and illustrations. *Teaching Business Ethics, 7*(1), 69-86.

Sims, R. R., & Felton, E. (2006). Designing and delivering business ethics teaching and learning. *Journal of Business Ethics, 63*(3), 297-312.

Stein, H. F. (1994). *Listening deeply: An approach to understanding and consulting in organizational culture*. Boulder, CO: Westview Press.

Taylor, C. (1992). *Multiculturalism and "the politics of recognition": An essay by Charles Taylor*. Princeton, NJ: Princeton University Press.

Walker, A. (1998). *By the light of my father's smile*. New York, NY: Ballantine Books.

Webber, A. M. (1993, January-February). What's so new about the new economy? *Harvard Business Review*, 24-42.

Wenger, E. (1998). *Communities of practice: Learning, meaning, and identity*. New York, NY: Cambridge University Press.

Whyte, D. (1996). *The heart aroused: Learning, meaning, and identity*. New York, NY: Cambridge University Press.

CHAPTER 6

ONCE MORE WITH FEELING

Integrating Emotion in Teaching Business Ethics—Educational Implications From Cognitive Neuroscience and Social Psychology

Christopher P. Adkins

INTRODUCTION

John Oliver of the *Daily Show* interviews a business ethics professor:

> Business ethics professor: "We teach cases about corruption and choices they have to make. We teach them tools by which they can say 'no' if they are asked to do something which is unethical."
>
> Oliver: "Well this sounds fantastic! When are you going to start teaching this?"
>
> Professor: "We have been teaching this for decades."
>
> Oliver: (Pauses) ... "Would you say you're good at your job?"

Experiences in Teaching Business Ethics
pp. 123–142
Copyright © 2011 by Information Age Publishing

Of course I laughed when I saw this segment on the *Daily Show*, but it also stung a bit too. Those of us who teach business ethics have been at this for a while now, and the scandals of the last decade call into question the effectiveness of teaching business ethics, and the larger question of how business schools are shaping future leaders. The debates surrounding "teaching ethics" are not new, and critics of business education have called for a renewed commitment to professional practice that embraces societal and environmental concerns (Khurana & Nohria, 2008; Samuelson, 2006).

Even if a new vision and commitment to business professionalism emerges, the challenge of effectively teaching ethical leadership remains. In many ways, teaching business ethics involves a unique set of challenges. First, our teaching is intended to produce behavioral change, and to so in a normative way. It is not sufficient to simply impart knowledge about ethical issues or develop one's analytical skills applied to ethical scenarios; ethical action in daily business practice is the ideal outcome. Second, the setting for our teaching is far removed from where the action must be practiced. In other words, our quiet classrooms are a far cry from the intensity of boardrooms and trading floors, and the anxiety of hiring and firing decisions. Without a naturalized context it is difficult to truly practice the proposed ethical behavior, let alone assess whether our students have been successful in practicing the behavior. Third, we often have one course, ranging anywhere from 6-15 weeks, to produce such behavior change. And lastly, the behavior we seek to influence involves not only one's thinking but also one's feeling and one's wanting, and for academics, emotion and motivation are usually considered beyond the scope of our educational efforts.

This chapter focuses on this last challenge of bringing emotion into the field of business ethics education. As the latest research in cognitive neuroscience and social psychology suggest, emotion fuels our first intuition in ethical situations, and in turn shapes our reasoning and motivations. The notion that emotions influence our decision making resonates with our everyday experience. Yet within the tradition of ethics education, emotion has at best been in the shadows while cognition claimed the limelight of center stage. The current resurgence of interest in moral psychology, sparked by insights from functional magnetic resonance imaging (fMRi) imaging, has now thrust forward emotion and intuition as the primary influencers of our ethical decision making. In light of these findings, I propose that we reconsider how we have circumscribed the scope of our teaching to cognition, and explore how we can integrate emotion in ethics education. Specifically, I will present several findings from the cognitive neuroscience and social psychology literature that illustrate how emotion is at work in ethical decision making, and in presenting these findings I will describe how these insights can be used in the teaching of business ethics. The concluding section will address the educational implications and approaches for integrating emotion in business ethics courses.

Before proceeding, let me, at the outset, clarify that I am not suggesting we replace cognition with emotion as our guide in making ethical decisions or in teaching ethics. Rather, I suggest that we expand our scope to include an understanding of emotion, lest we fall prey to its pitfalls or overlook its potential power in stimulating empathetic ethical action.

THE ULTIMATUM GAME: CHALLENGING THE RATIONALIST ASSUMPTIONS BEHIND BEHAVIOR

I am trained as a philosopher. When I first started teaching ethics, I focused on teaching my students ethical principles and frameworks they could apply to a range of scenarios. I often would have my students act as ethical consultants to the individual or organization in the case at hand, identifying the ethical considerations, legal obligations, and financial implications of the various options under consideration. After such analyses, students would offer a recommended course of action that followed from their logical application of an ethical principle or framework.

For many students, identifying ethical principles, let alone applying frameworks consistently and logically, proved difficult. Yet through our class discussions and small group meetings, they seemed to progress in their ethical reasoning. For his dissertation, a colleague of mine examined the ethical reasoning of my students and found that the students did indeed improve in ethical reasoning in taking my course (Schmidt, 2007). Improving moral judgment was not only possible, but I was finding success in doing so, even within a 12-week course. I wasn't satisfied with these results, however.

At the beginning of each semester, I ask my students a simple question: Who has known what the right thing to do is, but has failed to actually do it? Every hand goes up. We all seem to know that when it comes to ethics, knowing what to do is not sufficient; ethical deliberation must lead to ethical action. I wondered if my students applied the moral reasoning we developed in class in their own lives, and if such reasoning would transfer to the ethical challenges they would face as business leaders. I knew from my own experience that engaging in cool, logical analysis can be difficult, especially when one's own livelihood is at risk, or those for whom one cares.

Awareness of ethical issues and the development of moral reasoning have been considered essential goals of business ethics education. Understanding the psychological processes that shape such awareness and deliberation, however, has not. This is an unfortunate oversight, for we are missing how easily our emotions can influence reasoning. To illustrate this, I often begin my course with several rounds of the ultimatum game:

In the Ultimatum Game, two players are given the opportunity to split a sum of money. One player is deemed the proposer and the other, the responder. The proposer makes an offer as to how this money should be split between the two. The second player (the responder) can either accept or reject this offer. If it is accepted, the money is split as proposed, but if the responder rejects the offer, then neither player receives anything. In either event, the game is over (Sanfey, Rilling, Aronson, Nystrom, & Cohen, 2003, p. 1755).

The undergraduate business majors I teach arrive having taken prerequisite introductory classes in microeconomics and macroeconomics, and thus are familiar that traditional economic theories often assume that humans behave as "rational decision makers" seeking to maximize utility. Thus, according to this perspective, the responders should accept any sum of money, no matter how small, for they now have more than they would have otherwise. Yet Sanfey and colleagues note that "considerable behavioral research in industrialized cultures indicates that, irrespective of the monetary sum, modal offers are typically around 50% of the total amount. Low offers (around 20% of the total) have about a 50% chance of being rejected" (Sanfey et al., 2003, p. 1755).

This simple game lends itself to in-class demonstration, and I often will recreate the experiment as a short, simple, yet powerful discussion starter for lessons in neuroscience and social psychology. Before using money as the reward, I begin using pieces of candy. One can predict what happens: the proposer will offer to share the candy evenly, or may even offer most of the candy to the responder (particularly if that type of candy is not a favorite of the proposer). I then take out ten $1 bills, and ask the two students to repeat the experiment. Here my class experience is consistent with the findings summarized by Sanfey and colleagues. The proposer usually offers $4 or $5 to the responder and the responder accepts the deal. Yet in some cases, the proposer will offer only $1 or $2, upon which the responder usually rejects the deal.

Recreating the experiment in class, first with candy, then proceeding to real money, illustrates an obvious point: individuals behave differently depending on the stakes. One does not need an experiment to teach this point, but the demonstration engages students in active reflection on how various circumstances influence decision making. Of course, the in-class experiment does not indicate how they might behave in an experimental setting of the research studies, and in our class discussion students easily recognize the differences: (1) the two participants can see each other (in other words, there is no anonymity); (2) they will see each other again (thus reputation is a concern); (3) their peers are watching (again, reputation and social perception weighs heavily). The influence of being watched (social influence) and of being remembered (memory influence) foreshadow two themes I build on throughout my business ethics course: accountability and credibility. Moreover, it highlights the importance we place on fairness as a value in our social interactions, and that when we feel we've been treated unfairly, we are willing to sacrifice reward, even monetary reward, in order to punish the one who treated us unfairly.

The power of this emotion to override our rational calculation of utility is further illustrated through the findings of Sanfey and colleagues (2003) who had individuals play the ultimatum game while under fMRi scanning. In contrast to fair or advantageous offers, unfair offers triggered significant activity in the anterior insula, a region correlated with negative emotions such as anger. They also examined the contrast in activation between the anterior insula and the dorsolateral prefrontal cortex (DLPFC), a region associated with "goal maintenance and executive control" (2003, p. 1757).

They found that when unfair offers were rejected, the anterior insula exhibited greater activation than the DLPFC, yet when unfair offers were accepted, the DLPFC exhibited greater activation than the anterior insula. It would appear that the brain regions were in conflict with one another, and that when the emotional brain (anger in the anterior insula) got the upper hand, the unfair offer was rejected. However, when the rational brain (goal planning in the DLPFC) reigned, the unfair offer was accepted, netting the financial gain.

The ultimatum game, supplemented by the brain imaging results, highlights the interaction between cognitive and affective processes in decision making. Students easily see that our emotion is powerful even in a simple game and can overpower our rational nature, but that we can control this emotion as well. Having illustrated this tension between cognition and affect, we proceed for a closer examination of the nature of dual processing in decision making.

A TALE OF TWO PROCESSES

Recall Aristotle's insistence that virtue requires knowledge; for perhaps one thing it requires knowledge about is our own psychology. (Appiah, 2008, p. 70)

When one attempts to teach any skill, one begins with underlying assumptions about the processes involved in that very skill. What are the processes that underlie ethical decision making? Neuroscientist Joseph LeDoux (2003) categorizes the neural processes engaged in decision making as the mental trilogy: cognition, emotion, and motivation (LeDoux, 2003). The cognitive developmental tradition of moral education, most notably the work of Lawrence Kohlberg and James Rest, elevated cognition as the primary area of concern for moral education. This tradition uses a four-step process to describe the sequence of ethical decision making: awareness, judgment, motivation, and action. Ethics education, including business ethics education, has focused primarily on the second step, moral judgment, using case discussions and philosophical frameworks as the primary way to examine ethical issues and advance ethical reasoning. A new generation of moral psychologists has revived the field by taking a critical look at the cognitive developmental tradition, emphasizing that the "cognitive" processes are preceded by (or perhaps intertwined with) emotional and intuitive ones, and these exert a powerful influence over one's thinking, decision making, and thus one's course of action.

Consider the last time you were facing a moral dilemma in the workplace. Should I keep my word to a colleague, or share what I know to help the organization? How did you arrive at your choice of action? If asked we can list our reasons why we chose one path and not another. Yet did our reasons really lead us to our conclusion? Psychologist Jonathan Haidt (2001) argues that while you may think that reasoning leads to your moral decision, you're likely deceiving yourself. Rather, you immediately have a sense of what you want to do, the choice appears quickly and seemingly out of nowhere, and then your reasons kick in to justify it to yourself. Haidt argues that moral reasoning is a post hoc exercise following intuition, that is, we search for reasons that support our initial intuition as opposed to the open, inquisitive, and deliberative process of searching for truth. He portrays reason as a lawyer seeking to defend a position as opposed to a judge that considers multiple arguments to determine the right judgment. His point is simple and striking: our motives often drive us to our conclusions, not our reasons (Haidt, 2001).

Suggesting that our emotional intuition, not our conscious reasoning, drives our moral behavior has sparked controversy in academic circles, but Haidt's theory resonates with Kunda's (1990) notion of "motivated reasoning" in the marketing management literature and the "biases and framing" research of the Nobel-prize winning economists Tversky and Kahneman (1974). Social psychologists such as Robert Zajonc (1980) and Jon Bargh (1999) have proposed that humans assess situations in two simultaneous, parallel ways: (1) very quickly, automatically and unconsciously via our affective and intuitive systems; (2) more slowly, cognitively, and consciously

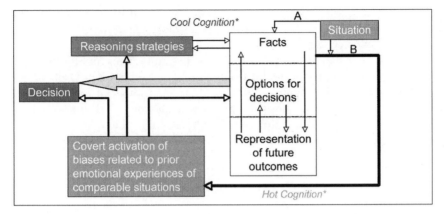

*The labels ("cool cognition" and "hot cognition") are the author's additions to Damasio's diagram.
Source: Damasio (2003, p. 149).

Figure 6.1.   Dual processing in decision making.

though controlled deliberation and reasoning. The affective system is deeply rooted in our evolutionary history, and is activated rapidly and powerfully in assessing situations. Neuroscientist Antonio Damasio (2003) offers the following model (see Figure 6.1) of how this emotional process runs parallel to our conscious reasoning when making decisions:

Path A is the path of cool, conscious, deliberate reasoning. It begins as we perceive the facts of the scenario and start making sense of the experience in terms of the options available and what the consequences of those various options might be. But as our cool cognition attempts to make sense of this situation, a parallel process has already begun. Path B is the path of "hot cognition" where our past emotional experiences from situations that resemble the current situation are reawakened outside of our conscious awareness of this process, at least initially (Path B). We may become aware of an emotional pull but may not know why, and this "gut feeling" may lead to our decision. Also, the emotional activation may unconsciously impact our understanding of options and consequences, as well as may influence our "reasoning strategies." Damasio (2003) suggests that the degree of influence and reliance on one or both paths depends on the situation and surrounding circumstances as well the individual's own background and development.

While complex at first sight my students comment that Damasio's dual process model and the emphasis on the power of past emotional experiences resonate with their own experience. They can identify "significant moral moments" from their past that were colored by powerful emotions, and they can recognize how these memories have influenced how they perceived later scenarios that were similar in nature. This highlights a secondary benefit of this model for teaching business ethics: it not only offers a framework for identifying how our "hot" emotions can influence our "cool" reasoning, but it engages students in personal reflection on how their perception of ethical situations might be shaded by their own subjective past.

UP CLOSE AND PERSONAL

Making ethical scenarios feel up close and personal is a primary challenge in teaching business ethics, particularly with undergraduates who tend to have limited work experience as points of reference. We tend to use vignettes or cases to evoke real-life scenarios for applying our ethical reasoning. Going further, we may attempt to identify with the protagonist and embrace the ambiguities and difficulties surrounding the decision at hand, but there is a comfortable distance in case discussions, temporally and spatially. Temporally, the urgency is missing (we need not act or decide quickly), and in many cases, the uncertainty is missing (we know the outcome of the situation). Spatially, we do not find ourselves in the office or boardroom, in the presence of coworkers or one's supervisor; rather we find ourselves in a classroom surrounded by classmates and the professor. Thus we are distant in time and space from the situation, and while attempts to experientially engage (such as role-playing) can shorten this distance, we remain third person observers and critics of what was a first person encounter.

Perhaps many faculty do not pause to consider this distance, or if they have do not consider it problematic, or simply accept it as a necessary condition for case method. There is a problem here, however, when it comes to teaching business ethics. Our class discussions and use of real-life cases intend to prepare students for the decisions and actions of real ethical scenarios, but do the mental processes we activate in class settings resemble the same mental processes engaged in real-life ethical encounters?

At about the time that my colleague was exploring educational approaches to moral reasoning, I discovered the research of Joshua Greene. Greene and colleagues were using fMRi to examine the brain activity involved in ethical decision making. His studies using trolley dilemmas have become a major source of discussion in the revival of moral psychology. In one of their first studies, Greene, Sommerville,

Nystrom, Darley, and Cohen (2001) noted a significant difference in the brain's response to moral dilemmas that were perceived as more or less personal. This distinction can best be illustrated by considering the scenarios offered to participants. The trolley dilemma exemplifies a moral-impersonal situation:

> A runaway trolley is headed for five people who will be killed if it proceeds on its present course. The only way to save them is to hit a switch that will turn the trolley onto an alternate set of tracks where it will kill one person instead of five. Ought you to turn the trolley in order to save five people at the expense of one? (Greene et al., 2001)

Greene and his colleagues note that most participants respond that they are willing to engage the switch and thus harm the one in order to save the five. Following this scenario, participants are offered a similar yet slightly altered version of the trolley dilemma known as the footbridge dilemma:

> Now consider a similar problem, the footbridge dilemma. As before, a trolley threatens to kill five people. You are standing next to a large stranger on a footbridge that spans the tracks, in between the oncoming trolley and the five people. In this scenario, the only way to save the five people is to push this stranger off the bridge, onto the tracks below. He will die if you do this, but his body will stop the trolley from reaching the others. Ought you to save the five others by pushing this stranger to his death? (Greene et al., 2001)

This "moral-personal" dilemma asks the individual to personally engage in a direct ethical violation that causes serious harm to another person. They hypothesized that the "moral-personal" dilemmas would be more likely to activate an emotional response. The fMRi scores supported this hypothesis, showing increased activity in those areas of the brain that previous research has associated with emotion: the medial frontal gyrus (bilateral), the posterior cingulated gyrus (bilateral), and the angular gyrus (right and left). Moral-impersonal scenarios activated those areas of the brain associated with working memory: the dorsolateral prefrontal and parietal regions (Greene et al., 2001; Greene & Haidt, 2002).

That the brain responds differently, and is influenced by emotion in scenarios that require individuals to engage in direct harm, is not a surprising discovery when one considers theoretical decision making in contrast to naturalized decision making. It is much easier to consider doing harm in hypothetical situations as opposed to doing real harm in the live moment. Yet what is particularly striking about these neuropsychological studies is that even hypothetical situations can trigger an emotional response in the human being. The participant knows that the footbridge dilemma is an imaginary scenario that one is likely to never encounter, but the brain still registers an emotional response. Clearly pushing a fat man does feel different than pushing a switch, even if the consequences are the same, and if the situation is far removed from reality.

What surprised me, however, had nothing to do with the moral-personal versus moral-impersonal distinction. In reading their results, I halted when I read this line of their article: "These data also suggest that, in terms of the psychological processes associated with their production, judgments concerning 'impersonal' moral dilemmas more closely resemble judgments concerning nonmoral dilemmas than they do judgments concerning 'personal' moral dilemmas" (Greene et. al., 2001, p. 2107) Moreover, "in BA 39 (bilateral), BA 46, and BA 7/40 (bilateral), there was no significant difference between the moral-impersonal and the non-moral condition (20, 21)." And "in Experiment 2 there was no difference in BA 9/10 between the moral-impersonal and non-moral conditions, and no differences were found for BA 46 (23)" (Greene et al., 2001, p. 2107). The distinction, or lack thereof, between the neural activations triggered by the moral-impersonal scenario and the nonmoral scenario, troubled me. If the brain activity suggested no meaningful distinction between hypothetical impersonal ethical scenarios and nonethical scenarios, then my efforts in using hypothetical ethical scenarios in class were likely similar to other non-ethical scenarios. Moreover, it did not seem likely that my moral-impersonal business scenarios, where the harm is indirect and one often does not feel the proximity to the individuals in the case, were evoking the emotional engagement that would occur when the situation was real.

These findings were consistent with my earlier suspicion: that teaching business ethics in the comforts of the classroom may not simulate or approximate the external environment nor stimulate the psychological processes involved when the ethical decisions were live and personal. After a few case discussions in my course, I share this study and its implications with my students as a way of amplifying the challenge involved in our study of business ethics. We observe how easy it has been to evaluate the cases thus far, and how difficult it is to truly immerse oneself in the scenarios.

KEEPING OURSELVES HONEST: THE POWER OF SELF-AWARENESS

Consider the following experiment:

> You are presented with two tasks. Task A has the potential for positive consequences: you can earn raffle tickets that may in turn lead to winning prizes.

Task B offers no such potential rewards. Also, task B, is rather dull and boring when compared with Task A.

One of the two participants in this experiment gets to assigns the tasks, and you have been selected as the "chooser" in this case. So you must decide who gets Task A and who gets Task B. The other participant will not know that you assigned the tasks, but will be told that the tasks were assigned by chance. Also, the two of you will never meet.

What task do you choose for yourself?

The choice may seem obvious: assign yourself the positive task (Task A). Why not follow your self-interest? But is this choice ethical? Is this even an ethical decision? One may contextualize this decision, thinking that it's only an experiment, and thus find it acceptable to privilege one's self over others. Or you may consider that the advantage you have was simply by chance, that you did not cheat the other person out of the rewards task, that you simply had the good fortunate to be the "chooser" in this case. You may expect that most other people would do the same if they were in the "chooser" role. In some sense, our moral intuition may not even be triggered, but for all us, our self-interest is immediately operative when we hear the options presented, pushing us toward the option best available for ourselves.

In their study of moral hypocrisy, Batson, Kobrynowicz, Dinnerstein, Kampf, and Wilson (1997) found that four out five participants assigned themselves to the positive consequences task. That 80% of the participants chose to follow their self-interest was not surprising, yet the researchers wanted to understand not only what choices individuals would make, but also how they understood their choices, and how they evaluated their actions. So after making the task assignment, they asked the participants how they felt about their decision (pride or guilt) and about the morality of their decision (right or wrong). Here is what they found: only 1 of the 16 who assigned themselves the positive task felt their decision was morally right and 12 indicated that assigning the other the positive task was morally right (which was the opposite of what they chose to do). Moreover, the majority felt guilty about their decision. It seemed that reflecting on the decision using a moral frame evoked some sense of regret and remorse.

To see if moral framing in advance of their choice would impact moral actions, the researchers conducted another study with a new group of participants, and added the following instruction:

Most people feel that giving both people an equal chance—by, for example, flipping a coin—is the fairest way to assign themselves and the other participant to the tasks (we have provided a coin for you to flip if you wish). But the decision is entirely up to you. (Batson, Kobrynowicz, Dinnerstein, Kampf, & Wilson, 1997, p. 1341)

So would the "fairness" frame, and the opportunity to apply it by flipping a coin, change the choices made? Here's what they found: half the participants flipped the coin, half did not. For those who *did not* flip the coin, all but one assigned the positive task to themselves. For those who *did* flip the coin, all but one assigned the positive task to themselves. So unless the laws of probability were suspended in this one study, flipping the coin did not make a difference. Why not? Why even bother flipping the coin if they simply intended to reward themselves? Here's what the questionnaires revealed this time: those who flipped the coin felt their action was more moral than those who did not, even though all but one chose to reward themselves over the other.

Batson and colleagues speculated that perhaps the coin flippers had not clearly defined what each side of the coin meant in terms of the consequences (what does heads mean again?) and thus could use this ambiguity to assign themselves the positive task while still feeling good about how they had made the decision. To make it harder for the participants to deceive themselves, they labeled the coins, placing a sticker for "self to pos" on one side and "other to pos" on the other. The result? It made no significant difference, with the majority of coin-flippers assigning themselves the positive task. What is interesting is that the fairness frame and the methodology for applying it seem to allow individuals to deceive themselves, thinking that they've acted morally. It appears that we may be more concerned with *feeling* moral that *acting* morally.

The researchers did find an approach that had some influence: they placed a mirror in front of the participant while making a choice. The mirror did not necessarily make more participants want to flip the coin or immediately assign the other the positive task, or even change their opinions on the morality of how to make the decision. But it did impact their action, how they assigned the task once they flipped the coin. Half of those who flipped the coin in front of the mirror assigned the positive task to the other, consistent with statistically probability for flipping a coin. Seeing themselves in the mirror made it more difficult to ignore the outcome of the flipped coin.

Why was the mirror such a powerful influence? Batson and colleagues suggest that seeing oneself made the decision to act deceitfully more explicit in one's consciousness, and thus interrupted any rationalization or abstraction that may have occurred in one's thinking. In other words, the mirror facilitated an external, visual self-awareness, which seemed to make it more difficult to internally rationalize not following the coin toss. Self-awareness and explicit attention to moral standards has been high-

lighted previously in the psychology and moral decision-making literature as a means for fostering consistency in values and behavior (Diener &
Wallborn, 1976; Duval & Wicklund, 1972; Langer, 1989). Raising self-
awareness is a tough challenge, considering that it seems to require an
internal willingness to reflect on one's behavior. However, as the mirror
provided an external source for reflection, reminders of one's moral commitment may prove effective. In a recent study of cheating behavior with
students, Mazar, Amir, and Ariely (2008) found that in situations where
students were given the opportunity to cheat, reminding individuals of
their university's honor code on the very sheet where they could cheat significantly reduced cheating behavior (my students are surprised by this
effect!). The researchers suggest that such codes may provide reminders
of one's own moral commitment.

There was another way to get participants to look beyond their immediate self-interest, without a mirror, and even without needing to flip the
coin. How? The answer lies in engaging our emotions through empathetic imagination.

SEEING AND FEELING AS OTHERS: EMPATHETIC IMAGINATION

Empirical moral psychology can help us think about how to manage our
lives, how to become better people. Situationism rightly directs us to focus
on institutions, on creating circumstances that are conducive to virtue.
Virtue theorists have sometimes directed us toward an excessively inward
model of self-development; situationism returns us to the world in which
our selves take shape (Appiah, 2008).

In many ethical dilemmas, business or otherwise, we know some of the
stakeholders who will be affected: those closest to us, our friends, colleagues, and families. And if the experiment involved assigning tasks to a
family member or close friend, we would likely act differently. Studies on
empathy highlight the importance of closeness or proximity in sparking
empathetic concern. Hoffman (2000) argues that we feel empathy toward
those familiar to us (family, friend, kin or tribe), those in front of us, and
those having an experience that resonates with an experience we've had.
The closer the situation is to home, the easier it is to empathize, and the
more motivated we may be to assist another.

Yet often the situation includes those not close to home. Complex business ethics decisions offer some anonymity in the sense that we do not
personally know all those who might be impacted. Consider global outsourcing. We may engage in stakeholder analysis and attempt to consider
the interests of all involved parties. In the face of competing interests and

unknown consequences, we're likely to pay attention to self-interest or privilege those we know.

In Batson's experiment, the participants did not know the other individual, so perhaps they found it difficult to feel empathy. Batson and his colleagues wanted to see if they could trigger empathy using a simple reflection exercise. In one scenario, after explaining and providing the background on the task assignments, the researchers asked the participant "to imagine how the other participant likely feels ... while waiting to hear which task he or she will be assigned ... when told which task he or she is to do" (Batson et al., 2003). While not every participant was moved by this exercise they saw a significant increase in individuals assigning the task to the other. Moreover, many decided to assign the positive task to other from the outset, not even needing to flip the coin, suggesting that the imagination exercise had a powerful influence in focusing concern toward the other. This exercise of considering how another both sees and feels the impact of a decision taps into a skill I call empathetic imagination, a technique that both students and leaders can use to enhance their understanding of impact on stakeholders.

How might empathetic imagination work? Imagining another's condition may bring to mind images that may provoke an emotional, empathetic response. As Hoffman (2000) notes, the moral sentimentalism of David Hume and Adam Smith suggested that imagination of another's emotions may cause us to feel similar emotions in ourselves:

> By the imagination we place ourselves in the other's situation, we conceive ourselves enduring all the same torments, we enter, as it were, into his body, and become in some measure the same person with him, and thence form some idea of his sensations, and even feel something which, though weaker in degree, is not altogether unlike them. (Smith, 1759/1965, p. 261, as cited in Hoffman, 2000, p. 53)

Smith's assessment is surprisingly rich in foreshadowing some of the latest findings in cognitive neuroscience on how empathy arises. The idea that in seeing another's or imagining another's situation we enter "into his body" and experience similar sensations has been explored by neuroscientist Antonio Damasio (1994, 2003). He argues that sympathy (feeling for another) can be transformed into empathy (feeling as another feels) through the work of mirror neurons and a body-mapping process that results in an "internal brain simulation" of another's feelings. Mirror neurons allow us to represent in our brain the same or similar movements we observe in another. The other individual need not be directly present; Damasio suggests that an "as-if-body-loop" mechanism allows us to "mirror" such experiences even if the other is not present, that is, simply imagining another's situation may trigger a process where our feelings attempt to match another's. These particular mirror neurons act as an emotionally competent stimulus that in turn sends signals to the "body-sensing" regions of the brain where one feels as if one were experiencing the sensation in one's own body. The "internal brain simulation" is not a direct match of the other's feelings, however. As Smith suggests above, the experience is likely weaker. Damasio goes further and calls such sensations "false body states" in that they are constructions based on perception of the other's possible sentiments as opposed to stimulated through the body. While falling short of an exact match of another's feelings, Damasio highlights the power and influence of such feelings, and argues that it is in this way that we empathize with others and may in turn be motivated to act on their behalf (Damasio, 1994, 2003).

THE IMPLICATIONS OF INTEGRATING EMOTION IN TEACHING BUSINESS ETHICS

In this chapter I have presented several studies that illustrate how emotion can influence our ethical decision making. Many more could have been offered to further this position, though I have found that in my conversations with fellow faculty (as well as students, family, and friends) few fail to acknowledge the powerful influence of the emotions in making ethical decisions in their own lives. Yet ethics courses often do not explain how our emotions influence our decision making, or offer ways for harnessing our emotions for ethical action. To conclude this chapter, I will offer specific suggestions in designing and delivering business ethics education, by way of revisiting the themes and studies discussed above.

Identify Dual Processes in Class Discussions

Faculty can begin by simply identifying when emotion emerges within one's class discussions. For example, many of us use the case method to teach ethics. Our discussions prompt a range of the responses as students identify the various ethical issues, their causes, the stakeholders involved, and the consequences of various courses of action. To foster ethical reasoning, we ask students to defend their position, stating their assumptions and articulating the line of reasoning that follows from these assumptions. On the surface, these discussions may seek to follow the "cool" path of logical, philosophical analysis, yet those of us who teach ethics know that these conversations become heated, often triggering quick, emotional responses to the issues at hand. Faculty can seize these moments to raise awareness of the two processes at work in ethical decision making by directing students' attention to the emotionality of the conversation. Simple questions, such as, "You seem to feel strongly about this. Why?" shift the focus of reflection from the rational to the emotional. As my course progresses, I become more direct in challenging the students in such moments, particularly those students who respond immediately with an answer to the case at hand. Using the lawyer-judge analogy (developed by Haidt and Wright mentioned above, which I include in the students' course reading), I will ask, "Your answer came so quickly, and you sound so certain. What gives you such certainty? Are you approaching this case as a lawyer or a judge?" Such a simple inquiry not only helps the student identify the emotional intuition that may underlie his or her response, but also helps the entire class develop the habit of stepping back from the line of discourse to explore from where the ideas and reasons are emerging. In other words, they can learn how to slow down and catch their own as well as other's intuitions and determine the emotions that may have aroused the immediate intuitive response.

Harness the Power of Proximity

While the trolley-footbridge dilemmas do not simulate the scenarios our students will see firsthand in the workplace, they illustrate how proximity to the individual or individuals under consideration can trigger a powerful emotional response that significantly differs when the individuals are more removed from our direct action or frame of view. The use of empathetic perspective-taking (as illustrated in the Batson study) to make the other participant proximate by imagining how he or she will feel offers another example of how the perception of proximity can influence decision making, in this case to promote prosocial behavior. Faculty can harness the power of proximity through case selection and by engaging students in reflections on significant moral moments from their past.

Choose Cases That Resonate With Students' Past Experiences

The cases included in many business ethics texts drop students into organizational contexts that can be unfamiliar to many (particularly undergraduates). These contexts are not only environments or situations they have never encountered, but they involve decisions made at the executive level, a position far removed from the current undergraduate or MBA student. In other words, these cases lack a sense of personal proximity for most students, and thus are more likely to be experienced as "moral-impersonal" encounters as opposed to the more emotionally-charged "moral-personal" scenarios.

Consideration of complex ethical issues such as global outsourcing or chief executive officer compensation have their place in the business ethics curriculum, but such issues are not representative of the day-to-day ethical decisions our students are likely to encounter. In my courses, I gradually build toward these more complex cases by beginning with cases that resemble scenarios students may have previously encountered. One might begin within the university context with cases of cheating, stealing, deception in career search, or team conflicts. These themes can easily move from college settings to corporate contexts, with the instructor illustrating the similar challenges and biases (i.e., pressure from authority or peers, loyalty to one's colleagues, lack of transparency) involved in ethical decision making. By beginning with cases closer in proximity, faculty can increase the likelihood of evoking students' past moral experiences, and the thoughts and emotions that accompanied these experiences.

Engage Students in Autobiographical Reflection on Significant Moral Moments

Returning to Damasio's dual process model, I ask students to recall significant moral moments, or episodes, that they think may have had a lasting impact on how they make ethical decisions and influence how they view future ethical situations. Usually such "moments" are "significant" due to the emotional power of the moment itself and the residual emotions that followed from the decision (elation, pride, disappointment, anger). After having students jot down a brief version of the story in class, I ask that they write a reflection on this experience that includes (1) a factual depiction of the ethical episode; (2) a rich, detailed description of the thoughts and feelings they experienced in this situation; (3) an identification of the reasons, emotions, and motivations they found most powerful (and least powerful) in this moral episode. The exercise facilitates a metacognitive reflection on students own experience as opposed to analyzing a hypothetical case scenario. As a result, students can see Damasio's dual process model at work in their own ethical decision making, and begin identifying how emotions and reasons can both help and hinder their ability to act ethically.

Apply Empathetic Stakeholder Analysis

When I share Batson's coin-flipping experiment in class, and the power of empathetic imagination in stimulating prosocial behavior, students begin to see how we can stimulate our own "hot" emotions, and thus warm up our "cooler" reasoning. We explore this approach by bringing empathetic imagination into our stakeholder analyses for the cases under discussion.

Stakeholder analysis is the usual approach for gathering new perspectives, but often it is performed on the surface level, examining the immediate physical and financial implications of a decision. Considering these consequences, however, is not always sufficient in helping an organization understand how stakeholders may react. Also, there's a tendency to limit stakeholder analysis with a "how would I think or feel if this were happening to me?" approach. But this approach has a significant shortcoming: we're still seeing the world through our own eyes. We may be bringing our own stereotypes to the case, or failing to see issues that are not part of our everyday concern but are important to others. If we're all likely to think from our own biases, from a "motivated reasoning" approach, then it is extremely important to step outside one's self and take the other's perspective.

Of course, this is not a new idea in decision making, but the notion of empathetic imagination is a particular approach to stakeholder analysis that strengthens one's moral perception and triggers new intuitions from multiple perspectives. Truly understanding stakeholders requires "standing under" their particular situation, that is, seeing not only your world from where they stand, but seeing *their* world from their eyes, as much as is possible. Rich and imaginative stakeholder analysis requires that we ask "How would they think or feel about this decision?"

Why should we encourage our students to develop empathetic imagination? How can empathetic perspective-taking prove valuable for their future as business leaders? In a complex, global business environment where the impacts of one's decisions can have far-reaching consequences for those we've never seen, companies can't afford *not* to misunderstand their many stakeholders' views. Empathetic imagination helps leaders understand the values important to each audience, and seek value congruence for effective negotiations, customer service, or human resources. It can spark new ideas for connecting with consumers and deepening one's brand. It can enhance cultural understanding in international partnerships. In particular, empathetic imagination, when supported by conversations with key stakeholders, can help companies move beyond their own perspective and get the feedback that they may not *want* to hear but *need* to hear. And lastly, empathetic imagination helps organizations consider the long-term impact of decisions of diverse constituencies, and enhances their understanding of what it means to be global corporate citizens.

CONCLUSION

Integrating emotion in the teaching of business ethics should be readily received by both faculty and students. After all, we don't need neuroscience or social psychology studies to remind us that our emotions are active, powerful, and persuasive influences in our everyday decisions. We have felt anger in the face of an unfair transaction, and the resulting vengeance that impacts future interactions with this party. We know it is much harder to harm someone we can see and touch than someone that remains unknown, as a mere bystander or number on a page. We can recognize how our emotional past shapes how we perceive ethical situations in the present. Yet with the acknowledgement of emotion's role comes an awareness of subjectivity and humanness, two frames of thinking that some students may consider unbecoming of a business professional. Often I will hear, "It's not personal, it's business," when we use empathetic stakeholder analysis for an ethics case discussion. Both seeing and feeling another's point of view makes the situation at hand more complex, introducing issues that make the situation more difficult to address, and some students simply want to avoid this added complexity. Here the faculty member has an opportunity to demonstrate how leaders can balance empathetic concern with principled moral reasoning. As Hoffman (2000) notes, empathy can help awaken our moral principles and fuel our reasoning with an affective charge, increasing the likelihood of taking action. Moral principles, in turn, can help stabilize and refocus our empathetic concern when it has become over-aroused emotionally or too narrowly focused toward any one individual or group. The ability to find such balance as a business leader is not only necessary, but must be rehearsed within our ethics courses if we are to better approximate the real-life scenarios our students will encounter. Our emotions influence our ethical decision making in varied and powerful ways; those of us who teach business ethics should find ways to explore the nature of these influences in our courses.

REFERENCES

Appiah, K. A. (2008). *Experiments in ethics.* Cambridge, MA: Harvard University Press.

Bargh, J. A., & Chartrand, T. (1999). The unbearable automaticity of being. *American Psychologist, 54,* 462-479.

Batson, C. D., Kobrynowicz, D., Dinnerstein, J. L., Kampf, H. C., & Wilson, A. D. (1997). In a very different voice: Unmasking moral hypocrisy. *Journal of Personality and Social Psychology, 72,* 1335-1348.

Batson, C. D., Lishner, D. A., Carpenter, A., Dulin, L., Harjusola-Webb, S., Stocks, E. L., et al. (2003). "As you would have them do unto you": Does imagining yourself in the other's place stimulate moral action? *Personality & Social Psychology Bulletin, 29,* 1190-1201.

Damasio, A. (1994). *Descartes' error.* Boston, MA: Norton.

Damasio, A. R. (2003). *Looking for Spinoza.* New York, NY: G. P. Putnam and Sons.

Diener, E., & Wallbom, M. (1976). Effects of self-awareness on antinormative behavior. *Journal of Research in Personality, 10*(1), 107-111.

Duval, T. S., & Wicklund R. A. (1972). *A theory of objective self awareness.* New York, NY: Academic Press.

Greene, J., & Haidt, J. (2002). How (and where) does moral judgment work? *Trends in Cognitive Science, 6,* 517–523.

Greene, J. D., Sommerville, R., Nystrom, L. E., Darley, J. M., & Cohen, J. D. (2001). An fMRi investigation of emotional engagement in moral judgment. *Science, 293,* 2105-2108.

Haidt, J. (2001). The emotional dog and its rational tail: A social intuitionist approach to moral judgment. *Psychological Review, 108,* 814-834.

Hoffman, M. L. (2000). *Empathy and moral development: Implications for caring and justice.* New York, NY: Cambridge University Press.

Khurana, R., & Nohria, N. (2008). It's time to make management a true profession. *Harvard Business Review, 86*(10), 78-84.

Kunda, Z. (1990). The case for motivated reasoning. *Psychological Bulletin, 108,* 480-498.

LeDoux J. A. (2003). *The synaptic self.* New York, NY: Macmillan.

Langer, E. J. (1989). Minding matters: The consequences of mindlessness-mindfulness. In L. Berkowitz (Ed), *Advances in experimental social psychology* (pp. 137-173). San Diego, CA: Academic Press,

Mazar, N., Amir, O., & Ariely, D. (2007). *The dishonesty of honest people: A theory of self-concept maintenance.* Retrieved from http://papers.ssrn.com/sol3/papers.cfm?abstract_id=979648

Samuelson, J. (2006). The new rigor: Beyond the right answer. *Academy of Management Learning & Education, 5*(3), 356-365.

Sanfey, A. G., Rilling, J. K., Aronson, J. A., Nystrom, L. E., & Cohen, J. D. (2003). The neural basis of economic decision-making in the ultimatum game. *Science, 300,* 1755-1758.

Schmidt, C. D. (2007). *Promoting the ethical development of undergraduate business students through a deliberate psychological education-based intervention* (Unpublished dissertation). College of William and Mary, Williamsburg, VA.

Tversky, A., & Kahneman, D. (1974). Judgment under uncertainty: Heuristics and biases. *Science, 185,* 1124-1131.

Zajonc, R. B. (1980). Feeling and thinking: Preferences need no inferences. *American Psychologist, 35,* 151-175.

CHAPTER 7

USING WRITING TO TEACH BUSINESS ETHICS

One Approach

Ronald R. Sims

INTRODUCTION

Developing and practicing ethics is an active life-long process for business students and continues throughout their careers. Students bring their personal ethics to business school and hopefully continue their ethical development. They read about business ethics, they discuss them in their courses, and they see the individual differences in how they are reflected in their own and others' lives and work.

In business schools committed to ethical awareness and development students face questions like: How central ethics is to whom they are and what they will do during their business careers? Are the ethics they are exposed to in business schools consistent with their own deepest values that they lived by before they entered business school, with the formal ethical standards they are exposed to while in business school, and with the realities of the broader world of work they hope to enter after graduation?

Experiences in Teaching Business Ethics
pp. 143–169
Copyright © 2011 by Information Age Publishing

Ethics are meaningless unless they fit well with what students will actually do in business situations. A main premise of this chapter is that business schools should create as many opportunities as possible for students to reflect on and learn about their own ethics. And one way I have recently found useful to accomplish this charge is through the use of writing in the form of journals. This chapter describes my recent experiences in incorporating writing via journals in my business ethics course. More specifically, the chapter describes the method of using journals that I have worked with over the past 2 years in teaching business ethics. The chapter will include conclusions which I and my students have drawn from this experience and offer some practical advice on how others might use journals as a tool for fostering reflection (i.e., learning) in a business ethics course. The chapter will also discuss some of the advantages and disadvantages of using journals in teaching business ethics. The chapter concludes with some practical suggestions or recommendations I have found helpful for using journals in teaching business ethics in my undergraduate course.

JOURNALS

Many educators have attempted to encourage critical thought, application of knowledge, and an attitude of intellectual curiosity through journal writing. The pedagogical benefit of journal writing is touted by many. For example, more than 2 decades ago Fulwiler's (1987) *The Journal Book* contained many examples of the ways teachers use journals to improve student learning in such diverse disciplines as physics, chemistry, political science, and geography. Fulwiler stated, "Journals are useful tools for both students and teachers. They can help students prepare for class discussion, study for examinations, understand reading assignments, and write formal papers" (p. 6).

Journals can facilitate reflection and allow students to express feelings regarding their educational experiences. The format of this writing can vary depending on the students' needs and the teacher or instructor's goals. Walker (2006) has noted that journal writing assignments can benefit students by enhancing reflection, facilitating critical thought, expressing feelings, and writing focused arguments. It has been the author's experience that journal writing can be adapted into any business ethics course to assist students with bridging the gap between classroom and real-world knowledge. In addition, journals can help students with exploring different options for handling daily ethical dilemmas or experiences.

There are many uses of writing like journals that could be used in teaching business ethics (Sims, 2002). The different names applied to them capture something of their variety or diversity. There are portfolios, record books, diaries, verbatim, dossiers, logs, and sociological diaries. And what they all have in common is that they can be used by those teaching business ethics for writing in the service of students' learning. However, their differences can be considerable, and they can by no means simply be understood in terms of the word used to describe them. Each particular use of writing needs to be examined in its own context by those responsible for teaching business ethics.

Writing in teaching business ethics not only requires thought, but also actually organizes thought, thereby facilitating analysis and synthesis (Sims, 2002). Observers report that in a journal, "learners will have written themselves toward understanding" (Fulweiler, 1980). Academics affirm that journal writing remains a valuable tool because it is a means to "teach learners to write" and encourages learners to share their experiences (Hettich, 1980, 1990). Researchers report that the use of these journals not only helps learners with comprehension and completion of assignments, but also actually teaches them to be better thinkers. Bromley (1993) has noted that student journals have proven simple, yet effective. All of these scholars express the view that writing, and specifically journal writing, is an effective learning technique (Carter, 1998; Walker, 2006).

Journals can have many different applications based on the goals of those responsible for teaching business ethics, for example, and students. As noted earlier, one common use of journals is to promote reflection and thought through dialogue between students and the business ethics teacher. Journals provide guided opportunities for students to "think aloud" on paper and reflect on their own perceptions or understandings of the situations or experiences encountered in and outside the business ethics teaching initiative. Hahnemann (1986) felt that journal writing assignments encourage exploration and risk taking on the part of the student. Before trying solutions to problems in real life, the students can be creative and express feelings and frustrations on paper. Students through their journals can be expected to apply knowledge gained from classroom content and literature to their experiential learning exercises. Journals can be used for student reflection to emphasize connecting business ethics content with thought processes and self-awareness.

Holmes (1997) stated that by recording and describing experiences, feelings, and thoughts, students are able to recreate their experiences for additional exploration. A student who had a difficult ethical dilemma to deal with could write in the journal about the situation and think about what happened (Sims, 2002). She could describe why certain decisions were made and actions taken, along with feelings and future thoughts and directions. As those responsible for teaching business ethics, we must push our students to reflect more deeply. Pushing students to continuously ask themselves why a decision was made or why they feel the way they do about a topic or situation will cause them to look deeper for answers. Why did they perform a certain action? What changes should they make to their action or decision in the future? In such instances journals can provide students with an opportunity to return to their experiences in an attempt to develop new perspectives that can guide future ethical decisions or actions. For example, a student, after participating in an experiential learning exercise and discussing it with his fellow students and/or business ethics teacher, could later write about the entire experience. What would he do differently? What did he learn? Writing encourages and provides an opportunity for students to reflect on an experience, connect, and think critically about ideas or situations.

ONE METHOD FOR USING JOURNALS IN TEACHING BUSINESS ETHICS

No true definitions of journals or journal writing exist due to the vast number of ways journals can be used. In the literature, as suggested earlier, journals or journal writing is described and explained in many different ways. For the purposes of this chapter, journals refer to any writing that students perform during either a business ethics course or classroom experience (i.e., particularly an experiential learning exercise) that challenges them to reflect on past situations, as well as consider how they might do something differently should similar situations arise in the future. The goal of any journal assignment, in my view, should guide the written content for the student. For example, a student could reflect on the challenges of introducing a controversial chemical plant in a third-world country as part of an organization's growth strategy. Students can also return to their struggles with matters such as ethical dilemmas during any aspect of their class or work experiences. Both assignments encourage the student to reflect on an experience, whether that experience be from business ethics classroom content or their work.

With journals, a student in my course is expected to write about personal experiences, problems, learning, and growth. So, for me the goal of the journal is to significantly extend the learning process in my business ethics course and in-class experiences. In my experience to date, the journal not only substantiates learning, but it enhances analytical learning. I have also found that a journal can provide a quiet or reserved student with a mode of communication. They are able to share thoughts and ideas that they feel are private. For the shy student and sometimes the foreign student who is not used to the active and aggressive dialogue that one sees in U.S. business schools journals at times seem to be a better means of communication.

Through journals each student can relate many more personal experiences from experiential learning exercises than are shared in oral discussion. Students bring their own backgrounds and cultures in their perceptions of business ethics issues and any accompanying experiential learning exercise. The journal allows for an in-depth analysis from each student's perspective. In the end, journals have allowed my students to record their experience, the relevant concepts and future application of concepts to out-of-class situations. The method that I describe in this chapter is intended to foster that important and essential counterpart to experience: reflection.

I have found this method of using journals within the context of a one-semester business and society course with a particular emphasis on business ethics, ethical awareness, and ethical development for the students quite useful to date. Most of the students in my course are between the ages of 20-23, and were, for the most part, well-motivated and anxious to take the course. The journal was used to assist students with the whole course, rather than as an aid or assessment for any one class within it, although it was principally used in conjunction with experiential learning exercises.

The precise focus of the course was to provide students with an introduction to business ethics, sensitize them to ethical awareness and ethical development. At the conclusion of the course students are expected to understand what is meant by business ethics and corresponding organizational and individual challenges. The knowledge and skills necessary to achieve this are presented to them within the context of their own personal, ethical awareness and ethical development. Therefore, within the course special attention was given to the increased self-understanding and ethical growth of each student. The course was directed to helping students come to an appreciation of ethical awareness and ethical development or growth by assisting them in reflecting on these realities in their own lives. The students themselves are recognized as being the most important resource to the course, and they are encouraged to interact with each other beyond the classroom, and share their learning about ethics, ethical awareness and ethical development that they believe takes place within them. The aim of the journal was to aid reflection on their own ethical awareness and ethical development and to encourage them to share this with others. The following goals for the journal were presented to the students in the course syllabus and during the first class.

1. To provide a record of the significant learning experiences which have taken place during the course.
2. To help the students come into touch and keep in touch with their own ethical awareness and the ethical development process that is taking place for them.
3. To provide the students with an opportunity to express, in a personal and dynamic way, their increased ethical awareness and ethical development.
4. To foster a sharing and creative learning interaction:

   • between the student and the ethical awareness and ethical development process that is taking place;
   • between the student and other students who are also in the process of increasing their understanding of ethical awareness and ethical development; and
   • between the student and the professor (learning facilitator) whose role it is to help foster such increased ethical awareness and ethical development.

5. To provide a means of reflecting on one's commitment to, and involvement in, the business and society course and their own increased ethical awareness and the ethical development process.

Identification of Journal Expectations and Planning

Before assigning the journal I have found that it is especially important that I convey to the students all expectations with regard to completing and grading (where applicable) the journals. Some of the questions that I have asked (and colleagues recommended) when contemplating whether to assign a journal in my business ethics course are:

• What is the purpose of the journal?—Critical thinking, reflection, ethical awareness, increased confidence in ethical decision making, et cetera.
• What is the expected format of the journal?—Typed, handwritten free form, full sentences required.
• On what will the students write?—Assigned ethics topics, daily ethical dilemmas or experiences, experiential learning exercises, decided by students.
• How much writing is required?—Page limit, word limit, paragraph limit, decided by students

- When will the journal be due?3Weekly, biweekly, monthly, set day of the week
- How will students be given feedback on their journals?—Written into the journal, a feedback instrument, conferences with the business ethics professor, feedback meetings with a team the student is assigned to (and then reviewed by the business ethics professor)
- When do the students need to pick up the journals? —Next day, set number of days after being turned in, or when meeting with the business ethics professor or after the professor reviews the results of the team feedback meetings
- How will students be graded?—Pass/fail, a grading instrument, self- and/or input from their assigned team members
- Who will read the journals? Business ethics professor, fellow students

To date, it is clear that these questions provide focus to enable the students to concentrate on the writing and not feel insecure about how I will grade the journal.

It is important that I make every effort be to ensure that the journal is seen as nonthreatening and satisfying. I have found that identifying expectations in the syllabus and during the first few classes before starting the first journal prevents any unnecessary confusion. A colleague of mine who has used journals over a number of years emphasized to me the importance of considering many facets of the journaling process. Some of these she recommended that I consider when planning for the use of journals included factors like: setting clear student expectations, identifying appropriate topics, journal utilization strategies, and grading systems. While all of these factors are important to the success of using journals in teaching business ethics I have found that some of the most important introductory advice on how to approach the journal came from students who had previously completed my business ethics course. The suggestions that follow on what students would say to someone just beginning to use a journal is drawn from my former students and from my own experience. The views expressed will not always be in quotations, but frequently will reflect the language of the former students.

1. In the end, the journal is meant to be a very personal document: there is no right or wrong way to keep it. You should seek out the method that suits you best. It is very important that you keep the journal personal. It is to be shaped by your own views, experiences and needs (of course you have to take into consideration the purpose of the course—business ethics and ethical develop-

ment). You need to view the journal as an extension of yourself, not something outside of you. In it you can and should say what you feel and think. It is important to be yourself (and especially be honest with yourself); that what you write is important to you, not just what the professor or others say is important.

2. Don't just be honest; be brutally honest in your entries. One student put it this way: "Write it as it is, not as you would like it to be, nor as you think or feel it should be. You should always commit to being open and sincere in what you write in your journal."

3. You should have a positive approach to the journal. Recognize the potential that it has for your own ethical development and learning, and approach it as something that can give you a rich return. You should not be afraid of the exercise. One student put it well: "Treat it as a close friend—not as a stranger or enemy."

4. Be assertive and if necessary aggressive in approaching the journal. You should not overly worry about how you are going to do it; get down and do something. Or as one student said: "Follow the Nike motto—Just do it!" A number of students advised to just let it flow, uncensored, and in whatever order it comes. These same students said that it is just simply best to write, write, write, and then to reflect on what has been written.

5. You should feel free to express yourself in whatever form it takes. Like symbols (i.e., diagrams, pictures, etc.) which can express what you are trying to say better than your words may at times.

6. You should be spontaneous and use your own words. It is important that you say what you feel, and if that makes you feel guilty, write that down and work through it further later on. It is not important for you to always be concerned about how you write and you should not look for style or literary eloquence, or worry that your writing does not seem to always be "on spot."

7. You should not be rigid in the way you keep the journal, but rather be prepared to change if necessary. You should feel free to try different methods, so that you can mould the journal exercise to your personal needs while also meeting the demands of the business ethics course. One student noted "It became easier and more meaningful once I discovered my own style of keeping the journal."

8. You should persevere in the face of initial difficulties in keeping the journal. You should be faithful to it and "stick at it," was perhaps the most common advice given by past students.

9. It makes the most sense to record your thoughts, feelings, opinions, and experiences as soon as possible, after a class, an experi-

ential learning exercise or a situation outside of the classroom. One student testified about the value of carrying a little notebook with him "So I could jot down my feelings, thoughts, or behavior that occurred throughout the class or during or after an exercise." There appears to be a definite advantage in being able to record or keep track of things as quickly as possible, even though one may not immediately write them down or develop them fully.

10. You should try to find a regular time to write in your journal, and a fixed time (daily or weekly) to reflect back on it. One student emphasized the fact that "To use it to fullest advantage, it is important to read over it frequently as it is not just writing in it that is important, but the continuing reflection on what has been written." I have found that one of the great enemies of the journal is procrastination. As a result I believe it is best to recommend to the students that they have fixed times and then try hard to stick to them, without necessarily making them absolutely exclusive.

11. A number of students suggested that important issues (i.e., experiences in handling ethical dilemmas, difficulties in making ethical decisions, "aha" moments or learning about one's self, etc.) in the journal need to be shared with others. Talking about one's ideas, thoughts, feelings and reflections should result in feedback that can help deepen them. This increased understanding or deepening should then be recorded in the journal.

12. You should be selective. Many students recognized that in the beginning they wrote a great deal more than was necessary. One student stressed that "Selectivity was a sign of experience and maturity in using the journal."

During the semester, I devote about 6-8 hours a week to assisting the students' work with the journal. I try to encouraged and help students to get comfortable with sharing with each other (students are assigned to teams in the course) what they are doing in the journal. This means not just sharing of the content, where that was appropriate, but also the method each was using. I found this helpful, as students learn from each other techniques that could help them, techniques which had not occurred to them personally. During these times, I would also provide exercises which would expose students to techniques they could use.

An important instruction that I give which goes counter to some of the advice I have received from my more experienced colleagues who have used of journals for a number of years was that the journal would not be confidential. Initially, this meant that students would be expected to hand in the journal (and share it with other team members) at any scheduled time during the semester. This was done to try to get the students to really use the journal to work on issues that were personally important to them but to also seek input and feedback from others. After some initial negative student reactions (and open class discussion) to the sharing or letting other team members read their journals, it was agreed that students would be asked to share from the journal with their team members. This meant that in team situations they would be called on to share with their team members some of the issues and learning (i.e., ethical awareness/ development) that they had included in their journal. I emphasized, however, that they would be fully in control of whatever was shared, and they would only share those things with which they were comfortable (a compromise on my end). In fact in the end, most of the students did share their journal with their team members, close friends, and others outside of the class. Going into my fourth year of teaching the course the emphasis on confidentiality versus complete sharing of the journals is an issue that I know still needs to be discussed and negotiated with each new group of students. One colleague from the school of "keep the journal confidential" has said that in his more than 2 decades of using journals he finds "confidentiality helps make the journal a more personal, and therefore a more creative and productive learning instrument and exercise."

Feedback from students over a 3-year period suggests that the journal is less personal since it has to be handed in to be checked or shared with fellow team members. More specifically, many of the students have said that because the journal had to be handed in (even to me as the professor) it tended to become something written for someone else rather than for themselves. I believe that indeed this takes away one of the journal's most important characteristics. A few students suggested that, since they viewed the journal as a self-reflection and learning experience, and that the obligation to hand it in did not change the way they kept it because they recognized the importance of getting feedback to their overall learning, growth, ethical awareness and ethical development.

Students' Use of the Journals

Even though there were some clear expectations and guidelines in my syllabus for the use of the journals as part of the overall student's learning experience in the course, students do have some freedom to use the journal in their own way and some common elements did appear in their use of it. There were some clear suggestions I made about what should be included in the journal: information from lectures and guest speakers, interpretations and applications of material (i.e. ethical theories, decision making models, etc.), affective responses to the experiential learning exercises, personal ethical behavior and personal decision making evaluation—when confronted with ethical dilemmas, for example. However, the suggestions were general enough to let each student proceed in his or her own way. The following paragraphs offer some insight into how the students used the journal, what they wrote in it, and how it helped them. Where the text appears in quotation marks I am using the students' words, taken from their postcourse evaluations of the use of the journal.

The journal was widely used to provide a lasting record of their personal journey during the business and society course, as a basis for continuing reflection. "I used the journal to record meaningful learning and experiences, which then became more meaningful after the first articulation—and led to further reflection and articulation. It helped me to surface a clearer understanding of my values, beliefs and behaviors in various situations where ethics was an issue at hand." "The keeping of a journal made it possible to knit the semester's progress (even though the semester isn't really long enough to focus on something like ethical development in all honesty) by reading back and considering what I had written in the light of the present and vice versa. It made it possible for me to step back and have a wider and different perspective at times."

The journal enabled the students to keep track of what was happening in their own ethical development and understanding, and gave them ongoing access to it. I believe it actually helped them appreciate the learning journey in the course. "The journal has helped me learn about the learning process itself. It has opened to me the possibility and given me the encouragement to explore my own values, ethics, and issues." It enabled them to see areas of ethical blind spots, growth, self-understanding and lack of growth, and to observe their own ethical development and questioning actually taking place. Changes in attitudes, values and behavior were apparent over the semester. In this context, I believe the journal provided a useful means of monitoring growth or self-understanding and evaluating it at various points throughout the business and society course, and, in a final way, at the end of the course.

Not surprisingly nearly all of the students mentioned that course content and the experiential learning exercise was included in the journal. Perhaps more accurately, it was responses to the course material that were written or recorded. "I used the journal to reflect further on business ethics in general and in relation to my own ethical development." "The journal has helped me learn about business ethics. It has put them in the perspective of my personal history and experience and provided an umbrella under which significant personal insights into my own values, beliefs, behaviors and ethics can be linked together." "The journal helped me to learn about business ethics. The journal led me to a reflection on my understanding and acceptance of the course content as it affects me here and now and in the future." "It helped me to correlate much of the lecture material; it was a link between the specifics of the course and life away from it; it showed me the value of reflection on my experience, and the articulation of my reflections."

It was the course material which touched them personally that was most often written about in their journals; that "which has moved me in some way, for example, to look at myself, my decisions, values and attitudes, and to challenge them at times." It did not matter whether the course material came from the formal lectures, or experiential learning exercises, or from their other personal life outside of the course, it was what was meaningful to them that came to be written and considered. It was the personal appropriation of the course material that was achieved through the journal. It was a vehicle that helped serious thinking or self-reflection: "any critical reflection or deep soul-searching that I needed to do, I found more beneficial if I wrote it into the journal." This helped to raise their level of ethical awareness, so that they came to be more observant in recognizing situations which might lead them to deeper reflection and accompanying insights.

For a number of students in the course the journal opened up insights into who they were and why they may have acted or not acted certain ways. "This is a most fascinating feedback for me. I could go right to the core. Things became clear in my head as I wrote things down. It helped me to put meaning to it." They found that they were able to look at themselves within this reflective sphere with fewer inhibitions and more honesty. "The journal helped me directly reflect on the most personally meaningful and important events during the course, by providing an objective avenue. It has to be honest otherwise I'm fooling myself and it is an utter waste of my own and others' time." Even though when writing for oneself in the journal one can tend still not to be honest, some students found it more difficult to be so within the framework of the journal. "I wasn't afraid to be honest—well, in all honesty I was afraid, but I tried to be honest just the same." "The journal did contribute to my experience in the course during the semester. I found it an enriching experience overall. I found it a very liberating experience to be able to express what I was feeling as I was feeling it—to be completely frank and honest. But I also thought it was a scary experience as I pushed away my initial defenses that might have kept a lot of strong feelings and thoughts at bay. Working through this was hard at times."

Some students used the journal to help them articulate their thoughts and feelings more concretely, and especially in their own words. This ability to put in their own words their deep feelings was particularly important for many. "Yes, writing down my thoughts and feelings, I became more conscious of what I am really feeling, and doing and 'being'—I have found words to describe myself (my values and ethics or what I stand for) and so it is much easier to speak about myself to others." It enabled them to identify and own these feelings and to appreciate them more once they had described them in a way that was personally meaningful to them. "Helped me remember and recall later many aspects of the experiential learning exercises in the business and society course that I otherwise would have forgotten. Many smaller issues would not have been 'looked at' as fully and a characteristic pattern of feelings/behaviors in certain ways would be less likely to have been identified or if already recognized, nothing more effective in terms of change or doing something different would have been done about what needed to be changed or may have been a better way to handle, say an ethical dilemma I might confront in the future."

In concluding this section I believe that the use of a journal in my business and society courses to date has provided students with the opportunity to express themselves and to embody their thoughts and feelings related to business ethics and their own ethical development in their own words. That is, there were many feelings and insights captured that might have otherwise been lost to the students. Not only were they captured at different points throughout the course when completing their journals, but they were embodied in a way that enabled the student to work more constructively and effectively with them.

SOME LESSONS LEARNED ON THE DISADVANTAGES AND ADVANTAGES OF JOURNALS

After teaching the business and society course for 3 years, getting feedback from students and through discussions with colleagues who regularly use journals in their teaching efforts I have identified a number of disadvantages and advantages to using journals in teaching business ethics (and for that manner are generalizable, in my view, to other business ethics teaching efforts). The remainder of this section highlights the disadvantages and offers some suggestions on how I think anyone can overcome them along with the important advantages in fostering the use of journals in a business ethics course.

Disadvantages of Journals

In my experience, there are two major disadvantages of using a journal in teaching business ethics. (1) The time required for me as the business ethics teacher to interact with every student (and the time it takes students to keep up with the journal), and (2) the lack of acceptance or active participation by some students in the value of or use of the journal.

Some students considered that the time taken by the use of the journal was a disadvantage. One student described this lack of time in the following way: "It takes a great deal of time to keep up with your journal, and I seemed to never have enough time to write all I wanted to. There was so much information, feeling and thoughts going around in my head that I had to end up being selective about what I wrote, thus leaving out some things I wish I had included." This student points to the need for selectivity by students in completing their journal. I think one of the most important things that the students have to learn in using a journal is to be selective. I have found that it is better for the student to select a few things to write, and work with them at greater depth, rather than record many things. At times, I have felt that the inclination of the students initially was to write as much as possible, and the recognition that they had to write less, and with it more, was a very important development within them. While the time it took did appear to be a disadvantage on the part of the student, in my eyes as the business ethics teacher the time devoted to the journal was often worthwhile and considered to be more important than the students had judged it to be. From my point of view, the journal certainly demands time, and this can be a disadvantage. Since students had to hand in their journal at various points during the course (five to six times on average), most did ask for assistance with it and time was by far the main issue we focused on in the early part of the course. In the end, this meant that I had to read and give careful consideration to the journals, so that a thoughtful response could be given which would help the students in its use. Despite the students' concern about the amount of time or how much time it took to work on their journals, I found it was worth whatever effort it demanded.

I would recommend that others who decide they want to use a journal in their courses on business ethics, and experience time as a constraint, consider the following time reduction strategies: (a) use less frequent journal entries; (b) randomly select a limited number of journal entries to be read each week; (c) periodically have students assess their peers' journal (i.e., assign students to teams for the duration of the business ethics course; (d) if journal entries are longer than one page, consider shortening the entry requirement to one page or less; (e) have students type all work to make it easier to read (but be prepared for some students to see typing the journal entries as an additional "hassle" versus being able to do the entries free hand); (f) have students submit group journal entries to reduce the total number of journals to be read, and (g) use e-mail and the Intranet to receive, respond and distribute students' entries. One of my colleagues recommended adopting a team journal entry process (which I have yet to try).

Another disadvantage of the journal highlighted the fact that it is not something that will appeal to all students. One of the goals of the journal was to have the actual entries or writing become a habit for students so that they saw the benefits to regularly writing in their journals about their in-class experiences and learning. Some students saw completing the journal as a job to be done, so that it lost the aspect of spontaneity, intense self-reflection and reluctance or their full participation in the journal writing process.

For those who saw the journal as more of a job to be done, the journal became a chore which dragged more and more as the semester went on. I found it necessary at times to suggest that individual students turn in their journals at unscheduled times, team them up with a fellow student, and have their assigned team members try to shepherd them through the process (i.e., peer pressure). I have to admit that in these situations I found myself being frustrated as I did not want to use the "grade" as a reinforcement and there were at least a couple of times that I was ready to suggest that individual students discontinue the use of the journal. While the journal is an important part of my business and society course, the journal or the use of writing often makes demands that many students are not willing to accept, despite the fact that writing across the curriculum is an important component of a student's education here in the Mason School of Business and at the College of William and Mary. This is a disadvantage from my point of view as the business ethics teacher since not all students recognize what I see as the value of a journal or writing to help facilitate self-reflection, learning, ethical awareness, and ethical development.

Like other things I have accepted that there will be some students who, even when you provide them with additional help, will not use the journal effectively or recognize its potential value to them. However, instead of simply giving up on the students, I believe that it is best to try to provide some other way for these students to achieve the goals that are established for the journal. Still, I would suggest that providing other ways for students to achieve the goals of the journal be the option of last resort. It has been my experience that by my spending additional time or partnering students with others in the course, most students are able to cope with it. However, the additional time it takes for me to interact with such students is one of the disadvantages for me and others.

I think I would be remiss if I didn't emphasize the fact that many students who have had difficulty with the journal in my course simply needed more individual time early on in the course. This means that I needed to design or provide some specific exercises which would help students work through the difficulties they were having. There were several types of participants who found significant difficulties in keeping the journal, but over the time I have taught the course they were a very small minority. Some focused exclusively on negative aspects of the way they handled ethical dilemmas or decisions they made or did not make both during experiential learning exercises and when making entries about related issues or experiences outside of the course, and needed to be guided to look for more positive elements. And of course there were those students who had blind spots when it came to the negative aspects of the way they handled ethical dilemmas or the implications of the decisions they made or the behavior they exhibited. Some students tended to become too introspective, and needed help to adjust their focus. There were also those students who were rather anxious or concerned about the issues that the journal could raise and simply needed some time to talk about their anxiety or concern. One student described the situation in these words: "I had difficulty at first keeping up with my journal because I seemed to be torn inside (in conflict) and wanted very much to avoid the issues which it raised. I found that it was much easier to direct my attention to the ethical or conceptual theories which were safe, and didn't stir up so many feelings inside me. It was initially very difficult to face some of the feelings I was having. For the first 2 weeks of the course I know I consciously avoided writing about these things." Talking through her concerns with several of her team members seemed to have helped her overcome her anxiety and concern. A safe, trusting and supportive learning environment in the business and society course was critical to students becoming more comfortable with the issues that were raised related their journals by myself and their classmates. Lack of active participation in completing the journals by some students defies the goal. To encourage active participation, I think it is important for those of you who are considering using journals in your business ethics courses to consider the following strategies: (a) attach graded points to the various stages of the journal—journal entry dates; b) set clear and nonnegotiable due dates; (c) encourage team sharing of journals (I have found that team involvement increases peer pressure to participate); (d) have students submit team journal entries that document "our" reactions; (e) encourage journal entries through office-hour feedback; and (f) use e-mail and the Intranet to foster the exchange of ideas and work products among students in the course.

Advantages of Journals

First, and foremost, I have found that the journal met the goals that were established by me and my colleagues at the beginning of the business and society course. Student feedback over the time that I have taught the course also suggests that the goals were met. One of the most important goals for the course was to facilitate the interaction between students and increase their understanding of ethics, attend to their ethical awareness and ethical development over time. The ability to express what was taking place in the student meant that each was able to share it in his or her own words with the other students and with me as the business ethics teacher. Students communicated better because they were able to write down their feelings, behaviors, thoughts and conflicts, for example, in their own words in the journals. This meant that they could speak about the ethics-related issues more easily in a classroom setting.

Of course, there are other advantages of journals. I found that students were able to use the journal to reflect on business ethics concepts and perceived ethical or unethical business practices. Journals offered an additional student assessment tool and provided an extra source of student feedback. The journals offered students who might not have participated in class as much as others an additional channel for expressing their knowledge and demonstrating knowledge and ethical skill attainment or development.

Additionally, the journal, improved student writing skills as evaluated by the College's writing lab and was an effective tool in bridging the gap to critical thinking about how to assess business organizations and oneself as they relate to ethics. Self-, other- and organizational ethical analysis, synthesis, and assessment are critical higher level thinking skills required of today's and tomorrow's employees, managers and leaders. And, the students seemed to gain an appreciation of these higher level thinking skills by the end of the course.

The journals also increased the students' ability to communicate. When students acquire better written communication skills, they are better able to articulate, elaborate, and dialogue about hot-button topics like ethics or their own ethical development. Students are more comfortable in engaging in a dialogue process in the business or self-ethics context. The dialogue they experienced in the business ethics course with me and their peers is similar to conversations they will engage in with other stakeholders throughout their lives. The use of journals improved their thinking skills as they reflected on their own actions or behaviors, feelings, and thoughts and received feedback to help them better understand themselves and at the same time improved their ethical decision making ability.

Based upon my experience to date I strongly believe that the journal is an excellent vehicle for helping to teach business ethics and more importantly getting students to reflect on their own and others' ethics and developmental challenges and opportunities. By way of using the journal

I recognize that as the business ethics teacher I am signaling to students the importance of writing skills, dialogue, discourse, feedback, and relationship building, and providing students with the opportunity to use the journal (or writing) to get things done. Journals are a mechanism for language functions and can include elements common to business ethics or self-actions or inactions. The journal allowed me to monitor student development on a timely basis and to personalize and individualize learning. It was an additional assessment and remediation tool. I also got responses and feedback on the course and was better able to detect both individual and common difficulties in learning material, and this helped me gain a new perspective on the topic of business ethics. I really think the journal process was invaluable in creating a supportive and trusting learning environment for the business ethics course.

Perhaps the best way to drive home the point of the advantages of journals is through the words of others as follows:

> The act of putting pen to paper (or finger to keyboard) engages our brains. To write we have to think (Smith, 2006). Mary Louise Holly argues that when we "capture our stories while the action is fresh," we are often provoked to wonder "Why do I do this?" or "Why did this happen?" (1989, p. xi).

Patsie Little makes a similar point about recording:

> By keeping records, I am able to monitor my practice. The act of writing something down often crystallises a particular problem or issue or enables me to see where a particular piece of work has not achieved its objective ... Through this process I can identify my strengths and weakness, and areas in which I could benefit from further training. (1995, p. 36)

Journal writing encourages engagement and reflection.

> "It isn't just that writing a journal stimulates thought—it allows us to look at ourselves, our feelings, and our actions in a different way. By writing things down in a journal the words are now "outside" of us. They are there in black and white on the paper or on the screen. We can almost come to look at them as strangers—"Did I really think that?", "How does this fit with that?" In other words, our words may become more concrete—and in this way we can play with them, look at them in another light. (Smith, 2006)

One final advantage of using journals is that it allowed me in a sense to create a communal class experience during discussions with a student. Discussions often really ended up being highly individualized conversations with each student through the sequence of journal entries and responses. While the individualized responses were quite time-consuming

I believe it was essential to the nature of the course. Students were challenged, intrigued, and sometimes intimidated by the ideas generated in the course; the individualized responses allowed the affirmation, clarification of confusions, and freedom to develop ideas in directions that interested and made sense for each student.

In the end, I found the journal to be a very helpful learning tool. It has increasingly become an important part of my approach to teaching business ethics. I hope to include the use of journals into my regular and executive Masters in Business Administration courses. It has been rewarding to see students recognize the value of a journal to their own self-learning and growth. I hope that you the reader will also see the value of including the journal in your own efforts to teach business ethics, as I have over the past 3 years.

RECOMMENDATIONS: GETTING THE MOST OUT OF JOURNALS IN TEACHING BUSINESS ETHICS

As the purpose of this chapter is to provide my first-hand experience in using journals I will conclude with some further practical recommendations or suggestions in no particular order, arising from my own experience, which might help others to facilitate its introduction in their own initiatives in teaching business ethics.

1. The journal process should be well planned and have explicit student expectations. You should plan on how you are going to introduce students to the use of the journal by emphasizing that they need to write, write, and write from their experiences in (and outside where appropriate) the business ethics course. The writing should create the dynamics that are operative in the use of the journal. The key to success in students' using the journal is for you as the business ethics teacher to encourage the students to write. It really seems to make a difference when I provided some practice examples of writing in the journal during the first few classes and the examples seemed to be an excellent vehicle for getting the point across to students.

2. Encourage the students to establish a definite time each day or class or after each experiential learning exercise in which they work with the journal, and a definite duration of time. I have found that students will not work with the journal successfully if they only pick it up when they feel like it. So, your encouragement in this area will make a difference.

3.   Related to No. 2 above, one way to show that writing in the journal is valued is to set aside some classroom time for the students to write. One of my colleagues sets aside 10 to 15 minutes of each class for students to write in the journal. My colleagues asked students to write about what they learned from class that day, as well as what had been learned from previous classes. Although allocating 10 to 15 minutes of class time for this purpose may not be feasible in a 50-minute class period (and is more applicable for an hour and 20 minute class like the one I taught), this method can be adapted to 2 to 5 minutes every class period or whatever fits your schedule.

4.   Be clear on how long you want the journal entries to be without stifling the students' ability to communicate their reflections (i.e., learning). As I have learned by surveying my colleagues, journal entries can vary from less than a page to five or more pages, and may be submitted once a week or four or five times in a semester (this seems to be the norm according to my colleagues who use journals more often than I do). I have found that the length and creativity of journal entries grow dramatically as students realize that their ideas are responded to in depth and with empathy.

5.   It is not enough to simply do a lot of work at the beginning of the course and then leave the students to work with the journal when they want to throughout the course. I have found that periodically (i.e., on a schedule that is communicated to students both in the course syllabus but also discussed during the first day of class) I needed to review how the journal was going and to provide exercises and opportunities that assisted the students with it. In fact, one of my colleagues suggests that the exercises should be graded so that later exercises to which the students are exposed should be more demanding than those which are presented early in the business and society course.

6.   It is critically important to build rapport and trust between the business ethics teacher and students; a classroom culture that will allow the student to openly discuss and share the journal with the professor is extremely important. In my experience, this personalized response to what students are doing is a major help to them in working with the journal. However, it requires a good rapport between the student and the business ethics teacher, because of the personal nature of what students write in the journal.

7.   I would encourage those of you who wish to use the journal with your students to begin, and not wait until the students have a

completely well-developed system in place for working on the journal (however, such a system does help smooth the transition and introduction of the journal into the business ethics course). Even though you may not be adept in the use of writing as an aid to reflection and learning, I believe there is much that the students can gain as they work with the journal and this will help you to come to greater experience its use. As one of my colleagues initially reminded me "I found that it was better to get in and give it a try, than spend a lot of time trying to develop the 'perfect system' and finding out about the journal and writing as the process moved along until I had found out all about it before starting." I think this is good advice that I have followed myself!

8. I think it is important that you mould the use of journals to your own talents, needs, interests and goals for your teaching business ethics initiatives. Given my experience to date, I don't believe it is necessary just to use someone else's model in your own course. Instead, it is critical that you look to the principles that are involved in writing, and commit to putting together something that will be tailored, a natural part of your own approach and an integral part of your business ethics course. Whatever you do needs to fit with who you are and what feel best to you, your style and your approach to teaching business ethics.

9. You need to constantly encourage students to work with their in- and out-of-class experiences that they enter in their journals over time. This means that you have to accept the fact that sometimes students will need encouragement or a nudge to keep working with their experiences and writing in their journal. It has been my experience that there is a tendency for some students to think that, once an experience has been reflected upon, it is worked through and complete. As a result, I have found that it is sometimes necessary for me to point out to the students that an in-class experience can be reflected on and worked through again and again as students get better at developing their skills in reflection. Students need to understand that they are be expected to develop a definite time at regular intervals to devote to going back over an event or incident beyond just writing or entering it in their journal.

10. Emphasize to students the importance of their taking the time at definite intervals to read their journal as a whole. Not to just work with particular experiential learning exercises, for example, but actually sit down and read their journal as a whole from beginning to end. And, in doing so they should pay particular attention

to trying to make sense of any possible themes, learning, insights, interpretations, and so one. In my experience, this gives the students something of an idea of the learning, growth and development that has taken place and very often will help them to relate different experiences and reflections that they have entered into their journal.

11. You should view the journal as a work in progress or a process by which students learn to reflect and get better at it as time goes by during the course. Simply, the goal is for students to evaluate their actions and reflect on how they could handle the situation(s) differently in the future. As the business ethics teacher you should be prepared to adapt the journal experience to enhance assignment goals, whether they are reflection, learning, and so on.

12. Emphasize to students the importance of their writing less and reflecting more in their journals. In the three times I have taught the business ethics course I noticed that there is a tendency for students, at the beginning of the course, to enter many things in their journal which cut back on the time they had available to reflect on what they did or could write. The more a student is able to be aware that it is the depth of reflection on their various experiences rather than the number and length of the entries of their experiences that is important, the better it will be, in my experience. Students have to learn to be selective.

13. Unfortunately (or maybe fortunately depending on whose perspective one is thinking about), the single most important factor for students is how the journal will be graded so you must make this clear in the syllabus and discuss this during the first class. Questions in need of answers related to grading in my experience include: How can a student be graded for writing about feelings and reactions to specific issues and topics? How does the business ethics teacher know whether a student is really trying to reflect? Although they should be graded for their thoughts and feelings, it is important the students be informed by the business ethics teacher as to how the journal will fit into their grades. What percentage of their grade will be affected by their journal? How will the journals be graded? One method of grading to consider according to a colleague of mine is if the student achieves all the goals for the journal, then he or she earns an A or passes that portion of the business ethics course the journal fulfills. Another option is to weight the journals as 10-20% of a grade in a course. However you decide to integrate journals into a course, unless the journal has an effect on the grades, it has been my experience

that students will put very little effort into their journals. Adding a grade to the journal puts value to it and establishes its importance.

14. When completing some journal assignments, allow students to write using what some researchers refer to as a free-form style (see for example, Hahnemann, 1986; Paterson, 1995). It was important for me to realize after the second time I used the journal in my business ethics course that the focus needed to be on the thought process and reflection, and that grammar and punctuation should not be a part of my evaluation of the journal. If the focus of the journal is to reflect, then the journal should be a forum where students can write and not worry about punctuation, grammar, and spelling. As stated by Hahnemann (1986) journals are a means by which students should be allowed to experiment and test their wings. When I focused too much attention on grammar and punctuation it led students to misinterpret the purpose of the journal. Instead, the attention should be on the content of what is written and not how it is written. In reality, good spelling, good grammar, and appropriate logical argumentation could be modeled by my responses to the journal entries, but the purpose is not for me to judge the ability of students to "stay within the lines." Students need encouragement, and perhaps some gentle guidance, as they become engaged in the business ethics course material and the different experiences.

15. After writing their first two entries give students feedback before they write their third journal entry. Feedback can be given in various ways. You can use both oral and written feedback. Student conferences, also known as debriefing sessions, either individual or group, can be set up to discuss the journal's relationship to the business ethics course content, reflection, critical thinking, etc. In my experience, student conferences allowed me to sit down with the students to discuss the journal along with feedback goals for upcoming future journal entries. In addition, team discussions early in the business and society course and/or throughout conserved my time, promoted the exchange of ideas, and helped synthesize information for the students. Another way to conserve time is to only grade at random a percentage of the journals that are written after a few weeks of feedback have been given. All of these types of feedback have strong points and limitations. It is up to you to decide what is appropriate and to modify as needed. Lastly, if a student inquires as to why or how the journal was graded, it is important for you to be able to explain all comments

and methods of grading. These grading points are not only justification but can help guide the student to further reflection.

16. Maintain a balance between giving too many comments and nudging the student into new ways of thinking. Correcting misinformation written by the student is encouraged, but no criticism or judgment should be made of the student's feelings. Annotations might pertain to future questions and comments to expand on in the next journal entry, but you need to try to avoid excessive grammar and spelling corrections as noted in recommendation No. 14. Some basic questions I think are helpful to have students ask themselves—and I have found are easily incorporated in feedback conferences with students—include:

- Are there any particular parts of the experiential learning exercises, situations or understandings that stand out for you? What is it about them that is catching your attention?

- Does what you have written in your journal still "ring true" after further reflection? Have you been fully honest and do the interpretations you made at the time still stand up? From your present standpoint and understanding are there things to question in your writing?

- What is missing? Has there been evasion? Complete honesty?

- Does what you are writing in your journal relate to what you know about business ethics, yourself, etc.? Can you see any connection with any of the broader ethical theories we have explored in the business and society course?

17. I would recommend that you do not let the journal be confidential or simply be kept as a personal document by the student. I believe there is a lot to be gained from having access to a student's journal, even though some colleagues stress the fact that the consequences of this access are very often that the student spends more time writing the journal for the business ethics teacher, and avoids writing about the more controversial or insightful feelings, thoughts or behaviors. It has been my practice to use the journal as a means whereby I as the business ethics teacher can gain insight into the ethical views, thoughts, behavior, learning and life of the student to help increase their ethical awareness and assist in their ethical development.

18. Work toward fostering continued interaction among the students using the journal. This can be done in two ways: on the method they are using in the journal and how it is helping them. This helps others to appreciate what can be achieved through the jour-

nal, and in my experience gives them some ideas on how to use it. In addition, students gain further reflection and feedback on what they write in the journals and their reflections. In my experience, students work seriously in their teams on the use of journals and their working together motivates each other and helps sustain interest in the course, experiential learning exercises, and what they enter in their journals.

19. Introduce an element of having fun into students' keeping their journal: sharing of amusing and insightful learning or reflections that have emerged. Where appropriate some lighthearted activity can successfully impart the important ethical principles of the course, foster interest in the journal, and their own ethical awareness and development.

20. Use experiential learning exercises in your teaching business ethics efforts and have students write about their experiences in the journal. A general guideline for journal entries based upon experiential learning exercises I have used are as follows:

    • Experience: Reflect on and explain what happened during the exercise. Include your observations of others and how you felt about these interactions.

    • Theory: Based upon the ethics readings and class and guest lectures, what theories apply or would be helpful to implement in the exercise?

    • Application: Considering the objectives of the exercise and your performance, how could you change the experience for a better outcome? How do you think the outcome would have changed and why? In what situations could this strategy be used? What situations call for a backup strategy?

21. At the end of a business ethics class or activity consider having students complete a personal application assignment (PAA)—a form of journal developed by Kolb, Osland, and Rubin (1995)—on how they will apply what they have learned from the business ethics teaching effort (or experiential learning exercise) to parallel or other related situations.

CONCLUSION

Writing in the form of journals in teaching business ethics allows for uninhibited expression, the opportunity to reexamine written ideas, and the ability to proceed through all learning stages in a structured manner

(Sims, 2002). It also provides the opportunity for the faculty member to comment and enhance each individual's needs and goals (Petranek, Corey, & Black, 1992).

The purpose of this chapter was to provide an introduction to how I use journals in teaching business ethics to undergraduate students. I have used this approach for 3 years in a business and society course. To date, I have found the experience rewarding for me and based upon the feedback received thus far students have also had positive experiences with the journals.

The teaching approach I use is not offered as some "magic wand" for teaching business ethics. It is an approach which takes time to develop and involves heavy effort on my part, yet it appears to have significant positive effects on my students to date. It stimulates self-reflection, tolerance for ambiguity, and leads to an acceptance of business ethics as a valued subject.

As with any teaching method, there is no right or wrong way to use a journal. As the students grew in self-confidence and gained trust in me as their business ethics teacher, they began to reflect and write about their experiences, thoughts, feelings and behaviors in the course. I believe this led to their being more open to the feedback I and their fellow students provided them on their journals. Reflection and learning about business ethics, increased ethical awareness and development and themselves was a critical goal of the course, and I believe both I and the students were rewarded via our experience with the journals. The journals allowed the students to reflect and enabled them to develop a better understanding of the course material and themselves.

In concluding this chapter the question I believe we all as business ethics teachers must ask ourselves is: Isn't our real goal in teaching business ethics to enable all of our students to give thought to their actions and behaviors with the utmost ethical self- and other awareness, ethical skill, knowledge, and confidence that they will do the right thing at the right time and in the best possible manner? If the answer is yes, then in my view, using a journal in teaching business ethics is one way to help students develop what Schon (1987) refers to as "reflection-in-action"[1] or "thinking on our feet." In my business ethics course the journal provides the opportunity for students to look to their experiences, connect with their feelings, and attend to their theories in use. It entails students building new understandings via reflection and writing in their journals to inform their actions in ethical or other situations as they unfold. Journals allow the student to write up their experiences, share and talk things through with their peers and me as the business ethics teacher. The act of reflecting-on-action via a journal enables students to spend time exploring why they acted as they did, what was happening in a situation and so on. In so doing the students hopefully develop sets of questions and ideas about their own actions or inactions. This is how meaningful learning takes place.

NOTE

1. Reflection-in-action occurs when an individual reshapes what he or she is doing while doing it.

REFERENCES

Bromley, K. (1993). *Journaling: Engagements in reading, writing, and thinking.* New York, NY: Scholastic.

Carter, C. W. (1998). The use of journals to promote reflection. *Action Teach Education, 19*, 39-42.

Fulwiler, T. (1980, December). Journals across the disciplines. *English Journal, 69*, 14-19.

Fulwiler, T. (1987). *The journal book.* Portsmith, NH: Boynton/Cook.

Hahnemann, B. K. (1986). Journal writing: A key to promoting critical thinking in nursing students. *Journal of Nursing Education, 25*, 213-215.

Hettich, P. (1980). The journal revisited. *Teaching of Psychology, 7*, 105-106.

Hettich, P. (1990, February). Journal writing: Old fare or nouvelle cuisine? *Teaching of Psychology, 17*, 36-39.

Holly, M. L. (1989). *Writing to grow: Keeping a personal-professional journal.* Portsmouth, NH: Heinemann.

Holmes, V. (1997). Grading journals in clinical practice: A delicate issue. *Journal of Nursing Education, 36*, 489-492.

Kolb, D. A., Osland, J. S., & Rubin, I. M. (1995). *Organizational behavior: An experiential approach* (6th ed.). Englewood Cliffs, NJ: Prentice Hall.

Little, P. (1995). Recording. In P. Carter, T. Jeffs, & M. R. Smith (Eds.), *Social working* (pp. 33-36). London, England: Macmillan.

Paterson, B. L. (1995). Developing and maintaining reflection in clinical journals. *Nurse Education Today, 15*, 211–220.

Petranek, C., Corey, S., & Black, R. (1992). Three levels of learning in simulations: Participating, debriefing, and journal writing. *Simulation and Gaming, 23*(2), 174-185.

Schon, D. A. (1987). *Educating the reflective practitioner.* San Francisco, CA: Jossey-Bass.

Sims, R. R. (2002). *Teaching business ethics for effective learning.* Westport, CT: Quorum Books.

Smith, M. (2006). *Keeping a learning journal.* Retrieved from the Informal Education website: www.infed.org/research/keeping_a_journal.htm

Walker, S. E. (2006). Journal writing as a teaching technique to promote reflection. *Journal of Athletic Training, 41*(2), 216-221.

CHAPTER 8

REFLECTION THROUGH DEBRIEFING IN TEACHING BUSINESS ETHICS

Completing the Learning Process in Experiential Learning Exercises

Ronald R. Sims and William I. Sauser, Jr.

INTRODUCTION

Our interest in using experiential learning (Kolb, 1984) exercises in teaching management and business ethics has spanned the past 25 years (Sims & Sauser, 1985). Over that time we have become convinced that it is important to draw upon students or learners' experience to provide opportunities for them to be engaged actively in what they are learning about business ethics. We have also accepted that experience alone is not the key to learning business ethics. Too often we have seen and heard students subjected to half-digested (and half-baked) or inappropriate academically oriented learning under the guise of effective or best practices teaching of business ethics. As a result of our own and others' missteps in

Experiences in Teaching Business Ethics
pp. 171–203
Copyright © 2011 by Information Age Publishing
All rights of reproduction in any form reserved.

teaching business ethics we now clearly realize that if one is to be effective in efforts to teach business ethics it is important that one begin by asking and answering questions like: What is it that turns experience in the business ethics classroom into learning? What specifically enables students to gain the maximum benefit from the experiential learning situations in which students find themselves in the business ethics classroom? How can students apply their learning in the business ethics classroom to new contexts? Why do some students appear to benefit more than others from experiential learning exercises or activities in the business ethics classroom?

The more we read and thought about our own and others' experiences related to the above issues, the more it became clear how important reflection and debriefing are to the effective teaching and learning of business ethics. Based on his own and others' experiences in teaching business ethics, Sims (2002) first wrote about debriefing and reflection almost a decade ago. Likewise, Sauser (2004) included aspects of reflective learning in his approach to teaching business ethics to professional engineers. Over the past 10 years we have continued using experiential learning exercises as techniques for promoting students' (i.e., undergraduate, graduate, and professionals) learning while constantly reflecting on the nature of learning as encouraged by the use of experiential learning exercises. Our views continued to be reinforced as we increasingly worked with fellow teachers and trainers to understand more about the nature of learning and of the possible role that experiential learning exercises, reflection and debriefing can play in effective efforts to teach and promote business ethics.

This chapter builds on our own and others' experiences in teaching business ethics and offers a more up-to-date view on the role that reflection and debriefing can and should play in the effective teaching of business ethics. More specifically, this chapter focuses on the process of reflection and debriefing and the postexperience analysis of experiential learning exercises in business ethics education. The purpose of reflection and debriefing is to use the information generated during the experiential exercise to facilitate learning for students and other participants. After students and other participants have engaged in an experiential learning activity, reflection and debriefing provide insight into the exercise. In addition to discussing reflection and debriefing, the chapter provides a conceptual model for debriefing using Kolb's (1984) experiential learning cycle and model of the learning process in teaching business ethics. We also offer practical ideas for applying the model to reflecting on and debriefing experiential learning exercises used in business ethics courses. Special attention is first given to a brief discussion of experiential learning exercises as a teaching tool. We also discuss the importance of the business ethics teacher's role in providing structure, ambiguity, and a climate for learning in experiential exercises so that learners can personalize the learning. Mistakes to avoid in debriefing experiential learning exercises in teaching business ethics are discussed before the chapter concludes.

EXPERIENTIAL LEARNING EXERCISES AND TEACHING BUSINESS ETHICS

Experiential learning exercises in teaching business ethics can span a wide variety of functional areas and formats. Indeed, the variety of exercises available and the creativity involved in developing them is amazing (Sims, 2002). Experienced teachers and trainers typically rely on a variety of different methods in their teaching or training endeavors: lecture, case study, role-play, behavioral modeling, and simulations. This sequencing reflects the theory that active experience facilitates learning better than passive techniques. Students or participants seem to learn better through interactive methodologies that are action oriented.

Moral judgment is action oriented. Business students should participate in experiential (learning) exercises that require them to ask themselves: What is the right thing to do, or what is the wrong thing to do? Experiential exercises that expect students to respond to moral questions that are personal in nature and involve interpersonal relations require normative responses to determine the appropriate course of action (Sims & Sims, 1991). In this age of moral relativism, business school curricula— or programs or workshops for professionals—should provide students with continuous experience in examining the underlying moral issues. What are managers', leaders' or employees' responsibilities or obligations to an organization, work group, themselves, family, and society? And what will be the possible consequences of a particular action if they make an immoral decision and knowingly harm others?

Many ethical problems or dilemmas do not have specific "correct" solutions like those problems presented in a number of courses and examinations in business schools (i.e., accounting, operations, statistics, etc.). Furthermore, an emphasis on factual rules important to success on professional examinations can create a classroom expectation that is especially unwelcoming to the unstructured and ill-defined ethical problems that students will face. Thus, the problem is two-fold: the emphasis on mastery learning of facts to produce correct solutions to examination problems is too narrow a focus; and, the pedagogy customarily applied to analyze ethical issues is not the right approach when the objective is to develop the ability to make independent ethical judgments.

To address these two problems, business students or professionals need to have an experiential awareness of the types of ethical dilemmas they will face (i.e., relevancy), and they need to be able to evaluate and identify possible courses of action when confronted by ethical dilemmas (Sims, 2002). As noted by Maglagan and Snell (1992), reliance on information-transfer approaches to ethics should be complemented by experiential methods. The use and value of experiential methods or exercises as a teaching medium are well recognized and have been widely reported (Sanyal, 2000). For example, Hemmasi and Graf (1992) show that experiential exercises have the following positive attributes: students retain material longer over time, students are actively involved in the learning process, actual work environments are simulated, and students enjoy them. Sanyal (2000) recently noted that experiential exercises serve as an effective training and teaching tool to prepare students to understand and cope with the ethical minefields they are likely to encounter when entering the business world.

Black and Mendenhall (1989) have noted that experiential training methods such as simulations, field trips, and role-plays are more rigorous and engage participants more fully than methods such as lectures and videotapes. Simulations, for example, can provide students with hands-on experience and a better understanding of the concepts discussed in the classroom (Teach, Christensen & Schwartz, 2005). In simulations designed for teaching business ethics, students can face ethical dilemmas that encourage them to react and act on the problems as though they were in a real-life situation (Haywood, McMullen, & Wygal, 2004; LeClair, Ferrell, Montuori, & Willems, 1999). Role playing also provides students with the opportunity to participate with a high level of personal involvement (Sims & Felton, 2006). Students could be asked to develop a code of ethics for an organization (Sims, 2003). Similarly, field trips can provide another pedagogical vehicle to actively engage students in analyzing ethical problems and identifying creative resolutions. Finally, Lampe (1997) has noted that requiring students to provide some form of community service also offers the potential for personal and emotional impact that may be difficult to capture through traditional classroom learning. As a result of the service learning experience, many students begin to see the relationship of business to society, eventually understanding that it is an open system, not a closed one (Carey, 2005). The movement toward experiential service learning has gained considerable momentum in business education since the early 1990s (Zlotkowski, 1996). These pedagogical approaches all emphasize high participation and active rather than passive learning.

Role-playing is one of the experiential learning techniques advocated for teaching about ethical issues (Baetz & Carson, 1999). In particular, it has been noted that role-playing might help students transfer their ability to reason ethically into the business context (McDonald & Donleavy, 1995). Role-playing leaves a memorable impression and actively engages all players in the learning process. Role-playing also provides students with the opportunity to participate with a high level of personal involvement.

Experientially oriented business cases and field-based applications can provide another pedagogical vehicle to actively engage students in analyzing ethical problems and identifying creative resolutions (Sims, 2002). Providing business students with experiential learning exercises that focus on problems involving improper gifts, kickbacks, and conflicts of interest will develop their ability to analyze unstructured ethical dilemmas and discern alternative courses of action. Requiring students to participate in some form of community service also offers the potential for personal and emotional impact that may be difficult to capture through traditional classroom learning (Hill & Stewart, 1999; Kohls, 1996).

Another familiar experientially oriented pedagogical approach that we have found to be highly effective is to schedule discussions that are focused on current events that have ethical ramifications (Phillips & Clawson, 1998). Reports and individual journals can be prepared from current periodicals based on recent headline-making fraud and embezzlement cases, and class discussion can focus on how these problems could have been avoided. (This also opens the door for a discussion of white-collar crime.) It is equally valuable to ask undergraduate business students to examine the ethical code of their college and student body (e.g., honor code, harassment policies) and query graduate business students on the ethical codes of their current or former employers.

There are several studies that have explored quantitatively the impact of experiential learning on student perceptions and performance (Hunt & Laverle, 2004). The use of experiential learning is related to students reporting higher levels of self-confidence in their discipline-based knowledge (House, 2002). Furthermore, experiential learning is empirically related to increases in learning involvement and motivation (House, 2002; Udovic, Morris, Dickman, Postlethwait, & Wetherwax, 2002), improvements in problem solving abilities (Zoller, 1987), and enhancements in creativity and social skills (Livingstone & Lynch, 2002). When compared with students in a comparison section of a course taught with passive methods, students in a section of a course taught with an experiential approach developed a deeper conceptual understanding of the material, a superior logical reasoning, and a greater appreciation for the discipline (Udovic et al., 2002). Studies show that experiential learning enhances cognitive advancement, a critical consideration of course material, critical thinking in general, the ability to work with others, and the tolerance of others (Abson, 1994).

Because experiential learning involves a learning process that is action-oriented, it is well-suited for preparing students for the kinds of job situations they will encounter that pose ethical issues and concerns (Sims, 2002). Most education focuses on a closed loop approach in which students are first presented with material, after which they attempt to understand it and repeat it back. However, experience is a crucial element in teaching marketing ethics for effective learning (Sims, 2002).

The brief look at pedagogical approaches and relevant research presented above emphasizes the value of experiential learning, high participation and active rather than passive learning. It is critical that experiential learning exercises are carefully designed and thoughtfully executed to include time spent on reflection and debriefing what actually occurred during the exercise or learning experience. In the end, an experiential learning exercise is a complex event in business ethics education. It needs to provide students with the basis for understanding why and how the new knowledge they acquire is related to what they already know. It must convey to the students that they have the capability of using this new knowledge not only in the classrooms in which they learn it but in other settings as well (Lederman, 1992).

When rigorously administered, experiential learning exercises can be a powerful form of teaching in which participants acquire new knowledge, skills and abilities by internalizing theory through guided practice. Of crucial importance in experiential learning is reflection and debriefing, as we highlight in the next sections of this chapter.

REFLECTION

What typically comes to mind when you think of reflection? In the physical sense one might think about mirrors and reflected images, of looking and seeing a parallel version of the world. However, from a human view one might imagine thinking quietly, mulling over events in our mind or making sense of (for example) ethical dilemmas or experiences we have had. Groups of people might also come to mind: people engaged in reflection of a particular event or issue in their organization or actively discussing recent organizational events or issues. Comparing notes, views and opinions; roundtable discussions related to particular events or issues; carrying out an after-action review; having an informal group discussion—all these are used to describe activities with which we are familiar and which have some relation to "reflection."

If one were to take a poll of a group of people the results would undoubtedly show that they all recognize the importance of these activities in their lives. We have all said that we need time to take stock of a situation, to make sense of what has happened, or to share other peoples' ideas on an experience. In reality, these are so commonplace that we regard them as a natural part of our daily lives—as natural as breathing. We know intuitively that we need to do these things in order to learn from our experiences and often to deal with our expectations.

The activity of reflection is so familiar that those of us in the learning or education business often overlook it in formal business ethics learning settings. We make assumptions about the fact that not only is it occurring, but it is something which we cannot directly observe and which is unique to each learner. However, as Daley (1982, p. 611) points out: "The skill of experiential learning in which people tend to be the most deficient is reflection." If we can get students and others who are involved in teaching and learning business ethics to sharpen their consciousness of what reflection in experiential learning can involve and how it can be influenced then we may all be able to continue to improve the practice of teaching and learning with respect to business ethics.

At a minimum, reflection should provide students who are engaged in experiential learning exercises in business ethics with a belief that they are engaged in important work and that such reflection can make a difference. Reflection can serve as a springboard for students to share different perspectives, understand nuances, appreciate alternative points of view, employ self-monitored learning practices, pursue new information, and clarify values and attitudes. For, example, the use of reflection in business ethics-oriented service learning courses enables students to explore beyond standard educational outcomes that may include technical, academic, personal and professional development to gain an appreciation of the "importance of reciprocity" (Zlotkowski, 1999, p. 107), as well as the skills necessary for democratic discourse (Brookfield, 1995). Faculty can use carefully structured reflection assignments to help students further develop and refine their ethical decision-making habits as they seek to understand and analyze cultural, social, and economic issues affecting our society. This will help students become caring, contributing citizens in a democratic society.

Through reflection those who use experiential exercises in teaching business ethics can ask students to describe their experience (what?), discuss what it means (so what?), and identify next steps (now what?). Reflection also helps those responsible for teaching business ethics to view the various experiences through students' eyes and thus teach more responsively or effectively. Thus reflection can accrue substantial educational rewards in teaching business ethics. Through experience, we have learned that reflection must be approached with considerable sensitivity in any experiential learning-specific content, and especially when content in business ethics is concerned. Through carefully structured reflection activities, experiential learning exercises and the business ethics course content can complement, affirm, and extend each other. For example, as students draw inductively from direct personal experiences and observations via general lessons and principles to resolve a simulated ethical dilemma, they strengthen and affirm both their general knowledge and their skills in wrestling with issues in business ethics. When structured reflection is integrated into experiential learning exercises, whether written or oral, it can be a major component of a strategy for teaching business ethics that connects the experiential learning exercise to other course content. When students share their personal experiences in experiential learning exercises, they inform and reinforce classroom instruction, provide depth and understanding to the actual exercise, draw on accompanying readings, and make both the exercise and their own learning more meaningful.

It has also been the authors' experience that reflection encourages change by providing opportunities for individuals to consider their own behaviors in light of their espoused theories and commitments. Reflection takes as a starting point personal experience and assumes that this provides a foundation for learning. In doing so, the reflective approach differs from one that is grounded on conceptual frameworks and theory-based empirical evidence as the necessary material for productive business or professional preparation.

Like others we contend that experiences are good fodder for ethical growth and personal and professional development. Experiential learning theorists, including Dewey, Lewin, Piaget, and Kolb, maintain that learning is most effective—most likely to lead to behavioral change—when it begins with experience (Sims, 2002). These theorists, joined by Knowles (1990), McCarthy (1990) and others, also point out that grounding learning in the realities of students' lives and experiential learning exercises is quite consistent with insights derived from the growing body of research on adult learning. Because reflection invites—and, indeed, often depends upon—a consideration of actual experience, its use as a pedagogical strategy suggests that the knowledge of practice is considered a valid and important part in teaching business ethics. In summary, reflection as a part of experiential learning exercises in teaching business ethics efforts should be structured to challenge both students and those responsible for teaching business ethics to explore questions and issues related to business ethics and one's approach to knowing or learning. Reflection should be pursued with intent as part of experiential learning exercises in teaching business ethics.

One caveat before we turn to our discussion of debriefing: It is essential that reflection be honest and genuine if it is to lead to personal growth. False reflection that consists only of a parroting of the instructor's viewpoint—or that of influential others involved in the discussion—will not lead to effective reflective learning. Thus it is essential that the business ethics instructor allow students *honestly* to express their own viewpoints in experiential exercises. It is only through the testing of one's actual beliefs that reflection provides the insight that leads to personal growth. Thus, the effective business ethics professor will typically refrain from judging students' reflective comments while the exercise is proceeding.

DEBRIEFING: NATURE AND DEFINITIONS

The historical roots of debriefing lie in military campaigns and war games (Pearson & Smith, 1985). Debriefing was the time after a mission or exercise when participants were brought together to describe what had occurred, to account for the actions that had taken place, and to develop new strategies as a result of the experience. This function of debriefing in relation to military action and training still continues today and in a number of ways the original purposes are directly relevant to teaching business ethics via experiential learning exercises. However, debriefing in regard to experiential learning exercises in teaching business ethics is more than simply describing events or accounting for actions. Debriefing provides the opportunity for structured reflection whereby experiential learning exercises are used for teaching business ethics (Sims, 2002).

Debriefing is sometimes identified with other terms such as "publishing" and "generalizing," which are used in experiential learning models. These terms refer to steps in the debriefing process. Similarly, the whole process of debriefing is sometimes referred to as "processing." Pearson and Smith (1985) note point out that "whatever the terms, purposeful reflection by an individual or group takes place" (p. 70).

While a number of authors write about the debriefing process, not all use the term "debriefing" to mean the same thing. For purposes of this chapter, *debriefing* is defined as the postexperience analysis designed to provide insight into the cases, journal keeping, role-plays or other experiential learning approaches used in teaching business ethics. Pearson and Smith (1986) offer the following insight into the relationship between the experience of learning and the debriefing phase: "Active experience is involving and interesting, even exciting. Debriefing means the cessation of this experiencing and the deliberate decision to reflect on action" (p. 156).

In his model of experiential learning, Thatcher (1986), drawing on the earlier work of Kolb (1984), emphasizes that reflective observation (debriefing) is the crucial link between experience and the process of change that makes the elements of the experience a part of the conceptual foundation of the learner. Thatcher (1986) notes:

> Debriefing is the part of the process in which the reflection takes place and from which the change in the person will occur, because it is the part of the activity which focuses on the complex processes which took place in each individual and in the group as a whole. (p. 151)

Debriefing has always been a key component of successful experiential learning exercises. The link between objectives, course materials, and the experiential learning exercise seems rarely, if ever, crystal clear to the participants. In the organizational world, this is even more relevant because some participants resist experiential learning exercises or games when they are "played" with Tinkertoys, Lego blocks, dolls, puppets, or other toy-like materials associated with childhood.

When debriefing is structured to promote reflection, encouraging students to analyze their own assumptions and think about how to enhance or develop more skills in handling (for example) ethical dilemmas, reflective practice should be involved. Like reflective practitioners who engage in introspection learn to self-correct and assimilate new experiences with prior ones and thus improve their professional competence (Rudolf, Simon, Rivard, Dufresne, & Raemer, 2007), students engaged in experiential learning exercises in business ethics classes can also improve their understanding and ability to address ethical dilemmas or make better ethical decisions. Debriefing provides opportunities to foster reflective learning, encompassing the ability to think-in-action as well as think-on-action (Schon, 1983).

Debriefing supports a constructivist theoretical framework within problem-based learning experiences (Dreifuerst, 2009). Constructivist learning is a contextual and experiential process where knowledge is individually constructed and thought about as learning occurs (Richardson, 1997). With the preponderance of simulation used throughout nursing programs and other professional curricula, educators need to understand and develop best practices for debriefing to facilitate significant student learning during these experiences.

The process of experiential learning in teaching business ethics requires active engagement. To facilitate meaningful, active learning, students must have opportunities to "reflect on their experience in the (exercise), have a period of emotional release, receive behavioral feedback, integrate their observations, behavior and feedback into a conceptual framework and create mechanisms and pathways for transferring learn-ing to relevant outside situations" (Warrick, Hunsaker, Cook, & Altman, 1979). These attributes—reflection, emotion, reception, and integration and assimilation—are the defining attributes of successful experiential learning debriefing in efforts to teach business ethics.

As noted earlier, reflection is the opportunity to reexamine the experi-ence. It can be a chronological review or simply thinking upon what comes to mind first and working through the experience from that start-ing point. It is time specifically set aside to engage *thinking processes* that makes for effective debriefing during experiential learning exercises used in teaching business ethics.

Emotion and emotional release are also important. Student engage-ment in the experiential learning exercise can cross boundaries of reality and call out significant emotional response (Dreifuerst, 2009). Emotion enhances learning by the way it frames the experience (Schon, 1983), but it can also inhibit learning if it distracts from engagement in the experi-ence. Facilitating the honest expression of emotions acknowledges the power of the learning experience to set the frame for embedding it in the learner's memory. Emotional release can redirect the attention of the learner to reflection and ultimately to learning during the debriefing pro-cess.

Integration of the experiential learning exercise and the facilitated reflection into a conceptual framework is one of the most challenging and least common attributes of debriefing. To be successful, those responsible for teaching business ethics must model framing and embed the elements of the experience into scaffolding that the students in the business ethics teaching effort are familiar with and can call upon when experiencing future situations. Pesut (2004) suggests that framing is attribution of meaning to a set of facts. In business ethics there are numerous frames, but the most common emphasized in teaching business ethics is the deci-sion making process. In most business ethics exercises emphasis is placed on making a sound decision related to the ethical dilemma presented. Integrating the elements of the ethical decision making process into debriefing sets the stage for assimilating knowledge, skills, and attitudes into real-world ethical situations, thus providing a path for accommoda-tion and transference into future work or other situations that require eth-ical decision making.

Integration using (for example) the ethical decision making process should be an important component of postexperiential learning exercise debriefing. Assimilation and accommodation to equip our students to deal with real-world ethical dilemmas are the ultimate goals of our efforts in teaching business ethics, and thus they must also be the essence of reflection during the debriefing portion of the experiential learning exercises we use. Those responsible for teaching business ethics want students to demonstrate successfully that they can transfer what they have learned and experienced from one situation to the next. In addition, assimilation and accommodation involve anticipation. Anticipation and reflection are related. While reflection is often considered looking back or looking at, as in "reflection on action" and "reflection in action" (Schon, 1983; Tanner, 2006), it can also be looking forward, or "reflection beyond action" (Dreifuerst, 2007). This critical aspect of reflection builds upon the work of Klein (1999), who describes "seeing the future while seeing the past" as a component of decision making (p. 289). Klein's work thus supports the anticipatory nature of reflection (Dreifuerst, 2009) as an essential part of debriefing in any experiential learning exercise used to teach business ethics (Sims, 2002).

DEBRIEFING EXPERIENTIAL LEARNING EXERCISES IN BUSINESS ETHICS

Every business ethics teaching activity should have a closing, and experiential learning exercises used in such efforts are no exception. Hunt and Laverle (2004) note that experiential pedagogies need to be combined with a debriefing stage where students are asked to reflect on the experience to complete the learning process. After students finish some business ethics education activity—a case, role-play, or simulation, for example—then what? What you do with the final few minutes of each class, module or—in our case—experiential learning exercise in teaching business ethics is very important.

Why Are the Last Minutes Important?

The closing portion of an experiential learning exercise in an effort to teach business ethics usually serves at least three purposes, and sometimes has a fourth as well. The final minutes can serve to:

Relieve Emotional Intensity

Experiential learning activities can be stressful. Students can be put into new, artificial, and somewhat uncomfortable roles. Often, the experiential learning activities involve competition (even if it is only a matter of two groups playing a game and then reporting their results or two groups working through a number of issues and decisions on a particular ethical problem), and for many students any form of experiential learning exercise is taken very seriously. Furthermore, most experiential learning exercises, no matter how enjoyably designed, deal with serious issues. Individual and organizational performance and success, or the future mission and course of the organization, may be on the line. As alluded to earlier, emotions will surface as students grapple with personal values, beliefs and morals; they need to be acknowledged and aired.

Even if the experiential learning exercise doesn't seem to involve stressful activities or highly personal issues, emotional release is needed. It has been our experience that students or professionals have the urge to share, to tell others what they did (or did not do), thought, and felt during the experiential learning exercise. Everyone needs the relief of debriefing, which means that everyone should have the chance to comment if they wish.

Solidify the Learning

During the experiential learning exercise in teaching business ethics students will have tried out a new idea, ethical framework, behavior, or skill. Having tried it, they may have questions that didn't arise earlier. Those questions should be answered now, so that the students are ready to move on to the next exercise, discussion, etc. Once questions are answered, it has been our experience that the instructor can then reinforce the learning by comparing and contrasting the experiences of individual students or groups. Discussing the differences and similarities, linking the students' experiences to the intended objectives for the experiential learning exercise or the ethical focus for the day's class, and highlighting any new insights allows students to draw for themselves lessons or conclusions.

Provide the Instructor Immediate Feedback

Listening to students' comments and questions, you know whether the intended learning objectives for the day or exercise are/were being achieved. In short, you'll learn whether or not the students are "still with you." Any concerns can be handled now, before they disrupt the flow of the class, module or course.

Bring the Total Class to a Decision by Consensus

Two points need to be made about consensus. First, not all experiential learning exercises in teaching business ethics lead to decisions, and not all decisions are reached by consensus. Nevertheless, consensus is most consistent with the goal when teaching business ethics of concluding the class with an agreed upon ethical principle, guideline, or major piece of learning to build on for the future. Ideally, there are times when the total class should be in accord, or at least the majority of students should agree while the minority accepts the outcomes, direction, or key ethical points expressed by the majority.

Second, consensus is not necessarily needed at the end of each business ethics class. Consensus may sometimes be important at appropriate times during an experiential learning exercise, at the close of an exercise, or at appropriate midpoints, such as at the end of a series of closely interrelated exercises that focus on a particular ethical issue or theme.

For these reasons, not every debriefing of an experiential learning exercise has or should have consensus as one of its purposes in teaching business ethics. If, however, decision by consensus is a goal for closing or debriefing an experiential learning exercise (or class) in teaching business ethics, then we have found that it is best to set such expectations at the outset of the class or exercise. In short, we tell students that we will be carrying out exercise X, with the goal of reaching consensus on Y. Or, if necessary, we tell them how a decision will be reached if other than by group consensus.

Hunsaker (1978) provides the following standards for debriefing:

> The main function of the facilitator during the debriefing is to insure an integration of the experiences with concepts and applications to outside situations so that appropriate generalizations can be made. It is also important that the facilitator encourage participants to exchange feedback and clarify strengths and weaknesses in their interpersonal behavior. Consequently, the facilitator should direct attention to both the content and process of the exercise with respect to both conceptual and personal learnings. (p. 3)

The debriefing phase can be conceptualized as a dialogue or conversation between the instructor (debriefer) and the students (Sims, 2004). For example, consider the case of a guest speaker in a course who views environmental pollution and adherence to legal restrictions as an economic problem of profit maximization. The event of the speech provides the opportunity for a follow-up session involving role-playing to make certain the issues focused on by the speaker were well understood. A debriefing phase following the speech and subsequent role-play provides the opportunity to address questions such as: "Is there a difference between legal authority and moral authority?" "What is the role of business in society?" "Should the university have censored the speaker's remarks?" "Now that the point-of-view of the speaker is known, should he be invited to speak again?" "What are the costs to society?" "What if all businesses followed the same practices?" A structured dialogue following such an activity offers valuable opportunities for students to learn and apply this learning to other situations. However, such dialogue can occur only if those responsible for teaching business ethics take the time to plan for debriefing.

PLANNING FOR DEBRIEFING

Debriefing can be structured to occur as part of only one experiential learning exercise, or it may occur over a number of exercises during a course in business ethics. If the business ethics teaching effort is an extended one, say over a semester-long course, debriefing may be needed at the end of any particular experiential learning exercise before going on to the next, as well as occurring at the conclusion of a series of exercises or at the conclusion of the entire teaching effort.

It is possible to draw a distinction between what might be called "planned debriefing" and "unplanned debriefing." Planned debriefing is that which is deliberately structured in some manner. Unplanned debriefing is that which occurs individually or after planned debriefing. What should be remembered is that the outcomes of unplanned debriefing may be just as important and powerful as those of planned debriefing of experiential learning exercises. One of the main aims of planned debriefing should be to stimulate students or other participants so they will continue reflecting upon their experience from the experiential learning exercise after the planned debriefing period has ended. The power to stimulate this continuing reflection by students and other participants in experiential learning exercises as part of business ethics teaching efforts is related on one hand to the careful planning and structuring of the planned debriefing period, and on the other to the effective management of the debriefing process so that it does not finish in such a way as to inhibit reflection by appearing to answer all questions and close all doors.

The debriefing stage must be planned so that it provides the student with continuity of the experience, as opposed to students losing the learning due to a lack of experiencing and understanding its application. For the experience to be maximally effective for students, therefore, the debriefing must be allocated an adequate amount of time or much of the potential richness of the experience is lost. No exact amount of time for the debriefing is recommended but the time has to be included in the planning of any experiential learning exercise in teaching business ethics. Those responsible for teaching business ethics can decide upon the length of the debriefing session. Some of the factors faculty may want to consider when determining the length of the debriefing session include purpose, complexity and level of intensity of the exercise; responsiveness of the students; and format of the debriefing session.

As noted above, time for debriefing must be included in the planning of any experiential learning exercise in teaching business ethics. Too often it is the debriefing phase of an experiential learning exercise which is cancelled or considerably shortened by the extension of the exercise itself. Thus, in our experience, the commitment to the importance of debriefing must be accompanied by a commitment by those responsible for the instructional initiative to allow sufficient time for effective debriefing to occur. A colleague of ours has suggested that in order to complete debriefing effectively it takes more time than the experiential learning exercise in teaching business ethics. We tend to agree, as this is especially the case with students (or even professionals) in experiential learning exercises in business ethics where often *all* the participants desire to be involved and "have a say," which necessitates even more time.

In the end, more important than the instructions and guidelines provided at the beginning of an experiential learning exercise are the purposes and intentions of those responsible for the business ethics teaching effort. Although debriefing of the experiential learning exercise may well include the discussion of issues that were not anticipated, the debriefing phase should attempt to achieve the purposes and intention determined during the actual planning of the ethics course and the decision to use an experiential learning exercise in an effort to teach business ethics. In addition, time must be spent during the planning phase determining how to evaluate how successfully this has been accomplished. The closeness of the relationship between the planned or desired outcomes being sought and the actual outcomes gained will undoubtedly vary in some way but the goal is to minimize as much variance as possible.

DEBRIEFING EXPERIENTIAL LEARNING EXERCISES IN TEACHING BUSINESS ETHICS: A RECOMMENDED CONCEPTUAL MODEL

In pursuit of achieving a level in which students not only absorb the knowledge presented in an effort to teach business ethics, but also apply this learning in practice, it is helpful to consider the entire process of learning, and then to apply this learning process specifically to the debriefing session. Over the years, we have used David Kolb's (1984) experiential learning model (ELM) to inform and direct such considerations.

The heart of Kolb's ELM is a cycle of learning. Kolb's cycle or learning sequence has the underlying premise that learners learn best when they are active, take responsibility for their own learning, and can relate and apply it to their own context. Kolb's cycle of learning proposes four learning modes: concrete experience, reflective observation, abstract conceptualization, and active experimentation. Learning occurs most effectively when all four modes in the cycle of learning are completed.

According to Kolb, we all learn from the experience of doing a task and the results of that learning can be used constructively and even assessed. But it is not sufficient simply to have an experience in order to learn. Without reflecting on this experience, often through discussing it with others (but we will suggest other methods below), it may be rapidly forgotten or its learning potential lost. The feelings and thoughts emerging out of this reflection can fit into a pattern that starts to make sense such that generalizations can be made and concepts can be generated, and relationships can be formed with existing theories. And it is generalizations and theories that give the learner the conceptual framework with which to plan and tackle new situations effectively.

What has this to do with the process of debriefing experiential learning exercises in teaching business ethics? Debriefing is the part of the Kolb' learning cycle in which reflection takes place and from which learning and change in individuals will occur, because it is the part of the activity which focuses on what took place in each individual and in the group as a whole. Thus debriefing is an important point of learning in Kolb's experiential learning cycle. It is the process by which the *experience* of an experiential exercise is examined, discussed, and turned into learning.

Kolb, Osland, and Rubin's (1995) model of adult learning defines each stage of the learning process and is presented here for application to debriefing. For each stage, key questions are provided that may help faculty members progress through the stages, applying each to the debriefing of experiential learning exercises in their efforts to teach business ethics (see Table 8.1). Additional questions are offered by Gaw (1979).

Although students may naturally proceed through some of the stages in Kolb et al.'s (1995) model during a debriefing exercise, often the progression does not result in active experimentation (doing). For example, the faculty member's or trainer's goal may be to ultimately motivate a student or participant to use learned ethical concepts or theories in new situations, yet some students or participants may merely conceptualize and not chance practice, while others may try different methods of practice without integrating learned concepts in a meaningful fashion. Through the application Kolb et al.'s model to the debriefing session, however, faculty or trainers teaching business ethics can guide students or participants through the stages to achieve active experimentation.

What should occur during the application and transfer stage seems more clearly found in the active experimentation stage as described by Kolb et al. (1995). The focus in the debriefing is to influence people in an active way and to transform situations in a dramatic fashion. It emphasizes practical applications as opposed to reflective understanding, a

**Table 8.1.   Debriefing Experiential Learning
Exercises by Using the Kolb Model**

Stage in Kolb's Model of the Learning Process	Description of Kolb's Stage	Questions for Application of Learning Stage to Stages in Debriefing Session
Concrete experience (feeling)	The students objectively describe the experience in terms of who, what, when, where, how. They also subjectively describe their feelings, perceptions, and thoughts that occurred during (not after) the experience. They tell their story. If the event is stressful, emotional or disturbing, the students can gain composure.	• Did you complete your assignment? • Were the objectives of the assignment clear? • How did you feel?
Reflective observation (watching)	At this level, the experience is viewed from different points of view that add more meaning and perspectives to the event. This approach values patience, impartiality, and considered, thoughtful judgment.	• Did you make assumptions about X, Y, Z? • What was happening for you during the exercise? • What did you observe in others? • What did the exercise mean for you and in relation to others? (Clarify differences of opinion).
Abstract conceptualization (thinking)	The debriefing relates ethical concepts, theories, or models from the readings and lectures to the experience in the activity. An original model or theory can be created.	• What policies/rules could you make based on your experience in this exercise? • With what variables would the rules/policies not apply? • Given such variables, what would be a better rule or policy?
Active experimentation (doing)	The students apply what has been learned in the experience of the activity to the parallel- world outside the classroom. "What if" scenarios may be explored.	• How would you change aspects of the experience for a better outcome? What new strategy would you use? • In what real world/practical work situations could this new strategy be utilized? • What situations would call for a backup or alternative strategy?

pragmatic concern with what works as opposed to what is abstract; an emphasis on doing as opposed to observing. Here, the focus is on getting things accomplished and achieving objectives. Impact and influence on the environment are valued. Active experimentation allows for testing the implications of ethical concepts and theories in new situations by students or other participants. These hypotheses are tested on future action, which, in turn, leads to new experiences.

The Debriefing Model in Action

The following is an example of how one of the authors (Sims) used the debriefing model to debrief a modified version of the experiential learning exercise, "Instructor/Participant Interviews" (Kolb et al., 1995). This exercise was used by Sims in the first two classes of an undergraduate Business and Society course. Briefly, the modified goal of this experiential exercise is for the instructor to learn from the students their expectations for the course regarding what they hope to learn; any concerns or fears they might bring into the class; and the virtues, values, or characteristics that they admire and by which they would like an organization (i.e., course) of which they are a member to be guided. An additional goal is to try to learn what students feel they can contribute to the achievement of their expectations and to the learning process.

During the exercise the instructor first interviewed the students, representatives of the class then interviewed the instructor, and finally, before the debriefing discussion, the total group compared the interviews and identified potential pinches (differences that will influence the learning process). It should be noted that the exercise was preceded by reading, lecture and in-class discussion on Kolb's (1984) ELM, and Sherwood and Glidewell's (1972) psychological contract and pinch model (see chapter 3 for a more detailed discussion of the Sherwood and Glidewell model). Briefly, Sherwood and Glidewell have developed a simple but powerful model, the pinch model, which describes the dynamic quality of psychological contracts and suggests ways of maintaining the potentially dysfunctional consequences of shifting expectations. In preparation for the first two classes the students also read a summary paper on traditional and contemporary ethical theories and models. All of these are intended to begin to develop a classroom climate of trust, openness, and sharing. More will be said about the classroom environment and the role of the business ethics teacher or trainer in the next section.

In the first step (concrete experience) of debriefing the exercise, students are asked to take 3-5 minutes to write down their individual feelings, perceptions, and thoughts that occurred during the exercise. The instructor also completed the task at the same time. The students were then asked to take ten minutes to share their work with other members of the groups in which they were working during the exercise. Following the group discussion the instructor then asked members of each group to share some of the information gathered in their group discussion with the total class.

Some of the comments generated by students were, "We weren't sure what we were supposed to learn from the first two classes and we all agreed that these classes were very different from other classes we had taken here at the college." "We weren't sure whether or not you really care about our fears, concerns and expectations, but time will tell!" At this stage of the debriefing process it is important to remember that as the instructor, Sims was concerned with getting as many students' feelings, perceptions, and thoughts expressed as possible. To accomplish this goal he asked students, "Are there any more questions?" and, "Did other groups have similar feelings, thoughts, etc.?"

After spending about 10-15 minutes on the first stage of the debriefing process, Sims made a transition to the reflective observation stage by asking students to take a few minutes as a group to look back over what had occurred during the exercise and to reflect on the questions they raised during the first stage of the debriefing process. In particular, Sims asked them to think about what ways their group's concerns, fears, virtues, values, or characteristics for an organization—and expectations and contributions—agreed or disagreed with his own. One of the key questions Sims posed to students during this stage was "In looking back over today's exercise and your group's discussion, what did you observe?" "Did you make any assumptions about what I and your other class members expect of you, and of this course?" "What are the virtues, values, or characteristics you admire and would like an organization (i.e., course) to be guided by?" "What did the exercise mean for you and others?" With these questions Sims tried to concentrate on encouraging students to reflect on their experiences during the exercise and articulate their perspective so that the total class could explore these understandings and learn from them.

Some of the students' points that came out of this reflective observation stage of the debriefing were: "No course we had ever taken had asked us questions like—What were my learning objectives for this course?" "Was I willing to participate actively in the setting of those objectives and in their attainment?" "What values or norms we wanted to use to guide this course?" "Several of us think this is what the exercise was all about."

As Sims reflected upon the comments made by the students not only in this course but also in previous courses, he recognized that students have been conditioned to listen and accept objectives, to take a passive role in the learning process, and to not be expected to share their concerns (or fears). Thus, when they were asked during Sims' first class to participate actively in objective setting and in an active learning process, many of them were unprepared to respond in a meaningful way. As a result, Sims has found that he has become increasingly sensitive to the need for himself, in his role as an instructor, to recognize and appreciate how much diversity there is within the class in students' ability to understand and respond to a different learning expectation and environment.

In the next stage of the debriefing process (abstract conceptualization), Sims asked the students first individually to think about, and then in their groups to discuss, the following question: "What ethical theories/models or course concepts that you heard in the lecture or read in preparation for class relate to your understanding of today's exercise?" While all the groups seemed to respond effectively to the question once the total class discussion began, one group's comments (with a little prodding from Sims) were clearly on target with the learning and insight he wanted to come out of the exercise and the first two classes. The following comments highlight the result of this debriefing stage: "First, this is to be an active learning experience. This sounds almost trivial but it is the basis of the psychological contract between you (the instructor) and the class (the organization) and furthermore is fundamental to learning in this course." A member of another group followed with:

> To be active learners means that I and the rest of the class will learn about business ethics by not only reading but by also actively experiencing situations that require some ethical decision making, etc. We must scrutinize the functioning of individuals, groups and organizations of which we are members, observe important situations, behaviors, etc., make hypotheses about these interactions, and actively test these hypotheses within the group in order to learn.

Finally, after some generous discussion amongst the students Sims pointed out that these comments almost directly flow from the first element (students are active learners) and the second element (a psychological contract between Sims as the instructor and they as students).

It has been our experience not only that conversations will be enhanced during the course through dialogue but students will also have opportunities to apply various ethical theories themselves. Finally, working through the direct application of various ethical theories or models provides a challenging learning experience for the students and the instructor. Students and faculty who seriously work through the application of the material together discover new insights. The elements directly concerned the learning process in which Sims engaged them in this course and fostered the substantive learning and teaching of business ethics itself.

These comments were intended to make a transition in the debriefing discussion from relating concepts and theories of the experience in the activities to focusing on the specifics (or rules of thumb) for students to be active learners in the remainder of the course. Both Sims' and the students' comments about active learners in his course were the main focus of the active experimentation stage of the debriefing model for the first two classes.

To continue the discussion on active learning, Sims then asked the students, "What will you need to do in future classes to meet your own and my expectations for this course?" He specifically asked the students to think about and generate rules of thumb or action resolutions. In response, one group commented, "In the future you (as the instructor) and we as students must take responsibility for raising a pinch (a point of disagreement in the model of psychological contracts) if and when it develops. We thought that pinches could either be raised via written comments or informal discussion, say at the end of class."

As evidenced in this debriefing example, the richness and strength of using the debriefing model presented above can be enhanced if debriefing proceeds through all of the stages: from concrete experience to reflective observation to abstract conceptualization and, ultimately, to active experimentation. The model allowed for testing implications of course concepts and theories in new situations which, in turn, led to new experiences and learning.

An important learning point as related to the above example is that the two elements (i.e., the psychological contract between the instructor and students and, that the students have some responsibility for setting the learning objectives), in combination, lead to a higher motivation to learn, provide students with a much better grasp of how the course will be conducted, and help them realize that knowledge can allay student's fears (i.e., uncertainty as to material, what is expected of students, and the invasiveness of dealing with "personal" values) often brought into an ethics course. Additionally, when the class agrees to the specific virtues relevant to the conduct of the course, students are provided with assurances of what norms are prescribed and what kind of classroom conduct is expected. Finally, the foundation is established for building a climate of trust and sharing in the classroom. In point of fact, Sims has found that both his attitude and that of his students toward learning—and the subsequent behavior of all—have reflected these efforts. As a result of using the debriefing model, we believe students are more inquisitive, more committed to learning and open to learning about business ethics, and in short, more involved in the learning process. It has been our experience that this involvement has resulted in large rewards for both the instructor and the students.

DEBRIEFING: COMPLETING THE ENTIRE LEARNING EXPERIENCE

Equally important to the effective planning of a debriefing exercise is providing an environment that is conducive to completing the entire learning experience. We think it is helpful to those responsible for teaching business ethics to understand the need for ambiguity and the need for structure in the experiential learning exercise. In addition, providing ground rules in which students will be able to experience all phases of the experiential learning cycle is helpful for keeping the effort to teach business ethics—and particularly the experiential learning exercise—focused and effective. Finally, it is important that the business ethics teacher or trainer commit to developing a supportive learning or sharing climate.

Encouraging an Environment of Ambiguity

As mentioned earlier, skills and knowledge gained from the exercise will differ for each student. Thus, the debriefing session will be perceived with some degree of ambiguity. For example, in the debriefing model in action discussion above, many of the students were unprepared to respond to an objective setting and active learning process. The questions made no sense to some of the students! Ambiguity is necessary so that individual's minds are personally stretched to apply ethical concepts and theories to real world situations. It may seem paradoxical that the pursuit of a conceptual model for debriefing is urged, yet ambiguity is also urged to meet the subjective needs of individuals and the reality of the ethical situations they will encounter outside of the classroom. Both requirements (structure and ambiguity), however, can be met if the faculty member or trainer is cognizant of each of the steps of the debriefing model and uses it as a road map to facilitate discussion so that all learning stages are experienced.

When adult learners reach the level of active experimentation (doing), they will use new skills, having experienced their usefulness/meaningfulness and will feel capable of using the skills, having experienced the competency to do so (Bandura, 1977; Kolb et al., 1995). The challenge for those responsible for teaching business ethics is to encourage the necessary amount of ambiguity in the experiential learning exercise so students can apply theories in practice. Faculty or trainers must provide guidance, by assisting students and other participants in keeping focused and effectively translating abstract conceptualization (theory) into active experimentation (practice). For example, in the debriefing model in action, students generated rules of thumb or action resolutions as part of the psychological contract. In the end, working through the direct application of ethical theories/models provides a challenging learning experience for the students and for us as professors.

This is similar to the notion of self-efficacy in Bandura's social learning theory, where human beings acquire new skills vicariously. Bandura (1977) argues that human beings think about and interpret their experiences as opposed to absorbing them blindly. From self-directed learning experiences, one gains a sense of self-efficacy in which new skills are used because the individual (a) has experienced their usefulness/meaningfulness and (b) feels capable of using the skills, having experienced the competency to do so. The instructor must encourage individuals to give and to get so that they develop their own meaningful applications of theory and will be more likely to experience their usefulness (Kolb et al., 1995). You will recall from the discussion of the exercise above that students soon recognized Sims' role in the debriefing in action as facilitator even though some had not experienced this situation in other classes.

To provide ambiguity, it is necessary to create an environment of *mutuality* (two-sided exchange), where learning is self-directed. Although there is no set method of creating such an environment, it may be helpful for faculty teaching business ethics to consider the lecture-oriented environment, which is typically one sided, where teachers give and students get. In contrast, adult learning needs are best fulfilled in an environment conducive to two sided-exchange. As Kolb et al. (1995) state,

> In adult learning both giving and getting are critical. In getting, there is the opportunity to incorporate new ideas and perspectives. In giving, there is the opportunity to integrate and apply these new perspectives and to practice their use. (p. 58)

As a general rule, Thiagarajan (1992) recommends that the instructor take on a cooperative role (as opposed to hierarchical or autonomous), in which the balance of power is equal between instructor and students. This mutuality allows for the fulfillment of the "contract of reciprocity" (Kolb et al., 1995) where students take an active role, responsibility, and interest in their own learning.

Finally, Gunz (1995) suggests that the instructor provide a great deal of tutorial support. A tutor with a good understanding of the exercise can ask appropriate questions of the participants, guiding them to appropriate observations from which they can build more helpful hypotheses. If this is not done, there is a risk that students will not make any successful circuits of the Kolb (1984) experiential learning cycle, and learning will not take place.

The "Game Plan": Providing Structure for the Exercise

Once the format for the debriefing session (i.e., discussion, game, constructive feedback, etc.) has been decided upon, those responsible for teaching business ethics should consider explaining the game plan and ground rules for the session to the students. By game plan, we mean a specific description of events and timing of them during the session. In terms of the game plan, faculty or trainers teaching business ethics may choose to describe the game or discussion format to the group and how it will occur in the context of the stages. For example, if a constructive feedback session is used within the framework of Kolb's model, the business ethics teacher or trainer could describe that the experience will be discussed (concrete experience), followed by feedback from group members (reflective observation), followed by a conceptualization of rules that may apply to other situations (abstract conceptualizations), and concluded with practical applications of the concepts to work situations (active experimentation). In describing the stages, the business ethics teacher or trainer can set a time limit for discussing each to ensure that there is ample time for all stages. If the group becomes lost in a digression, the instructor can refocus the debriefing by redirecting the group back to the game plan that had been previously articulated. The business ethics teacher or trainer can ensure focus by asking the types of questions for each stage provided earlier in Table 8.1. Using Table 8.1, the business ethics teacher or trainer has a tool for guiding the experiential learning cycle at the pace, depth, breadth, and intensity that seems appropriate.

Following the explanation of the game plan, setting ground rules for the debriefing session is important since it will involve discussing the actions of others, especially during the concrete experience (feeling) stage. Specifically, the business ethics teacher or trainer should convey that feedback should be descriptive (as opposed to evaluative), nonjudgmental, and noncritical. The constructive (as opposed to destructive) purpose of the exercise must be underscored (Borisoff & Victor, 1989).

Planned debriefing of experiential learning exercises in teaching business ethics is likely to be more effective when the purposes of an exercise are clearly identified during the presentation of the game plan, or what Pearson and Smith (1985) refer to as the *briefing* phase. These purposes form a focus for the *debriefing* of an experiential learning exercise so that the beginning and the concluding phases of the exercise provide an integrated context for the exercise or experience itself. It is important for those responsible for teaching business ethics to realize that the game plan is the time when students or other participants are oriented to the experiential learning exercise.

Creating a Supportive Environment
for Understanding and Sharing

Those responsible for teaching business ethics should use experiential learning exercises aimed at developing understanding and interpretation which in our experience involves a high degree of interpersonal action, sharing, dialogue and conversational learning by students and other participants. Examples of such experiences are learning about one's own and others' differing ethical viewpoints or opinions, which centers upon the sharing of students' or participants' reactions, understandings and meanings.

The role of those responsible for teaching business ethics in this case is not one of an expert with power and authority but that of a facilitator who encourages the sharing of ideas, feelings, emotions, understandings and viewpoints. Where the role of those responsible for teaching business ethics is mainly to facilitate sharing, dialogue and conversational learning, debriefing of experiential learning exercises must be organized and structured in such a way as to promote feelings of comfort, safety, trust, risk and acceptance. A learning environment characterized by these features is essential for students and other participants to feel that they can share in a frank, open and honest manner. In this context those responsible for teaching business ethics will undertake a great deal of listening and encourage students and other participants to talk openly with one another. The framework for the dialogue will be clearly related to the originally established intentions, but those responsible for teaching business ethics should also be open to hearing the concerns of the students and other participants and directing the dialogue toward such concerns when appropriate. By example those responsible for teaching business ethics and using experiential learning exercises establish and strengthen an accepting climate conducive to openness, trust and sharing. It is very important that business ethics teachers or trainers remember that any initial discussion of an experiential learning exercise during debriefing needs to be nonjudgmental; this fosters the authentic, honest sharing of viewpoints essential for true learning. During this period of initial discussion the instructor should refrain from reinterpreting, for example, students' or other participants' contributions by paraphrasing or summarizing.

Once a supportive learning environment has been established, the role of the instructor in facilitating the sharing of students' or participants' feelings, viewpoints, interpretations, meanings, understandings and clarifying the feelings being expressed can involve a further development: that of *challenging* viewpoints expressed and the perceptions and ethical theories on which they are based. In our view, such confrontation is appropriate where the intention is to promote critical thinking and reflection. The major aim of debriefing an experiential learning exercise in teaching business ethics aimed toward critical knowing is to shift individuals' understanding of themselves and their own actions to a new level; to establish a base which can be used as a self-sustaining takeoff to further personal growth and action. The purpose of critical knowing is to provide the intellectual tools for individuals themselves to continue in the process of critical reflection without the support of the business ethics teacher or trainer or other students or participants in the exercise, to develop the commitment toward their own critical self-knowing and to have the ethical skills and tools necessary to achieve it. Yes, this may be a grand ideal in an effort to teach business ethics. However, it is our belief that this ideal *should* be an important aim of any experiential learning exercise in teaching business ethics, especially those which are concerned with educating and training students and others for ethical decision making and action. Otherwise the learning from experiential learning exercises in business ethics classes will not be transferred to the work, home or other postclassroom context.

EXPERIENTIAL LEARNING EXERCISE DEBRIEFING MISTAKES

The debriefing phase in experiential learning exercises in teaching business ethics is easy to design. Typically, each group (and very often each individual) reports on the process and/or the results of the experiential learning exercise. The business ethics teacher or trainer (or one of the students) in the role of facilitator captures key points on an easel or the blackboard and then leads a discussion.

Although this process sounds simple, we have found that four common mistakes are often made in debriefing experiential learning exercises in teaching business ethics.

Rushing. Under pressure to stay within the confines of a scheduled class period, a business ethics teacher or trainer hurries through the debriefing and fails to give the class enough time to explain what happened and what they learned. Obviously, the debriefing phase cannot run indefinitely, and every ethics class or exercise does not need to tell every detail of its experience. There are ways to eliminate repetition. For example, after two groups of students have reported in, you might ask later groups if they had a similar experience and encourage them to add to or contrast with (rather than repeat) what has already been said. Techniques to keep the debriefing phase well paced will work as long as everyone feels she or he has had the chance for self-expression.

To avoid rushing, you should schedule adequate time for debriefing. If the experiential learning exercise is simple and the class is small, five minutes may suffice. Larger classes and more complex exercises may take 20 minutes or more depending on the actual exercise and its purpose or intention.

Forgetting to Give Credit. We have found that students learn best and are more committed to ethical reflection and learning when they have made the key discoveries themselves. When summarizing, it often helps to point out what students have contributed and learned. Give credit for their insights, rather than making them feel they have "gotten the right answer" by reaching one of the ethical or other insights you expected.

For example: Instead of saying, "As I explained at the beginning, one of the keys to effective ethical decision making is ...", try saying, "As Group A discovered when it played the negotiation game, one of the keys to effective ethical decision making is ...." Or, instead of saying, "One of the conclusions from our discussion is that unethical behavior in organizations depends heavily on ...," try saying, "During our discussion, Ramona and Jackson pointed out that unethical behavior in organizations depends heavily on ...."

Suppressing or Ignoring Emotions or Feelings. Experiential learning exercises used in teaching business ethics bring forth emotions. Because emotions make some people uncomfortable, students may try to rein in their feelings, and business ethics teachers may be content to pretend those emotions don't exist. But they do exist and, left unaddressed, they can pull the class off track. Sims recalls one ethics workshop for professionals during which participants played a 2-day business game that included a major focus on sexual harassment. Pressed for time, the group didn't adequately discuss the professionals' emotional responses. Instead, the day's session ended where some participants refused to speak to others and the atmosphere became increasingly hostile through the evening. Talking about those emotions and feelings became the next order of business before the second day of the game began.

You should be sure that emotions and other feelings are expressed. We have found that if you sense that the class is tense, hostile, frustrated with one another or in any way "charged," open the door for a discussion by saying something like: "When I've used this exercise with other groups, people sometimes have been frustrated by how difficult it can be to find a really good solution. Are any of you feeling frustrated?" Or, "I'm sensing a little anxiety here. Are you comfortable in the roles we've been practicing? Are some of you uneasy?" Or, "When other students played this game, everyone was very competitive, and some people were angry with some of the ways others played their roles. How do you feel?" The goal is not to avoid tense or uncomfortable feelings in the students but to be sensitive to the fact that sometimes intervention in the form of a mini-debriefing might be necessary on your part to increase the overall learning for the ethics exercise.

Forcing Consensus. Some experiential learning exercises we use in teaching business ethics to students or professionals generate a lively, interesting discussion, but no clear-cut conclusion. A business ethics teacher or trainer who tries to force consensus risks alienating the participants.

When planning an experiential learning exercise, it has been our experience that one should anticipate the likely findings, insights, lessons, and conclusions that will result from the exercise. Consider these likely outcomes to be written in pencil, not carved in stone. During the actual debriefing phase, listen carefully and be sure your comments reflect what the class has really experienced, learned, and concluded. It is better to reach partial agreement or to "agree to disagree" than to force a conclusion or consensus.

How can you design a debriefing when so much depends on the student's actual experience in the ethics class and the experiential learning exercise? There are limits to how much you can plan an "online" event. Nevertheless, you can:

- Be sure you have scheduled adequate time for debriefing. As noted earlier, time for briefing has to be included when planning the experiential learning exercise.

- Mentally practice some of the comments you might make, to be sure you give credit to students for their insights (and in our experience they will have many) and that you encourage them to express honestly and authentically their thoughts, feelings and other reactions.

- Imagine how you will handle the situation if the students or other participants do not readily reach consensus on an important ethical point or issue or if it draws conclusions that are different from those you anticipated. How can you acknowledge the outcome, keep the class in a positive frame of mind, and move forward to the next experiential learning exercise, class or effort to teach business ethics?

CONCLUSION

Reflection and debriefing are important components of teaching business ethics and experiential learning exercises. Students and other participants form links between known and new knowledge during reflection and debriefing. Most business ethics teachers and trainers realize the importance of reflection and debriefing and build them into their business ethics teaching efforts. Both reflection and debriefing are necessary parts of the experiential learning process, which is crucial to completing successfully the *learning* in teaching business ethics endeavors. We have found Kolb's model of the learning process to be an effective vehicle for helping to achieve the ultimate goal of active experimentation from experiential learning exercises used in teaching business ethics.

Business ethics teachers and trainers must provide an environment in which sharing, trust, risk-taking and learning can occur, and be transferred to nonclassroom situations. To meet these goals, structure is required. It is also necessary, however, that ambiguity is allowed so students can personalize their learning and experience meaningfulness (usefulness) in its application. This makes learning relevant to the individual.

In conclusion, conducting successful experiential learning exercises in efforts to teach business ethics requires effective processes of reflection and debriefing. Reflection and debriefing are important to synthesizing, strengthening, and transferring learning from the experiential learning exercise to the context of "real life." Those responsible for teaching business ethics can enhance the learning of students and other participants by incorporating reflection and debriefing as part of the postexperience analysis designed to provide insight into cases, journal-keeping, role-plays or other experiential learning approaches to teaching business ethics.

REFERENCES

Abson, D. (1994). The effects of peer evaluation on the behavior of undergraduate students working in tutorless groups. In H. C. Foote, C. J. Howe, A. Anderson, A. K. Tolmie, & D. A. Warden (Eds.) *Group and interactive learning* (pp. 153-158) Southampton, United Kingdom: Computational Mechanics Publications.

Baetz, M., & A. Carson. (1999). Ethical dilemmas in teaching about ethical dilemmas: Obstacles or opportunity? *Teaching Business Ethics, 3*(1), 1-12.

Bandura, A. (1977). *A social learning theory.* Englewood Cliffs, NJ: Prentice-Hall.

Black, J. S., & Mendenhall, M. (1989). A practical but theory-based framework for selecting cross-cultural training programs. *Human Resource Management, 28*(4), 511-539.

Borisoff, D., & Victor, D. (1989). *Conflict management: A communication skills approach.* Englewood Cliffs, NJ: Prentice-Hall.

Brookfield, S. D. (1995). *Becoming a critically reflective teacher.* San Francisco, CA: Jossey-Bass.

Carey, W. P. (2005, November 23). *The hidden costs of dishonesty: Ethics is vital to business education.* Retrieved from http://knowledge.wpcarey.asu.edu/article.cfm?articleid=1137

Daley, J. S. (1981). Field experience education. In A. Chickering (Ed.), *The modern American college*. San Francisco, CA: Jossey-Bass.

Dreifuerst, K. T. (2009). The essentials of debriefing in simulation learning: A concept analysis. *Nursing Education Perspectives* 30(2),109-114.

Dreifuerst, K. T. (2007). *Reflecting on metacognition: Defining the concept map for a plan of research*. Unpublished manuscript. Indianapolis, IN: Indiana University School of Nursing.

Gaw, B. A. (1979). Processing questions: An aid to completing the learning cycle. In J. E. Jones & J. W. Pfeiffer (Eds.), *The 1979 annual handbook for group facilitators* (pp. 147-153). La Jolla, CA: University Associates.

Gunz, H. P. (1995). Realism and learning in management simulations. *Journal of Management Education, 19*(1), 54-74.

Haywood, M. E., McMullen, D. A., & Wygal, D. E. (2004). Using games to enhance student understanding of professional and ethical responsibilities. *Issues in Accounting Education, 19*(1), 85-99.

Hemmasi, M., & Graf, L. A. (1992). Managerial skills acquisition: A case for using business policy simulations. *Simulation & Gaming, 23*(3), 298-310.

Hill, A., & Stewart, I. C. (1999). Character education in business schools: Pedagogical strategies. *Teaching Business Ethics, 3*, 179-193.

House, J. D. (2002). The motivational effects of specific teaching activities and computer use for science learning: Findings from the national mathematics and science study. *International Journal of Instructional Media, 29*(4), 423-439.

Hunsaker, P. L. (1978). Debriefing: The key to effective experiential learning. In D. C. Berenstuhl & S. C. Certo (Eds.). *Exploring experiential learning: Simulations and experiential exercises* (pp. 3-4). East Brunswick, NJ: Nichols.

Hunt, S. D., & Laverle, D. A. (2004). Experiential learning and the Hunt-Vitell theory of ethics: Teaching marketing ethics by integrating theory and practice. *Marketing Education Review, 14*(3), 1-14.

Klein, G. (1999). *Sources of power: How people make decisions*. Boston, MA: MIT Press.

Knowles, M. (1996). *Teaching management*. Houston, TX: Gulf.

Kohls, J. (1996). Students' experiences with service learning in a business ethics course. *Journal of Business Ethics, 15*, 45-47.

Kolb, D. A. (1984). *Experiential learning: Experience as the source of learning and development*. Englewood Cliffs, NJ: Prentice-Hall.

Kolb, D. A., Osland, J. S., & Rubin, I. M. (1995). *Organizational behavior: An experiential approach* (6th ed.). Englewood Cliffs, NJ: Prentice Hall.

Lampe, M. (1997). Increasing effectiveness in teaching ethics to undergraduate business students. *Teaching Business Ethics, 1*, 3-19.

LeClair, D. T., Ferrell, L., Montuori, L., & Willems, C. (1999). The use of a behavioral simulation to teach business ethics. *Teaching Business Ethics, 3*, 283-296.

Lederman, L. C. (1983). *Intercultural communication, simulation and the cognitive assimilation of experience: An exploration of the post-experience analytic process*. Paper presented at the 3rd annual conference of the Speech Communication Association of Puerto Rico, San Juan.

Lederman, L. C. (1992). Debriefing: Toward a systematic assessment of theory and practice. *Simulation & Gaming, 23*(2), 145-159.

Livingstone, D., & Lynch, K. (2002). Group project work and student centered active learning: Two different experiences. *Journal of Geography in Higher Education, 26*(2), 217-317.

Maglagan, P., & Snell, R. (1992). Some implications for management development research into managers' moral dilemmas. *British Journal of Management 3*, 157-168.

McCarthy, B. (1990, October). Using the 4MAT system to bring learning styles to school. *Educational Leadership,* 31-37.

McDonald, G. M., & Donleavy, G. D. (1995). Objections to the teaching of business ethics. *Journal of Business Ethics, 10*(1), 829-835.

Pearson, M., & Smith, D. (1986). Debriefing in experience-based learning. *Simulation/Games for Learning, 16*(4), 155-172.

Pearson, M., & Smith, D. (1985). Debriefing in experience-based learning. In D. Boud, R. Keogh, & D. Walker (Eds.), *Reflection: Turning experience into learning* (pp. 69-84). London, England: Kogam Page.

Pesut, D. J. (2004). Reflective clinical reasoning. In L. Hayes, H. Butcher, & T. Boese (Eds.), *Nursing in contemporary society* (pp. 146-162). Upper Saddle River, NJ: Pearson Prentice Hall.

Phillips, R. A., & Clawson, J. G. (1998). Current events periodicals and business ethics. *Teaching Business Ethics, 2,* 165-174.

Richardson, V. (1997) *Constructivist teacher education: Building new understandings.* London, England: Falmer Press.

Rudolph, J. W., Simon, R., Rivard, R., Dufresne, R. L., & Raemer, D. B. (2007). Debriefing with good judgment: Combining rigorous feedback with genuine inquiry. *Anesthesiology Clinics, 25*(2), 361-376.

Sanyal, R. N. (2000). Teaching business ethics in international business. *Teaching Business Ethics, 4,* 137-149.

Sauser, W. I., Jr. (2004). Teaching business ethics to professional engineers. *Science and Engineering Ethics 10,* 337-342.

Schon, D. A. (1983). *The reflective practitioner: How professionals think in action.* New York, NY: Basic Books.

Sherwood, J. J., & Glidewell, J. G. (1972). Planned renegotiation: A norm setting OD intervention. In W. W. Burke (Ed.), *Contemporary organization development: Orientations and interventions* (pp. 35-46). Washington, DC: NTL Institute.

Sims, R. R. (2002). *Teaching business ethics for effective learning.* Westport, CT: Quorum Books.

Sims, R. R. (2003). Business Ethics Curriculum Design: Suggestions and Illustrations. *Teaching Business Ethics, 7*(1), 69-86.

Sims, R. R. (2004). Business ethics teaching: Using conversational learning to build an effective classroom learning environment. *Journal of Business Ethics 49*(2), 201-211.

Sims, R. R., &. Felton, E. L., Jr. (2006). Designing and delivering business ethics teaching and learning. *Journal of Business Ethics, 63*(3), 297-312.

Sims, R. R., & Sauser, W. I., Jr. (1985). Guiding principles for the development of competency-based business curricula. *Journal of Management Development, 4*(5), 51-65.

Sims, R. R., & Sims, S. J. (1991). Increasing applied business ethics courses in business school curricula. *Journal of Business Ethics, 10*, 211-219.

Tanner, C. A. (2006). Thinking like a nurse: A research-based model of clinical judgment in nursing. *Journal of Nursing Education, 45*(6), 204-211.

Teach, R. D., Christensen, R. L. & Schwartz, R. G. (2005). Teaching business ethics: Integrity. *Simulation and Gaming, 36*(3), 383-387.

Thatcher, D. (1986). Promoting learning through games and simulations. *Simulations/Games for Learning, 16*(4), 144-154.

Thiagarajan, S. (1992). Using games for debriefing. *Simulation and Gaming, 23*(2), 161-173.

Udovic, D., Morris, D., Dickman, A., Postlethwait, J., & P. Wetherwax. (2002). Workshop biology: Demonstrating the effectiveness of active learning in an introductory biology course. *Bioscience, 52*(3), 272-281.

Warrick, D. D., Hunsaker, P. L., Cook, C. W., & Altman, S. (1979). Debriefing experiential learning exercises. *Journal of Experiential Learning and Simulation, 1*, 91-100.

Zlotkowski, E. (1996). Opportunity for all: Linking service-learning and business education. *Journal of Business Ethics, 15*(1), 5-19.

Zoller, U. (1987). The fostering of question-asking capability: A meaningful aspect of problem solving in chemistry. *Journal of Chemical Educations 64*, 510-512.

CHAPTER 9

AUBURN UNIVERSITY'S MANAGEMENT ETHICS PROGRAM

Achilles A. Armenakis

INTRODUCTION

All too often, the business media report on numerous instances of unethical conduct by organizational decision makers. One can find websites that publicize unethical conduct by companies as well as websites that publicize ethical conduct of companies. Many colleges and universities have incorporated ethics programs in their curricula to create an awareness of ethics and challenge students to process information about ethical and unethical issues and the consequences of each. Auburn University established a formal management ethics program beginning in 1998. The purpose of this chapter is to describe this program.

THE EMINENT SCHOLAR IN MANAGEMENT ETHICS

Because of the publicity surrounding the numerous instances of unethical behavior of organizational decision makers and others subject to the scrutiny of the public, James T. Pursell, Sr.,[1] chairman and chief execu-

Experiences in Teaching Business Ethics
pp. 205–216

tive officer of Pursell Family Corporation (PFC), established an endowment in 1998 to promote ethics in the Management Department of the College of Business. The position of eminent scholar in management ethics was consequently created for this purpose. Earnings from the endowment are also intended to support a speakers program. Individuals who have distinguished themselves by contributing positively to the dissemination of ethical behavior and knowledge speak to students enrolled in numerous credit and noncredit programs on the Auburn University campus. As Pursell Distinguished Fellows in Ethics, each speaker describes real life scenarios in which the *right* decision was made when faced with an ethical dilemma, based on moral standards. This program does not host individuals who acted unethically, were convicted, and alas are interested in explaining the *slippery slope*, which led them to act inappropriately.

In 1976, Mr. Pursell began managing his company according to Christian principles. He has been an excellent role model for managers to observe and learn how to manage according to ethical principles. He has served on the Alabama Ethics Commission, was a founder of the Fellowship of Companies for Christ, International, and is a continuing contributor to numerous socially responsible projects, such as The First Tee Program. The College of Business at Auburn University began a continuing long-term mutually beneficial relationship with Mr. Pursell in 1981. Numerous projects have been completed for PFC, allowing for a practical laboratory for faculty, staff, and graduate students. Published materials are available in the public domain that describe this mutually beneficial relationship (cf. Armenakis, Brown, & Mehta, 2010; Armenakis & Burdg, 1986; Armenakis & Burdg, 1991; Armenakis, Burdg, & Pursell, 1991).

PURSELL DISTINGUISHED FELLOWS IN ETHICS

Roger Boisjoly: 2001 and 2006

Roger Boisjoly is the retired Morton-Thiokol, Inc., engineer who warned of the danger of O-rings not sealing on the space shuttle *Challenger*, especially in cooler temperatures. His warning memo sent to Morton-Thiokol executives several months before *Challenger*'s fatal launch was considered "company private" and not shared with NASA administrators. During his first visit to Auburn he agreed to an interview describing his experiences with Morton-Thiokol and *Challenger* (cf. Armenakis, 2002). This document is shared with students to discuss the ethics of the launch. In addition, Auburn University students analyzed a special case written on the *Challenger* incident (cf. Raju & Sankar, 2000) for which Mr. Boisjoly served as referee (see http://en.wikipedia.org/wiki/Roger_Boisjoly).

Dr. Jeffrey S. Wigand: 2002, 2004, 2008, and 2009

Dr. Jeff Wigand is the former senior vice president of Brown & Williamson Tobacco Company (B&WTC) who publicly revealed that executives at B&WTC knew the hazards of tobacco and that nicotine was habit forming. The movie, *The Insider,* described Dr. Wigand's experiences after going public with his information. He has been featured on *60 Minutes* three times and twice on *Frontline.* During his first visit to Auburn he was interviewed about his experiences with this issue (cf. Armenakis, 2004). This document serves as class discussion material on ethics. During his visits to Auburn, he discusses his experiences in following his "moral compass" as well as the social responsibility of all companies to be valued members of society.

One unique project was a one-credit hour elective, titled Ethical Decision Making, team taught by Dr. Wigand and Dr. Achilles Armenakis. During the semester, students viewed *The Insider, 60-Minutes, Frontline: Smoke in the Eye,* and *Frontline: Inside the Tobacco Deal,* and participated in class discussions about reasons why organizational decision makers make unethical decisions. Furthermore, Dr. Wigand explained in detail how cigarettes were manufactured, including what toxic materials were added to cigarettes (and pipe tobacco) to improve the taste, but to deceive users and nonusers. It is quite common for students who have participated in lectures and class discussions to present Dr. Wigand their tobacco products and declare "I will not continue using this product!"

Also, Armenakis and Wigand (2010) have analyzed publicly available internal documents from British American Tobacco & Cigarette Affiliated Companies (parent of B&WTC) and interview responses from selected Philip Morris executives (Rosenblatt, 1994). In this article the authors explain how tobacco executives used moral disengagement tactics in their decision making to justify marketing tobacco products. Dr. Wigand is the founder of Smoke-Free Kids, Inc. He currently devotes considerable time in working with ministers of health throughout the world in creating smoke-free environments (see http://www.jeffreywigand.com).

Major General Perry M. Smith: 2003

General Perry Smith (USAF, ret.) is author of *Taking Charge: Making the Right Choices* (Smith, 1988). He is former military advisor to CNN but resigned his position because the broadcast documentary "Valley of Death" incorrectly reported U.S. Air Force pilots dropped nerve gas on innocent civilians and U.S. troops. General Smith urged CNN to retract the story. However, when they refused he concluded CNN was unethical in not retracting the story immediately. However, subsequently, CNN did in fact retract the story (see http://www.charlierose.com/view/interview/4831).

Dr. Sharon K. Stoll: 2005, 2006

Dr. Sharon Stoll is the director of the Center for Ethics at the University of Idaho. She is coauthor of *Sport Ethics: Applications for Fair Play* (Lumpkin, Stoll, & Beller, 1999). Dr. Stoll is responsible for content and curriculum development for *Winning with Character*, a program designed to teach ethics to athletes. Dr. Stoll is well known for her expertise in teaching and methodology applied to morals (see http://winningwithcharacter.org/Leadershipteam/leadership_team.htm).

Dr. P. Roy Vagelos: 2007

Dr. Roy Vagelos is retired chairman and chief executive officer of Merck, Inc., and coauthor of *The Moral Corporation: Merck Experiences* (Vagelos & Galambos, 2006). Currently he is chairman of Regeneron Pharmaceuticals, Inc., and Theravance, Inc. Under Dr. Vagelos' leadership Merck was one of the most profitable and socially responsible companies in the world. One decision Dr. Vagelos made was to supply Merck's drug Ivermectin free of charge to treat individuals infected with "river blindness" (caused by the bite of a black fly) that infected an estimated 18 million people in West and Central Africa, the Middle East, and Central and South America. River blindness is a disease caused by a parasite which among other negative symptoms (like severe itching) can ultimately blind those infected. The drug was expensive and neither those at risk nor their governments could afford the treatment (see http://en.wikipedia.org/wiki/P._Roy_Vagelos).

Thousands of Auburn University students have benefited from participating in this speakers' program. Their learning about ethics has been enhanced by these distinguished individuals sharing their experiences.

AUBURN UNIVERSITY CENTER
FOR ETHICAL ORGANIZATIONAL CULTURES

The Auburn University Center for Ethical Organizational Cultures (AUCEOC) was established in fiscal year 2008 by a generous 5-year annual financial commitment from James T. Pursell, Sr. The logic in establishing such a research center is found in the popular business press attributing the high visibility unethical business cases, like Enron, to their corporate cultures. Furthermore, research findings released from the Ethics Resource Center reported that respondents to periodic national surveys observe misconduct within their respective organizations but refuse to report the misconduct for fear of reprisals or because of their opinions that it would do no good (Ethics Resource Center, 2010). This is clearly an indication of the impact organizational culture has on employee behavior.

The mission of AUCEOC is to develop a research methodology that can be used to assess organizational culture and determine the extent to which the culture is ethical. Upon determining the extent to which an organizational culture is ethical, organizational decision makers can conceive and implement an organizational change effort to develop an ethical organizational culture.

The funding for the center is used to support research projects conducted by faculty assisted by graduate students in the academic programs of Auburn University. Faculty members (i.e., Pursell Research Associates) are matched with graduate students (i.e., Pursell Graduate Assistants). Faculty members receive summer stipends for their efforts in designing and conducting scholarly research and for mentoring PhD students. In addition, PhD students receive financial stipends and the benefit of working with faculty throughout their academic programs developing ethics research and teaching skills. Upon graduation these students relocate to other universities and begin their academic careers. The findings from the ethics research projects are disseminated through scholarly journal articles and serve as supplemental readings in undergraduate and graduate management courses that have ethics components. Details of the research projects already completed and those currently underway can be obtained from http://business.auburn.edu/nondegreeprograms/ethics/.

The current projects being sponsored by the AUCEOC are as follows:

Professor Achilles Armenakis is directing Keith Credo's (Auburn University, PhD student) dissertation which is to develop a methodology to assess the ethics safety culture of a multinational oil drilling corporation. The end product of this research will be a quantitative scale that can be administered anonymously to a company's operative-level employees regarding ethical/unethical safety practices. The first phase of the study utilized a qualitative methodology to develop appropriate dimensions to assess. Subsequent phases utilized a quantitative methodology to develop a reliable and valid quantitative scale. Some preliminary finds from this research have been released (cf. Credo, Armenakis, Feild, & Young, in press; Credo, Ianuzzi, & Armenakis, 2010).

Professor Brian Connelly has been working in a mentoring role with Ashley Gangloff (Auburn University, PhD student) on a project that explores how morals diffuse throughout social networks. This research is particularly pertinent to today's organizations owing to the increased presence, and reliance, on an individual's social connections and the simultaneous increase in organizational ethical lapses. Work in summer 2010 focused on developing databases that would facilitate empirical investigation of complex social network phenomena and how these affect the likelihood that a firm would engage in unethical behavior. This resulted in the creation of two major databases: (1) a complete social network of nearly 40,000 company board directors, their interlocks, and the attributes of directors in the network, all compiled longitudinally over 11 years, and (2) a database of material financial restatements filed by all publicly traded firms over the same 11 year time horizon, meticulously culled from a variety of sources. Initial analyses have uncovered some intriguing findings about how various types of social networks affect the likelihood that firms will engage in unethical business practices.

Professor Connelly has also recently completed an international research project on executive-employee pay inequality. Not surprisingly, the growing pay inequality between executives and employees has been criticized in the popular press, by employee advocacy groups and in political rhetoric. According to equity theorists, when individuals perceive unfairness in allocation of resources and rewards, they may (a) engage in unethical behavior so as to increase their rewards, thereby resulting in an unethical culture, (b) decrease their efforts, or (c) leave their firms, thus leading to declines in firm performance. In this study, Connelly and colleagues test a framework of the determinants of pay inequality using longitudinal data on 130 firms from 29 countries spanning a ten-year period.

Professor Jacqueline Dueling directed Mr. Gregory Stevens' thesis (Auburn University, MS student) that investigated moral disengagement practices of students in various decision-making situations. Of particular interest were the situational factors that contribute and interact with individual differences of decision makers. Findings from this study can be obtained from Stevens, Dueling and Armenakis (2010).

Professors Alan Walker and James Smither (La Salle University) were assisted by Jason DeBode (Auburn University, PhD student) on a research project to investigate how religious motivation orientation, sanctification of work (i.e., perceived sacred qualities of work), and views of God (loving versus punishing) affected participants' judgments of ethically questionable vignettes. Participants in the study consisted of 220 working adults selected from a national population. Findings from this study can be obtained from Walker, DeBode, and Smither (2010).

Professor Alan Walker and colleagues investigated the association of religiosity on ethical beliefs. Utilizing latent profile analysis they found evidence, consistent with symbolic interactionist theory, that both extrinsic (versus intrinsic) religious motivation orientation, general religiosity (i.e., frequency of prayer, church attendance, and religiousness) and theism (agnostic versus theist) are key elements comprising one's overall religious identity which is, in turn, related to ethical beliefs. Findings from this study can be obtained from Walker, Farmer, DeBode, Smither and Smith (2010).

Professors Alan Walker and James Smither (La Salle University) apply the corporate ethics virtue model (Kaptein, 2008) to examine the relationship between an organization's culture and employees' self-report of ethical beliefs, values, and judgments. The findings from this study will add insights regarding the relationship between organizational culture and employees' tolerance of ethical dilemmas in the workplace. In another study Professors Walker and Smither are investigating the relationship between (a) religious self-identity, (b) religious identity salience, (c) sanctification, and (d) religious motivation orientation and (e) ethical attitudes, (f) ethical values, (g) ethical beliefs and (h) ethical judgments in the workplace.

Professors Achilles Armenakis, Steven Brown (PhD, AU 2009) and Anju Mehta (PhD, AU 2008) assessed the organizational culture of the PFC after the company was sold to Agrium International in 2006 (Armenakis, Brown, & Mehta, 2010). Using a qualitative methodology, data collection was guided by the organizational ethical practices audit, developed from an analysis of the *best practices* of the Baldrige National Quality Awardees from 1988-2006. PFC has a reputation for being not only ethical but being managed according to Christian principles. Using Schein's (2004) cultural elements framework the Christian culture of PFC was described. The case described the requirements for transforming an organizational culture.

Although the current work must be considered preliminary, the intellectual contributions produced so far from the AUCEOC contribute to our understanding of ethical and unethical employee behavior. The combined research projects can be used to assess the extent to which any organizational culture is ethical. Furthermore, we know what steps must be taken to transform an unethical culture to an ethical culture. Future research projects will be designed to refine our methodologies and to continue our understanding of the role of organizational culture on ethical employee behavior.

PROGRAMMATIC BENEFITS

Auburn University has realized numerous benefits from the ethics program. The benefits realized are summarized next as they relate to the instructional, research, and outreach missions of the university.

Instructional Benefits

Organizational decision makers who serve as external speakers present real-life experiences regarding ethics. This adds credibility to the course material. One class period is usually devoted to laying the foundation for the speaker. For example, when Dr. Vagelos lectured to the principles of management classes, material from his book (cf. Vagelos & Galambos, 2006) was summarized into lecture material establishing why he was an appropriate speaker to discuss the topic of ethics. Then Dr. Vagelos described why Merck Corporation was considered a moral corporation. The presentation format for external speakers is typically lecture and discussion.

Research findings produced by faculty researchers as described in scholarly articles serve as supplemental readings for ethics topics covered in courses. This is beneficial in that students get personal exposure to faculty engaged in research. For example, *stakeholder theory, corporate culture, decision making, and ethics,* are topics that are discussed in the Armenakis and Wigand (2010) article about tobacco companies. These topics are covered in the Principles of Management course and are integrated into an application case demonstrating how they relate to each other and impact the extent to which an organization is socially responsible. An analysis of critical incidents of tobacco executives (available from the public domain) revealed the application of moral disengagement tactics (Bandura, 1999; which is how managers rationalize their decisions in order to minimize guilt often associated with unethical actions). These moral disengagement tactics are examples of the espoused beliefs and values of organizational decision makers (one of the cultural elements of Schein's framework) From these moral disengagement tactics an assessment is made of how socially responsible the tobacco companies have been. The distinction between what is *legal* and what is *ethical* is described by pointing out that tobacco products are *legal* but are *unethical* because when used by consumers as the manufacturers intend, the products produce deleterious health effects. Thus, the underlying assumption (that is the foundation element of organizational culture; cf. Schein, 2004) of tobacco cultures of the two companies analyzed is inferred to be "let the smoker and nonsmoker beware"). The organizational cultures of these two companies are then labeled unethical.

Research Benefits

The funds from the AUCEOC are used to support faculty and PhD students in research projects that are published in scholarly journals. These activities contribute to the research mission of the College of Business, providing supplementary funding for faculty and stipends for graduate students. In addition to the financial support, the engagement of faculty and graduate students contributes to the professional development of each.

In some instances the involvement of external speakers contributes directly to the research program. For example, the relationship established with Dr. Wigand resulted in publication of the Armenakis and Wigand (2010) article on tobacco company cultures.

Outreach Benefits

The outreach mission of the College of Business is enhanced by inviting executives, managers, and the general public to participate in the presentations by external speakers. Thus, learning about ethics is shared with participants who are not enrolled in credit courses.

SUGGESTIONS FOR ESTABLISHING AN ETHICS PROGRAM

To establish such a program, the mission should be endorsed by the dean and embraced as a major initiative in the college strategy. Furthermore, development officers should be integrated in the effort to publicize the program and discuss the benefits of such a program with potential sponsors.

Some kind of sponsorship structure should be established so that various levels of sponsorship can be considered. The Auburn University ethics program consists of two parts. The James T. Pursell, Sr. Eminent Scholar Program, funded through a generous endowment provides funds for the external speakers program.

The AUCEOC is funded through annual commitments. Sponsors can select from three levels of sponsorship (see Table 9.1).

GOING FORWARD

The Auburn University ethics program is an integral part of the academic programs of the College of Business. Every academic year new Pursell Distinguished Fellows in Ethics, Pursell Research Associates, and Pursell Graduate Assistants are named, and new program ideas are generated. In this manner, ethics education is evolving and becoming more and more integrated into the fabric of undergraduate and graduate instruction in the Department of Management at Auburn University.

**Table 9.1.   Auburn University
Center for Organizational Cultures Sponsorship Levels**

A. Contributing Sponsor
    Benefits:
    a. Publicity as a sponsor for support of the AUCEOC on all AU College of Business media
    b. Contribute to developing the methodology to assess the extent to which organizational cultures are ethical
    c. Contribute to AU's reputation as a leader in disseminating "best practices" for improving ethical conduct in organizations
    d. Support for disseminating AU research findings on ethics to managers to increase their attention to ethical practices
    e. Support for disseminating AU research findings on ethics to university professors to teach ethics at their respective universities
    f. Support for disseminating AU research findings on ethics to AU students
    g. Support AU PhD students to conduct research on ethics
    h. Support for AU PhD graduates to teach ethics at the university level
    i. Receive all publications prepared by the AUCEOC
    j. For a 3-year period, participate as speakers in AU ethics educational events
    k. For a 3-year period, attendance by five sponsor representatives to all AU presentations by ethics speakers. Invitations to small-group functions (lunches, dinners, receptions) to interact with speakers.
    l. For a 3-year period, attendance by five sponsor representatives at AU conferences on ethics
B. Participating Sponsor
    Benefits:
    a. Same benefits as a Contributing Sponsor
    b. Participate in allowing AU personnel to assess the sponsor's organizational culture
C. Founding Partner
    Benefits:
    a. Same benefits as a Contributing Sponsor
    b. Participate in allowing AU personnel to assess the sponsor's organizational culture
    c. One-half day conference at sponsor's site to present research findings
    d. Faculty and graduate student summer fellowships named for sponsor

NOTE

1. James T. Pursell, Sr., is now retired chairman of the board of the former Pursell Technologies Incorporated (PTI). PTI, with Mr. Pursell's leadership, developed and patented the most scientifically advanced product for broadcasting fertilizers, herbicides, and insecticides. The product, POLYON, consists of multiple concentric layers of a compound which sandwich a fertilizer, insecticide, or herbicide and dissolves upon contact

with water. This POLYON is a controlled release product that slowly releases into the ground and maximizes absorption by plants.

REFERENCES

Armenakis, A. (2002). Boisjoly on ethics: An interview with Roger M. Boisjoly. *Journal of Management Inquiry, 11*(3), 274-281.

Armenakis, A. (2004). Making a difference by speaking out: Jeff Wigand says exactly what's on his mind. *Journal of Management Inquiry, 13*(4), 355-362.

Armenakis, A., Brown, S., & Mehta, A. (2010, August). *The assessment and transformation of an organizational culture.* Paper presented at the Academy of Management 2010 Annual Meeting, Montreal, Canada.

Armenakis, A., & Burdg, H. (1986). Planning for growth. *Long Range Planning, 19*(3), 93-102.

Armenakis, A. A., & Burdg, H. B. (1991). Commercial Fertilizer, Inc. (A). In A. Glassman & T. Cummings (Eds.), *Cases in organization development* (pp. 46-55). Plano, TX: Richard D. Irwin.

Armenakis, A. A., Burdg, H. B., & Pursell, J. T. (1991). Commercial Fertilizer, Inc. (B). In A. Glassman & T. Cummings (Eds.), *Cases in organization development* (pp. 59-67). Plano, TX: Richard D. Irwin.

Armenakis, A., & Wigand, J. (2010). Stakeholder actions and their impact on the organizational cultures of two tobacco companies. *Business & Society Review, 115*(2), 147-171.

Bandura, A. (1999). Moral disengagement in the perpetuation of inhumanities. *Personality and Social Psychology Review, 3*(3), 193-209.

Credo, K., Armenakis, A., Feild, H., & Young, R. (in press). Organizational ethics, leader member exchange, and organizational support: Relationships with workplace safety. *Journal of Leadership and Organizational Studies.*

Credo, K., Ianuzzi, A., & Armenakis, A. (2010, October). *Organizational ethics perceptions: Aqualitative and quantitative assessment.* Paper presented at the 2010 Meeting of the Southern Management Association, St. Pete Beach, FL.

Ethics Resource Center. (2010). *The 2009 National Business Ethics Survey.* Arlington, VA: Author.

Kaptein, S. (2008). Developing and testing a measure for the ethical culture of organizations: The corporate ethical virtues model. *Journal of Organizational Behavior, 29*, 923-947.

Lumpkin, A., Stoll, S., & Beller, J. (1999). *Sport ethics: Applications for fair play.* New York, NY: McGraw-Hill.

Raju, P., & Sankar, C. (2000). *Design of field joint for STS 51-L: Launch or no launch decision.* Anderson, SC: Taveneer.

Rosenblatt, R. (1994). How tobacco executives live with themselves. *Business & Society Review, 89*, 22-34.

Schein, E. (2004). *Organizational culture and leadership* (3rd ed.). San Francisco, CA: Jossey-Bass.

Smith, P. (1988). *Taking charge: Making the right choices.* New York, NY: Avery.

Stevens, G., Dueling, J., & Armenakis, A. (2010). *Successful psychopaths: Are they unethical decision makers and why?* Unpublished manuscript, Auburn University.

Vagelos, P. R., & Galambos, L. (2006). *The moral corporation: Merck experiences.* New York, NY: Cambridge University Press.

Walker, A., DeBode, J., & Smither, J. (2010). *The effects of religiosity on ethical judgments: The role of sanctification, religious motivation orientation, and views of God.* Unpublished manuscript, Auburn University.

Walker, A., Farmer, A., DeBode, J., Smither, J., & Smith, R. (2010). An examination of the effects of religiosity on ethical beliefs utilizing a symbolic interactionist perspective. Unpublished manuscript, Auburn University.

CHAPTER 10

TEACHING BUSINESS ETHICS AT A DISTANCE TO EXECUTIVE MBA STUDENTS

William I. Sauser, Jr.

INTRODUCTION

For over a decade the author has had the privilege of teaching business ethics to large classes of students enrolled in Auburn University's executive master of business administration (MBA) program, which was recently ranked among the world's leading executive MBA programs by *Financial Times* (2009, p. 10). The executive MBA program at Auburn University features several intensive classes taught in residence, a number of classes taught at a distance, and an international experience abroad during which faculty and students travel together from the United States to one or more other nations to learn first hand key lessons in comparative global business (Auburn University College of Business, n.d.).[1]

The business ethics course in this program is a one-semester-hour required course taught at a distance. This chapter describes the goals and content of a recent (fall semester, 2009) version of the course, the methods by which it was delivered to the students, efforts to maintain continuing contact among the professor and students despite asynchronous

Experiences in Teaching Business Ethics
pp. 217–229
Copyright © 2011 by Information Age Publishing
All rights of reproduction in any form reserved.

delivery across state and national borders, required graded student deliverables, and student reactions to the course. Since all the students enrolled in Auburn University's executive MBA program have considerable business and managerial experience to draw upon,[2] this course makes use of extensive self-reflection so students can come to understand and articulate their own ethical code and how it can be applied in the particular setting of their own work. Challenges and joys of teaching such a course at a distance are discussed from the author's point of view, and recommendations are offered to other faculty members who may be considering a similar endeavor. The course is appropriately rigorous and demanding of both students and the instructor.

COURSE OBJECTIVES, FORMAT, AND SCHEDULE

The student learning objectives for the course are fourfold and are stated on the syllabus as follows:

1. to become familiar with issues and terminology related to business ethics;
2. to consider the viewpoints of various experts in areas of business ethics;
3. to begin to formulate a personal code of ethics; and
4. to promote ethical behavior in business.

The course is not designed to be a didactic exercise in "teaching students what to think," nor is it an introduction to the moral philosophy of ethics, nor even a case-based study as is so popular in business instruction these days. Instead, it is an opportunity for mature students to explore and broaden their own thinking about ethical issues in business, to formulate their own personal code of ethics based on this exploration, and to examine how that code can be applied in the business context that surrounds them in their leadership roles.

The course consists of five modules, each containing a lecture, an interview, a reading assignment, and a writing assignment. The course is designed to be self-paced. Students may work through the five modules at whatever pace they desire (as long as all assignments are completed before grades are due by the end of the semester). All written assignments are posted to "EMBANet" (a proprietary distance education software system) so other students in the class may read them and learn from them.[3] Each written assignment is graded by the instructor, and individualized feedback and scores are sent to each student in confidence. Students are told that written assignments should be thorough but need not be lengthy, and they should be based on the student's own informed opinion. Students are also told that it is not necessary that the written assignments conform to the viewpoints of the various authors and interviewees to whom they are exposed in the course—or the professor's opinions—in order to earn a high grade; what matters is that each response expresses the student's informed opinion with respect to the question asked. By asking each student to formulate an informed opinion on each of the issues addressed in the questions, and to share these opinions in writing with their peers on interactive distance education software, the instructor simulates (across time and space) a high-level discussion among the class, while also giving individualized attention to each student's work.

COURSE PRODUCTION AND DELIVERY

The five lectures for a recent version (fall semester, 2009) of the course were professionally produced in the television studio operated by the Media Production Group of the Auburn University College of Business. The instructor spent 2 days in the studio (in late July 2009) under the care of a professional producer/director and associated media technicians. PowerPoint illustrations prepared by the instructor (using a template provided by the EMBA program staff) were integrated with head-and-shoulder shots of the instructor speaking to the camera as though he were in a classroom with the students, with appropriate gestures and facial expressions to "keep it real." Each lecture was approximately 60 minutes in length.[4] The lectures were digitized and provided to the students on a DVD the first day of their initial residency (in early August 2009), along with all other materials they needed for the course, including a carefully selected textbook, *Executive Ethics: Ethical Dilemmas and Challenges for the C-Suite* (Quatro & Sims, 2008), and several recent journal articles written by the instructor.

The commercially available EMBANet software system incorporates a variety of options to facilitate distance education across time and space. For example, each student has his or her own password-protected mailbox (as does each instructor) so information can be shared confidentially when necessary. The system also includes boxes for each class and small discussion group, plus a "chat room" for synchronous communication when desired. These options allowed the instructor to invite the students to share their written assignments with one another (which they did readily) while also communicating confidentially with the instructor as they progressed through the course. Students were encouraged to comment on one another's written assignments, and also to post current information about business ethics which they encountered during the course of the semester. The instructor—and many of the students—took part in this ongoing discussion, although such participation was not a requirement of the course.

The five interviews included within this course were similarly produced in either the Media Production Group's studio (using a "living room" set) or on location in the university president's conference room. Three of the interviews (those with Larry Fillmer, Dr. Jay Gogue, and Dr. Don-Terry Veal) were conducted in July 2008; the other two (those with James Pursell and Leann Barr) are "classics" that were produced some years ago. The five interviewees are leaders in the private, educational, and governmental sectors of our economy and hold positions from which they assert considerable leadership influence in the community. Each interview was roughly twenty minutes in length and consisted of the instructor asking a series of questions intended to explore the interviewee's perspective on business ethics, how that perspective is applied in organizational and community leadership, and defining events in each interviewee's life that influenced his or her worldview. The interviewees are diverse in terms of age, race, gender, and perspective. The five interviews are included on the course DVD along with the lectures, syllabus, and required readings.

COURSE CONTENT

Module One

The first module required the students to read three papers, then attend to the lecture and interview before writing a brief essay focused on the primary topic for the module.[5] The required readings were "Crafting a Culture of Character: The Role of the Executive Suite" (Sauser, 2008a), "Purpose Matters" (Bakke, 2008), and "The Inescapability of Worldview for Business Ethics: The Root of C-Suite Beliefs, Values, and Affections" (Nielson, 2008). The common themes among these readings are (a) the value system and behavior of the firm's leadership sets the tone for the ethicality of the organization, (b) a strong organizational culture can elevate the morality of the organization, and (c) the values and beliefs of the members of the executive suite are shaped by their personal experiences and worldviews. The lecture for this module, titled "Introduction to Business Ethics," reviewed a number of recent ethical lapses that have made international news, introduced several current ethical issues in business, and explored popular cultural viewpoints about business ethics (e.g., "Is the phrase 'business ethics' an oxymoron?" "Can 'business ethics' be taught and learned?" "Is 'business ethics' a manifestation of personal values?").

The instructor devoted about twenty minutes of the first lecture to his own "story" and how significant events in his personal history influenced his own worldview. The first interviewee, Larry Fillmer, is a former chief executive of several information technology companies and currently directs the Natural Resources Management and Development Institute at Auburn University. In his interview Mr. Fillmer also illustrated how significant events in his life influenced his worldview and approach to understanding and applying business ethics. For their first written assignment, students were asked to write a brief essay in response to the following question: "What is your 'story' (e.g., personal history)? How has your story shaped your own worldview?"

Module Two

The second module was similar to the first in terms of format (as were also the three that followed). The lecture, "Understanding Ethical Behavior," touched on such themes as (a) ethics has to do with behavior—what you actually *do*; (b) there are a variety of societal standards for appropriate behavior, including moral philosophies, codes of law, professional standards, societal norms, and personal values and beliefs—and sometimes these standards come into conflict with one another; (c) ethical decisions—some large, some seemingly small, many quite complex—must be made every day in business; and (d) issues of cultural relativism, universal values, and respect for human dignity must be considered as business is conducted across the globe. Assigned readings for module two were "Ethics in Diversity Management Leadership" (Kahn & Maxwell, 2008), "Job Design and Affect: Ethical Implications for the C-Suite" (Hawver, Pollack, & Humphrey, 2008), and "Business Ethics: Back to Basics" (Sauser, 2005a). The latter paper is a primer on ethics in business and lays out the author's basic philosophy on the importance of acting ethically when serving as a business leader. The former two papers explore important issues in business ethics and illustrate how the leader's actions can influence those of major stakeholders, including employees at all levels of the organization.

This theme is beautifully illustrated in a classic interview with Mr. James Pursell, former chairman of the board of Pursell Technologies, Inc., and now a leading philanthropist and proponent of ethics in business. Mr. Pursell—who served for several years on the Alabama Ethics Commission—describes how his worldview was shaped by events throughout his life, and how that worldview led him to position Pursell Technologies as a values-driven firm. He spoke of the actions he took to shape the philosophy of his organization and some of the tough decisions he had to make in order truly to "walk the talk" he espoused. The readings, lecture, and interview were designed to enable students to reflect on their own beliefs before writing an essay in response to the following question: "In your opinion, what are the major benefits and costs for businesses that seek to operate in a moral manner? Are the benefits worth the costs? Why or why not?"

Module Three

The lecture for the third module, "Ethical Challenges in Business," reviewed a number of specific examples of ethical temptations and challenges persons face in the business world; (b) touched on themes of "mixed messages" and rationalizations and their effects on ethical decision making; (c) explored the importance of organizational culture in shaping ethical conduct; (d) described specific actions a leader can take to create an organizational culture of character; and (e) provided a checklist for making ethical decisions, including seeking appropriate counsel and taking time to make "an ethics double check" before implementing any important decision.

Readings for this module, illustrative of the themes addressed in the lecture, were "A C-Suite Challenge: Preventing Ethical Breaches" (Sims, 2008), "Ethics and Corruption from the Perspective of the CFO" (Geary, 2008), and "Employee Theft: Who, How, Why, and What Can Be Done" (Sauser, 2007). The interviewee for the third module was Dr. Jay Gogue, president of Auburn University, a man with many years of high-level leadership experience in a number of institutions of higher education. Dr. Gogue shared his beliefs on the importance of ethics in business, government, and higher education, then described the process he takes when seeking to make sound decisions when faced with tough ethical dilemmas. The written assignment was designed to allow students to reflect on their own specific leadership contexts; the assignment was to answer the following question: "What do you believe are the five most critical ethical issues in your own field of endeavor? Why are they critical, in your opinion?"

Module Four

The focus of module four was "Social Responsibility and Corporate Performance." In the lecture portion of this module, the instructor contrasted classical with socioeconomic views of corporate social responsibility, then discussed four types of responsibility for business organizations: economic, legal, ethical, and discretionary (Schermerhorn, 2010, pp. 107-109). Statutes, government regulations, and case law affecting ethical business practices were discussed in the lecture, as were some of the consequences of breaking the law. Finally, the instructor provided twelve "best practices for business ethics" that can be followed by any organization seeking to operate responsibly in society.

Assigned readings for this module were "Global Stakes: Globalization's Challenges and Opportunities for Stakeholder Theory" (Wescher, 2008), "Environmental Ethics: Achieving Corporate Sustainability to Save the Planet" (Johnson, 2008), and "Regulating Ethics in Business: Review and Recommendations" (Sauser, 2008b). The latter paper was the source for the "best practices" recommended by the instructor during the final portion of the lecture for this module. The interviewee for this module, Dr. Don-Terry Veal, Director of Auburn University's Center for Governmental Services, reflected on his experiences in working with state and local governments and how they led him to interests in opportunities for public service and corporate involvement in the community. After considering the ideas offered in these readings, the lecture, and the interview, students were required to address the following question in a brief written essay: "In your opinion, what are the responsibilities of business to society? How can these responsibilities best be met?"

Module Five

The final module in this series of five was designed to lead the students to the capstone experience of the course, preparing their own individual, personal code of ethics. The assigned readings for this module were "Humility in Leadership: Abandoning the Pursuit of Unattainable Perfection" (Hoekstra, Bell, & Peterson, 2008), "Human Resources Management as a Champion for Corporate Ethics: Moving Towards Ethical Integration and Acculturation in the HR Function and Profession" (Gilley, Anderson, & Gilley, 2008), and "Ethics in Business: Answering the Call" (Sauser, 2005b). The third paper is an in-depth statement of the instructor's personal philosophy on business ethics, a philosophy influenced by such visionaries as Autry (2001), Baelz (1977), Greenleaf (2002/03), Jackall (1988), Novak (1996), Stackhouse (1995), and Zinbarg (2001).

The lecture portion of this module, "Business Ethics in Practice," was primarily an exposition of key ethical issues in various functions and sectors of business, a review of the instructor's research on employee theft (Sauser, 2007), recommendations for ethical practices in human resources management, and a discussion of Novak's (1996, pp. 134-159) proffered list of corporate ethical responsibilities.

The closing interview was a classic discussion the instructor had with Ms. Leann Barr, director of the Human Resources Division of ACIPCO—the American Cast Iron Pipe Company. ACIPCO is an internationally-recognized example of an employee-owned company. Its founder literally left the company to his employees in his will upon his death. Ms. Barr talked of the personal philosophy of the firm's founder and how his values have influenced the members of the ACIPCO workforce as they have sought to balance concepts of sustainability, profits, and corporate social responsibility in this heavy manufacturing firm. The instructor's intent in this final module—and indeed for the entire course—was to inspire the students to think deeply about their own beliefs and guiding principles so they would be ready to tackle the final written assignment, which was to address this important question: "What is your own personal code of business ethics? In a 'final essay' formulate (or at least begin to formulate) a statement of your own personal code of ethics. Use whatever format or approach is most comfortable to you. I'm interested in your own thoughts expressed in your own style."

OUTCOMES OF THE COURSE

The instructor was very pleased with the essays written by most of the 57 students enrolled in this course during the fall semester of 2009. They were honest and straightforward, and often very moving. This is a special group of students, of course, carefully selected for ability, maturity, and leadership experience. This cohort of students came from large corporations, small businesses, not-for-profit organizations (such as hospitals, educational institutions, and charitable foundations), government agencies, the military branches, and professional practice. They were able to express themselves well in writing and had considerable life experience to draw upon as they prepared their essays. They were willing to share their experiences with one another and to discuss openly their differences of opinion. Most of the students were citizens of the United States of America, but other nations were represented in the class, and many of the members of the class had completed international assignments or tours of duty. As a class, this group scored very well on the graded assignments.

Student reactions to the course, to the instructor's delight, were very positive. On a standardized multiquestion formal evaluation of the course, students scored it a 4.9 on a 5-point scale. Anonymous comments provided by some of the students on the formal evaluation confirmed that the instructor's objectives for the course were understood, appreciated, and—for the most part—met. One student observed that there was too much work for a one-semester-hour credit course, and the instructor readily acknowledges that the course was demanding. However, most students thought the time devoted to this course was well spent. Here are a few sample anonymous verbatim comments:

- [This course] allowed me to stretch myself and analyze my career and ethical challenges that I face every day.
- The class taught me a lot and caused a good bit of personal reflection regarding my career and my life.
- [The instructor] was very engaging and created an atmosphere of open and candid communication that spurred lots of productive class discussion.
- [The instructor] provided an atmosphere conducive to self-reflection and development of clear ethical boundaries.
- [The instructor] helped strengthen our personal code of business ethics.
- [The instructor] got me to confirm why I believe what I believe and why that is so important in business. Ethics in business is a must.

Confidential communications from many of the students reinforced these anonymous comments. Several of them wrote to the instructor about ethical challenges they were facing in their own career and how the ideas presented in this course helped them understand and begin to resolve the problems they were facing. Others observed that the course gave them an entirely new perspective on business ethics—not as a "dry and dull" subject for tiresome study but rather as a challenging aspect of their chosen calling.

CHALLENGES AND JOYS

The instructor was challenged by this course in a number of ways. Consider the following:

- Standing in front of a television camera for two solid days speaking to an empty room is not easy. The lights are hot, the voice is strained, the muscles are cramped, and the absence of any reaction from the invisible audience is disconcerting. *However, with practice these problems can be overcome.*

- Preparing a set of lectures for a class of students one has not yet met face to face is difficult. *However, this is a challenge dealt with by every instructor preparing a new course offering.*

- Carrying on meaningful class discussion is very difficult when students (and the instructor) are separated by time and space. When students are scattered across the globe, working a variety of schedules, and moving through the course at their own individual pace, it is not easy to maintain a unified class atmosphere. *Fortunately, distance learning systems like EMBANet can ease this problem somewhat by enabling continuing communication among class members and the instructor. This is only a partial solution, however, and faculty members who depend on synchronous class participation will need to modify a course like the one described herein to meet that need. This course was designed for maximum flexibility to meet the needs of the students.*

- A lack of face-to-face interaction with students makes it very difficult to get to know each one of them personally. *This challenge is very difficult to overcome in the current course format. The instructor was able to spend an hour with the assembled class during their fist residency week, but this short time was certainly not sufficient to get to know 57 students. One reason the students were required to "tell their own story" in their first assignment was to enable the instructor and their fellow classmates to get to know each student in his or her "own words." A photo directory of the students helps, but this challenge is not easy to overcome.*

- Finding (or making) the time the instructor must devote to a class like this is a highly demanding challenge. Preparing and taping all the lectures in advance requires a block of uninterrupted time, a luxury not often available to busy faculty members. Reading, grading, and providing individualized responses to $57 \times 5 = 285$ short essays—arriving at different times during the semester—was a daunting task. Faculty who cannot schedule their time with flexibility—or who are not willing to work long hours, often over weekends—should not attempt to lead a class like this. *The instructor is not on the "tenure clock" (having attained that privileged status many years ago) and, over the years, has learned how to schedule his time efficiently. It must be noted that the asynchronous structure of the class works in the faculty's favor in this regard. Course-related tasks can be accomplished after hours and on weekends—when many of the students are also doing their class-related work; this builds empathy with the students! Also, the work is not "place bound," meaning that it can be accomplished in the office, at home, or when traveling—anywhere there is a wireless connection to one's notebook computer.*

- Extra compensation earned by teaching this course does not really cover the instructor's opportunity costs. Classes taught in Auburn's Executive MBA program are additional assignments above and beyond the faculty members' regular assignment, and do generate extra compensation for the participating faculty. This additional compensation is a valuable reward, of course, but it must be realized that the instructor chose to spend at least ten clock hours per week (on average) communicating with these students. As with many classes, the amount of time spent on grading and providing feedback tended to increase as the semester drew to a close. *Extra compensation must not be the faculty member's only source of motivation if he or she is to achieve satisfaction from offering a course like this. Teaching this course is a labor of love for the present instructor. It is a joy to interact with highly motivated, mature, experienced, talented students like the ones this instructor works with every year when teaching this particular course.*

SUMMARY AND RECOMMENDATIONS

This chapter describes a one-semester hour required course in business ethics the author teaches on a yearly basis to talented and experienced students enrolled in Auburn University's executive MBA program. The course is updated each year, delivered at a distance, produced in a professionally staffed television studio, provided to the students fully packaged on a DVD during their first week of residency, and supported throughout the semester with a sophisticated proprietary distance education software system, EMBANet. The chapter describes the content of the most recent (fall semester, 2009) annual offering of this course, and shows how the instructor sought to meet four course objectives through five modules, each consisting of a lecture, an interview, three reading assignments, and a written essay assignment. As a capstone experience, each student prepared his or her own ethical code based on insights gained through the course.

While the course is very demanding for students (and the instructor), student reactions indicated that the time spent on the course is considered quite valuable by this special group of mature students. There are a number of challenges to be faced by anyone attempting to offer a course like this. It should not be attempted by anyone who does not have the time and technical support needed to "do it right." A desire to earn extra compensation cannot be the instructor's sole motivation to take on a task like this, because the time demands are considerable. The joy of interacting with highly motivated, mature, experienced, talented students who are able to share their insights regarding ethical issues in business must be the intrinsic motivator that drives a faculty member to accept an assignment like this. The author finds it to be a very satisfying teaching—and learning—experience.

NOTES

1. For more information about Auburn University's executive MBA program, visit the website at http://emba.business.auburn.edu/EMBA/.
2. A minimum of 8 years of progressively responsible managerial and professional leadership experience is required for admission to the program.
3. Since the written assignments are shared with their classmates, the instructor specifically warns students *not* to provide confidential information within them.)
4. Lectures are updated for every year's iteration of the course so fresh illustrations and current examples can be included for each cohort. Independent research was also encouraged for this and every module.

REFERENCES

Auburn University College of Business. (n.d.). *Auburn University executive MBA programs* (Brochure). Auburn, AL: Author.

Autry, J. A. (2001). *The servant leader: How to build a creative team, develop great morale, and improve bottom line performance.* Roseville, CA: Prima.

Baelz, P. (1977). *Ethics and belief.* New York, NY: The Seabury Press.

Bakke, D. W. (2008). Purpose matters. In S. A. Quatro & R. R. Sims (Eds.), *Executive ethics: Ethical dilemmas and challenges for the C-suite* (pp. 35-48). Charlotte, NC: Information Age.

Financial Times. (2009, October 19). *EMBA 2009: The top 95 executive MBA programmes* (Special report). *Financial Times*, p. 10.

Geary, W. T. (2008). Ethics and corruption from the perspective of the CFO. In S. A. Quatro & R. R. Sims (Eds.), *Executive ethics: Ethical dilemmas and challenges for the C-suite* (pp. 179-190). Charlotte, NC: Information Age.

Gilley, J. W., Anderson, S. K., & Gilley, A. (2008). Human resources management as a champion for corporate ethics: Moving towards ethical integration and acculturation in the HR function and profession. In S. A. Quatro & R. R. Sims (Eds.), *Executive ethics: Ethical dilemmas and challenges for the C-suite* (pp. 191-213). Charlotte, NC: Information Age Publishing.

Greenleaf, R. K. (2002/03). Ten characteristics of a servant leader. *Pastoral Forum, 20*(1), 6-7.

Hawver, T. H., Pollack, J. M., & Humphrey, R. H. (2008). Job design and affect: Ethical implications for the C-suite. In S. A. Quatro & R. R. Sims (Eds.), *Executive ethics: Ethical dilemmas and challenges for the C-suite* (pp. 263-278). Charlotte, NC: Information Age.

Hoekstra, E., Bell, A., & Peterson, S. R. (2008). Humility in leadership: Abandoning the pursuit of unattainable perfection. In S. A. Quatro & R. R. Sims (Eds.), *Executive ethics: Ethical dilemmas and challenges for the C-suite* (pp. 79-95). Charlotte, NC: Information Age.

Jackall, R. (1988). *Moral mazes: The world of corporate managers.* New York, NY: Oxford University Press.

Johnson, R. (2008). Environmental ethics: Achieving corporate sustainability to save the planet. In S. A. Quatro & R. R. Sims (Eds.), *Executive ethics: Ethical dilemmas and challenges for the C-suite* (pp. 159-177). Charlotte, NC: Information Age.

Kahn, A. E., & Maxwell, D. J. (2008). Ethics in diversity management leadership. In S. A. Quatro & R. R. Sims (Eds.), *Executive ethics: Ethical dilemmas and challenges for the C-suite* (pp. 247-262). Charlotte, NC: Information Age.

Nielson, N. B. (2008). The inescapability of worldview for business ethics: The root of C-suite beliefs, values, and affections. In S. A. Quatro & R. R. Sims (Eds.), *Executive ethics: Ethical dilemmas and challenges for the C-suite* (pp. 63-78). Charlotte, NC: Information Age.

Novak, M. (1996). *Business as a calling: Work and the examined life.* New York, NY: The Free Press.

Quatro, S. A., & Sims, R. R. (Eds.). (2008). *Executive ethics: Ethical dilemmas and challenges for the C-suite.* Charlotte, NC: Information Age.

Sauser, W. I., Jr. (2005a). Business ethics: Back to basics. *SAM Management in Practice, 9*(2), 1-4.

Sauser, W. I., Jr. (2005b). Ethics in business: Answering the call. *Journal of Business Ethics, 58,* 345-357.

Sauser, W. I., Jr. (2007). Employee theft: Who, how, why, and what can be done. *SAM Advanced Management Journal, 72*(3), 13-25.

Sauser, W. I., Jr. (2008a). Crafting a culture of character: The role of the executive suite. In S. A. Quatro & R. R. Sims (Eds.), *Executive ethics: Ethical dilemmas and challenges for the C-suite* (pp. 1-17). Charlotte, NC: Information Age.

Sauser, W. I., Jr. (2008b). Regulating ethics in business: Review and recommendations. *SAM Management in Practice, 12*(4), 1-7.

Schermerhorn, J. R. (2010). *Management* (10th ed.). Hoboken, NJ: Wiley.

Sims, R. R. (2008). A C-suite challenge: Preventing ethical breaches. In S. A. Quatro & R. R. Sims (Eds.), *Executive ethics: Ethical dilemmas and challenges for the C-suite* (pp. 123-140). Charlotte, NC: Information Age.

Stackhouse, M. L. (2005). Introduction: Foundations and purposes. In M. L. Stackhouse, D. P. McCann, S. J. Roels, & P. N. Williams (Eds.), *On moral business* (pp. 10-34). Grand Rapids, MI: Eerdmans.

Wescher, L. R. (2008). Global stakes: Globalization's challenges and opportunities for stakeholder theory. In S. A. Quatro & R. R. Sims (Eds.), *Executive ethics: Ethical dilemmas and challenges for the C-suite* (pp. 141-157). Charlotte, NC: Information Age.

Zinbarg, E. D. (2001). *Faith, morals, and money: What the world's great religions tell us about ethics in the marketplace.* New York, NY: Continuum.

CHAPTER 11

RETHINKING ETHICS TRAINING

New Approaches to Enhance Effectiveness

John C. Knapp

INTRODUCTION

When the office of the governor of Georgia asked me to develop an ethics training program for appointees to state boards and executive offices (see Appendix), I agreed to take the assignment but offered a word of caution: Don't call it ethics training. In many years of conducting executive education in this field, I have learned that few people are eager to participate in anything called ethics training. Some fear they will be subjected to a lecture on legal compliance or moral philosophy. Others just feel insulted, assuming they are being sentenced to some kind of character remediation.

These attitudes exemplify an irony of ethics education. That ethical behavior is essential to good personal and business relationships everyone will agree. And they will agree that their own organizations should uphold high ethical standards. Yet the suggestion that they personally have some-

Experiences in Teaching Business Ethics
pp. 231–245
Copyright © 2011 by Information Age Publishing

thing to learn about ethics is almost sure to meet with resistance. In my experience, this resistance tends to increase with rank and seniority, with top executives and boards less open to training than rank-and-file employees.

There are several possible explanations for this. For one, many people are skeptical about the potential for developing ethical sensitivity and judgment in adults. I have heard businesspeople and faculty colleagues erroneously assert that such development begins in early childhood and ends by adulthood. As one chief executive officer (CEO) told me, "By the time they arrive for their first day on the job, they've either got it or they don't. We just need to hire good people." While it is inarguable that an ethical workforce depends largely on good hiring, research and our own experience tell us that adults can continue to develop ethical competencies throughout their lifetimes. They can learn from their own mistakes and successes, from the examples and advice of others, and from training where they practice recognizing, analyzing, and resolving ethical problems.

Another reason for resistance is that few businesses have established a common language for talking comfortably about ethics in the workplace. In many organizations, ethics is a topic that comes to the fore only when something goes awry, and then usually at a time when fingers are pointing and tensions are high. A corporate executive shared with me that her company's CEO was taken aback by her proposal to train the sales force in ethics. He asked, "Have we had some problem in sales?" As she explained it, theirs was a culture where any talk of ethics was off-putting and uneasy.

People also resist ethics training because, frankly, it is often rote, dry and unimaginative, punctuated by reminders of the consequences of non-compliance. Much ethics training today is administered with a primary goal of ensuring that every employee has read the rules. This check-the-box mentality is an unfortunate consequence of legal developments that have caused many employers, often reluctantly, to require company-wide training. Is it any wonder the annual ethics training at some firms is a running joke among employees?

In this chapter we will consider how training programs can engage employees more effectively and contribute to a culture where conversations about ethics are commonplace and positive, not sporadic, off-putting, or threatening. We will explore trends in compliance management, including legal developments, and will identify some emerging best practices to enhance learning about ethics in the workplace. Three key factors will be discussed:

- *Strategic orientation*: a values focus versus a compliance focus;
- *Contextual learning*: training led by managers and supervisors; and

- *Functional relevance*: aligning training with the risks and opportunities pertinent to each employee.

THE EMERGENCE OF ETHICS AND COMPLIANCE MANAGEMENT AS A BUSINESS DISCIPLINE

It may be helpful to consider how ethics training became so commonplace. The formal concept of managing ethics and compliance first emerged in the 1990s as a recognized business discipline and function within organizations. Prior to this time, few corporations or other large organizations had formal programs supported by dedicated staff, budget resources, and policies, and only a minority of public companies had codes of conduct. The rapid development of this field is indicated by the membership of the Ethics and Compliance Officer Association (ECOA), founded in 1992 with a handful of members, and now comprising 1,300 professionals, and in the growth of the newer Society of Corporate Compliance and Ethics (SCCE), which has attracted 1,800 members in just eight years. Many of these professionals also participate in academic centers, online networks, and commercial conferences, most of which are less than a decade old.

To be sure, earlier ethics and compliance initiatives existed in the defense industry (e.g., Defense Industry Initiative of 1986) and some other heavily regulated sectors, but the broader impetus for formal programs came in 1991 when the U.S. Sentencing Commission, with Congressional approval, promulgated the federal sentencing guidelines for organizations, providing for significantly lower penalties for federal criminal violations if a convicted organization could demonstrate in federal court that it had in place an adequate compliance program at the time the crime was committed. In effect, an incentive was offered for any company to make a good-faith effort to prevent misconduct. The guidelines' criteria for effective compliance programs quickly became the de facto standard and framework for managing ethically, and this included employee training.

Five years later, in a landmark case involving Caremark, Inc., the Delaware chancery court held that directors of a corporation have a duty to ensure that a legal compliance program is in place and that failure in this duty can expose directors to personal civil liability to shareholders. The court defined a compliance program as a system reasonably designed to provide to senior management and the board itself timely, accurate information sufficient to allow management and the board to reach informed judgments concerning the corporation's compliance with law. Thus, Caremark established that corporate directors and senior management should be involved in the oversight of compliance, though it allowed that the level of detail that is appropriate for a compliance system is a question of business judgment. However, the ruling did give some guidance as to what constitutes an adequate program, including a code of business conduct, a designated compliance office, an internal audit plan, and, significantly, employee training (Caremark International, 1996).

By the late 1990s, formal ethics and compliance programs were common among large, publicly traded corporations. Although the sentencing guidelines applied to companies with as few as 50 employees, smaller public companies and most private firms were slower to adopt these practices, including formal training regimens. The 1991 *Sentencing Guidelines Manual* established specific criteria for determining a compliance program's adequacy for preventing criminal wrongdoing by employees or other agents of a firm. It also specified that a program, including training, should be relevant to the risks associated with a corporation's business type. In other words, a generic, off-the-shelf training course would not suffice.[1]

The guidelines were widely accepted by ethics and compliance professionals as best-practice standards until fraud at Enron, WorldCom, and several other major corporations raised questions about how these scandals occurred at companies with supposedly state-of-the-art compliance programs. Thus, after the U.S. Congress enacted the Sarbanes-Oxley Act of 2002, the Federal Sentencing Commission announced the formation of an *ad hoc* advisory group to revise the organizational guidelines, noting that despite the guidelines' startling impact on the implementation of compliance and business ethics programs over the last 10 years, they were deficient in "preventing large-scale corporate wrongdoing." Two years later, the commission announced revised guidelines for organizations, which were considerably more rigorous than the 1991 version and highlighted connections between compliance, corporate culture, and the tone set by leaders at the top. "Directors and executives of organizations who help to mitigate criminal fines now must take an active leadership role in the content and operation of compliance and ethics programs," the commission said. "They must also promote an organizational culture that encourages a commitment to compliance with the law and ethical conduct" (United States Sentencing Commission, 2004). In April 2010 the guidelines were again amended, largely in response to failures in the financial sector that led to governmental intervention in 2008 through the U.S. Treasury Department's Troubled Asset Relief Program (TARP). Two of the amendments have potentially important implications for ethics and compliance programs, though not necessarily for training.

Perhaps not surprisingly, many CEOs of large corporations are displeased with the costly and time-consuming regulations imposed by

Sarbanes-Oxley and other reforms, as they see these measures as requiring corporate America to pay penalties for the misconduct of a very few firms. This attitude makes it difficult to keep some CEOs engaged in matters related to ethics and compliance management. In my conversations with CEOs, it is not uncommon for them to ask, "Haven't we dealt with this enough?" It is therefore crucial for those responsible for ethics training to have a solid understanding not only of the legal requirements, but also of the managerial case for the benefits of training done well.

RATIONALE FOR ETHICS TRAINING

A 2008 survey of CEOs of U.S. corporations with more than $10 million in annual revenue found that 78% of publicly held companies had formal ethics and compliance training for employees. The practice was less prevalent among private companies, with 46% conducting ethics training. This discrepancy reflects the fact that public companies are more likely to have comprehensive ethics and compliance programs, principally because of Sarbanes-Oxley, Securities and Exchange Commission rules, and the listing requirements of stock exchanges. Also, private companies are smaller, with fewer employees than public companies in this sample.[2]

This survey notwithstanding, it is difficult to determine the extent of ethics training in U.S. workplaces. Ethics and compliance content is often included in other functional training, such as sales seminars and new employee orientation, in training on related topics (e.g., leadership, behavioral skills, diversity, etc.), and in informal communications. Also, external training delivered by professional societies and trade associations is not reported as employer-provided. Nonetheless, there is every indication that workplace training is on the rise in all sectors, and is increasingly common in smaller businesses. The following are often cited by employers as the primary purposes of ethics education:

- comply with USSC Guidelines and other compliance requirements (contract, regulatory, etc.);
- prevent illegal or undesirable conduct (reduce risk);
- establish values and expectations of right conduct;
- familiarize employees with sources of guidance and relevant policies, such as a code of conduct;
- demonstrate employer's commitment to its values and policies;
- sensitize employees to potential pitfalls before they encounter them in practice;

- heighten awareness of wrongdoing when it occurs in the workplace, thus making it more likely misconduct will be reported;
- develop critical thinking and moral reasoning skills;
- provide language and build competency for sustaining a workplace dialogue on conduct;
- establish clear performance standards for employee evaluation, rewards and disciplinary action;
- strengthen workplace trust and morale, as the best training is shown to reinforce shared values and equitable expectations; and
- improve relationships with customers, suppliers, communities and other constituencies by ensuring that employees understand what contributes to, or detracts from, company reputation.

STRATEGIC ORIENTATION: VALUES FOCUS VERSUS COMPLIANCE FOCUS

The amended sentencing guidelines recognize that compliance efforts aimed at preventing misconduct must be supported by organizational cultures that actually *encourage* ethical conduct. In other words, it is not sufficient to aim solely at staying out of trouble. To this end, organizations are required to promote compliance through a combination of positive incentives and appropriate discipline. Employees' incentives are often provided through performance evaluations, public recognition, or other rewards for exemplary behavior. For managers, some organizations tie incentives to demonstrated competencies, such as communication, employee development, and discipline.

By stressing ethical culture over bare compliance, the framers of the new guidelines were echoing a trend already under way in corporate America: a shift in focus from rules to values. Today's best ethics and compliance training covers all the bases for the prevention of misconduct, but its predominant thrust is the promotion of ethical values and desired conduct (see Table 11.1). In such programs, values provide the rationale and justification for rules of conduct and their enforcement. As an example of this shift in focus, employees must be taught that sexual harassment can place them and their employer at legal risk. This is the compliance message. But a values-based approach also emphasizes potentially more important reasons for not tolerating this behavior, such as being a workplace where every person is treated with dignity and respect.

Some who are accustomed to compliance-driven training may view a values-based approach as somehow less serious. But establishing shared values is no easy task. Management expert Jim Collins, author of books

Table 11.1.   Compliance Focus versus Values Emphasis

Compliance-Based Approach

Primary goal is to discourage unethical conduct; relies on rules and enforcement.

- Emphasis on prevention and restraint ("Thou shalt not ...")
- Technical, compliance specific
- Driven by program staff
- Externally defined (by law, regulation, contracts, etc.)

Values-Based Approach

Strives for compliance, but primary goal is to encourage ethical conduct; relies on leadership.

- Emphasis on encouraging right conduct ("Thou shalt ...")
- Aspirational, focused on broader principles
- Driven by leadership
- Internally defined

including *Built to Last* and *Good to Great*, cautions that the alignment of values and practice is one of the most difficult challenges facing leaders of large organizations. Collins (1996) believes executives spend too much time drafting, wordsmithing, and redrafting vision statements, mission statements, values statements, purpose statements, aspiration statements, and so on. In his opinion, they spend nowhere near enough time trying to align their organizations with the values and visions already in place. The difficulty lies in the fact that misalignments always exist, as tactical decisions frequently are made under time pressure with little attention to strategic vision or values. It is precisely this disconnection that breeds cynicism about ethics, leading employees and other stakeholders to question corporate commitment to principles. Training is where everyone from the top down should be challenged to apply the organization's espoused values to critical decisions.

CONTEXTUAL LEARNING: TRAINING LED BY MANAGERS AND SUPERVISORS

In response to the need for low-cost training and an audit trail showing that all employees have taken it, many new e-learning programs have been marketed in recent years. Workers no longer need be present for in-person training; they may logon at their convenience and complete a prescribed program that automatically records their responses, an obvious advantage for companies wishing to achieve 100% participation. "Consistency, cost effectiveness, proof of completion and automatic record keeping are some of the reasons why e-learning has been so popular with those responsible for compliance training," according to Overton (2007, p. 29).

A good example is Ernst & Young's 2-hour, web-based course, "Living Our Values," which is mandatory for 120,000 employees in 140 countries. As the name implies, the course focuses heavily on the firm's values, beginning with a 45-minute segment on the subject. Michael Hamilton, Ernst & Young's chief learning officer for the Americas, explains,

> We put employees in situations and ask them to take the firm's values and ethics to solve problems at the firm itself.... You can't expect people to exercise the right answers unless you give them a chance to apply them to real-life situations. (Quoted in Burke, 2007, p. 32)

Web-based learning is an easy way for employers to check the "ethics training box," leading them to abandon traditional face-to-face learning. But e-learning has inherent drawbacks, even with programs as advanced as Ernst & Young's. "Compliance e-learning may help save costs but it is in danger of giving e-learning a poor reputation that might one day be the death of it," writes Overton (2007, p. 29), who uses words like "dull," "legalistic," "uninspiring" and "boring" to describe the programs she reviewed.

Online programs can be substituted for human interaction in types of training, such as learning to use a new technology; but ethics is not solely about mastering the rules and building technical competencies. It is about how human beings behave in relationships with others. Ethics training, therefore, must bring employees together to discuss difficult issues, resolve disagreements, weigh conflicting priorities, and affirm shared values and expectations. Better decisions result when people seek the advice of others and take into account multiple points of view, and training is a place to practice collaboration and consultation.

The best use of e-learning is as a supplement to face-to-face training, a reinforcement of the rules of conduct and prior lessons. In some companies this takes the form of short problems that must occasionally be resolved by employees when they log onto the intranet. Research demonstrates, however, that adult learners make significantly greater gains in ethical judgment through interactive training than through methods where decisions are made without benefit of discussion (Izzo, Langford, & Vitell, 2006).

Even more may be gained from interactive training involving regular co-workers in their normal roles, led by their supervisors. This yields two valuable benefits: fostering a culture of ethical discourse within existing work groups, and positioning supervisors as leaders with responsibility for ethics within their scope of day-to-day influence. The Federal Sentencing Commission and the SEC have said much about the importance of setting the right tone at the top, which usually means the CEO championing and modeling ethical conduct. But this role is just as important, if not more so, for leaders throughout the organization—the many "tops" at the division and departmental level.

A good example of interactive, supervisor-led training is found at AGL Resources, a $2.5 billion wholesaler and retailer of natural gas serving more than 2 million customers in the Eastern and Southwestern United States. With 2,400 employees in multiple locations, AGL developed a program comprising compulsory e-learning covering the code of conduct, and periodic small-group sessions led by employees' own managers. The stated goals for the sessions are:

- to help employees understand what is in the code of conduct—and why;
- to encourage employees to talk with managers about ethics and compliance whenever they have questions or concerns;
- To create opportunities for employees to confront ethical questions *before* they arise on the job; and
- to promote a positive culture by bringing values to life regularly *and* consistently (Tkacs, 2008).

A user-friendly philosophy makes the materials easy for managers to use, with limited prep time or training. Initial training in how to lead ethics discussions is supported by a manual covering step-by-step instructions. A turnkey packet for each session contains a facilitator's guide, employee handouts and other materials. A session covers only one topic (e.g., using inappropriate language, accepting gifts from customers) relevant to the work of the particular group, and a follow-up captures feedback from the manager and participants. This year-round training is integral to a larger ethics and compliance program that includes posters and other communications to reinforce learning. It also has significant advantages over programs that require employees to go through annual training that attempts to cover every conceivable topic at once.

Interactive training need not be dull conversation about law and regulation. After all, ethics encompasses some of the liveliest issues that live and breathe within organizations. The best approaches encourage spirited dialog and use creative methods, such as role-play, that can even be entertaining.

FUNCTIONAL RELEVANCE: ALIGNING TRAINING AND RISK

Alignment of ethics training with corporate risks is a priority of the Federal Sentencing Guidelines which emphasize that each company needs a customized approach. This is a reminder that the generic, one-size-fits-all products offered by some vendors are less than effective. As we have discussed, exposure to various risks of misconduct varies by company type and industry. Likewise, individual employees face differing risk exposure. A production line worker in Milwaukee will never face pressure to bribe a foreign official in Moscow, so why distract her with a lesson on the Foreign Corrupt Practices Act? Training content should fit the needs of the learner, yet a surprising number of companies run every employee through the same course content.

This approach permits ethics content to be included in the context of other employee training. For example, a discussion of bribes and kickbacks may be addressed much more effectively within a sales-training program than as a stand-alone module bearing an "ethics" label.

A risk-based approach also can update and reorient training as developments expose the company and its employees to new challenges, as when laws change, new products are developed, operations are launched in other countries, or mergers or acquisitions are completed. As practitioners of enterprise risk management (ERM) know, not all risks involve potential criminal conduct, so ethics and compliance training must take into account all circumstances that may place the organization's reputation or relationships at risk. For this reason, educational programs may benefit from input from risk management, internal audit, and other units assessing corporate vulnerabilities (in addition to traditional coordination with human resources and legal counsel).

THE VALUE OF CEO LEADERSHIP

While working with a large insurance company to strengthen its ethics and compliance program, I conducted a firm-wide survey of employees and found that fewer than 20% agreed with the statement, "Our CEO is strongly committed to ethical business practices." The CEO was shocked to learn this and wanted to know what he could do to change this perception. We discussed a number of strategies, which he eagerly adopted, including having him participate in a visible manner in employee ethics training. Not only did he agree to participate, he decided to take part in every session held in departments throughout the company, not to make speeches, but to show employees that he was committed to learning alongside them. The effect was felt immediately as ethics training took on much greater significance.

CEO leadership is also essential because there are some messages that can only come from a CEO, such as a willingness to forego profit to do what's right; a commitment to rewarding ethical performance; or unwillingness to tolerate retaliation against employees who voice concerns. This must be integral to any training program, even if only through a video-recorded message. Such communication is more important than ever in today's climate where CEOs are confronted by unprecedented demands for internal accountability and transparency. Employee trust, once assumed to be reliable except in extraordinary circumstances, is now an elusive asset, difficult to acquire and easy to lose. Internal trust can be bolstered by a CEO-level, intentional focus on sincerely held and commonly shared values. Employee trust of leaders is highest when leaders are perceived to have integrity, modeling the organization's espoused values, and humility, participating enthusiastically in training. Employees who trust their leaders—from CEO to immediate supervisor—are significantly more likely than others to report misconduct to leaders and to conduct themselves in an ethical manner in relationships with coworkers and others.

We must be mindful that informal employee education can be even more powerful than any amount of formal training. In every organization, people constantly take their cues from what is spoken, practiced and rewarded, especially by those at the top. The director of the Securities and Exchange Commission's Division of Enforcement said in 2004, "Whenever your CEO is delivering a state-of-the-company address to company employees, or offering remarks at a company event, she should be talking about the company's values as well as its profits. Too many times in our cases, we've seen instances of senior managers demanding 'results,' and what employees heard was a demand for 'results at any cost—including noncompliance with the rules'" (Cutler, 2004)

A CONCLUDING SUGGESTION

In any organization, a crucial first step in strengthening ethics training is deciding what to call it. I am increasingly convinced the word ethics is an almost insurmountable obstacle, for it is so often associated with negative experiences, from lousy past training sessions to threatening memos from corporate lawyers to dismal college courses in philosophy. I would offer any employer the same advice I gave the governor of Georgia—*don't call it ethics training*. We described the program for gubernatorial appointees as a discussion of how to maintain public trust and confidence in the agencies of government. Nearly everyone saw this as important and worthy of their time. Each four-hour session progressed naturally from the challenges of governing in today's skeptical society to a dialog about what could cause a loss of public trust. We had moved into ethics training without the participants thinking of it as such. It should not be hard for any organization to describe its program in a more inviting manner. After all, what is more important about ethics in business than building good relationships and reputation?

NOTES

1. See http://www.ussc.gov/orgguide.htm
2. 2008 Survey of CEOs on Business Ethics, conducted by researchers John C. Knapp (Samford University) and Daniel Wueste (Clemson University), with grant support from UPS Foundation. A mailed questionnaire was completed by 300 CEOs of U.S. companies in more than 14 industry categories; average annual revenues were $200 million; 23 percent were public traded. The study examined practices in ethics management, management philosophy, perspectives on business issues, and other topics.

APPENDIX: TRAINING SESSIONS FOR GUBERNATORIAL APPOINTEES IN THE STATE OF GEORGIA, 2004-2007

At the request of Georgia Governor Sonny Perdue, a series of training sessions was conducted for senior appointees to leadership positions in state agencies. The trainees included members of governing boards and senior administrators of more than 40 agencies including the departments of transportation, corrections, education, human resources, natural resources, community affairs, public safety, pardons and paroles, technical and adult education, and the University System of Georgia.

The program was developed and led by John C. Knapp, then director of the Center for Ethics and Corporate Responsibility at Georgia State University, and Betty L. Siegel, president emeritus and chair of Leadership, Ethics and Character at Kennesaw State University. The following outline describes the development, format, and general content of this training.

Executive Order and Principles of Effective Board Governance

Prior to beginning the training program, the governor issued Executive Order No. 1, his first directive to executive branch employees and appointees, calling for high standards of ethics and legal compliance. For appointees to boards overseeing governmental agencies, he appended "Seven Principles of Effective Board Service," developed with the assistance of the training team. These principles (see below) were incorporated into training, with time for discussion of each.

Preparation and Program Design

- Participants were invited with a personal letter from the governor explaining the importance of addressing issues of public trust and confidence in government.
- Each 4-hour session was held in a specially scheduled meeting of each respective board and senior management team, when possible at an off-site location.
- Prior to each session, one of the educators conducted in-depth interviews with the board chair and agency director to identify specific issues and concerns to be addressed in training, as well as to allay any apprehensions about the nature of the program.
- The program was designed to be interactive throughout, with ample opportunity for peer-to-peer exploration of ethical issues.
- Resource materials for each group were customized to include pertinent bylaws, state statutes, and other relevant information.
- Board chairs were prepared in advance to participate in leadership of the program, especially as the groups identified ethical risks and developed consensus about how to minimize them through mutual accountability.

Training Content

- Section 1: *Establishing shared values.* Following introductions and an informal discussion about participants' backgrounds and interests, an exercise was conducted wherein each person responded in writing to the question, "What are five values that you hold that will direct the way you perform your work on behalf of this agency?" These values were captured and placed on large sheets at the front of the room, showing that there is much consensus about the ethical foundation of public service.
- Section 2: *The threat of eroding trust.* A presentation was made on the decline of public trust in government, supported by charts showing trends and causes of the trust deficit based on state and national

opinion surveys. A facilitated discussion followed, exploring the implications of low trust for the effective functioning of government institutions, and considering how adhering to the group's espoused values may be essential to maintaining the trust and confidence of the public.

- Section 3: *Identifying risks and means of prevention*. Participants were asked to complete two sentences in writing: (1) "Our agency's effectiveness and credibility would be weakened if a board member or senior administrator were to _____." (2) "To encourage good governance and prevent this from happening, we should _____." A group discussion followed to examine each hypothetical scenario and develop consensus on how the participants themselves may prevent undesirable conduct. In many cases the issues identified were not hypothetical, but current concerns needing attention.

- Section 4: *Sources of guidance and principles governance*. The last hour of the training session included an overview of relevant provisions of agency bylaws and policies, state legal statutes, and other sources of guidance, as well as a more extended discussion of the governor's Seven Principles of Effective Board Service, with participants contributing examples to illustrate each point:

Pervasive Principle:

1. *Board members are expected to adhere to the highest ethical and professional standards.* Through members' individual behavior and through the collective behavior of the Board, conflicts of interest should be avoided at all times.

Expectations of Board Members:

2. *Board members must understand the central purpose of the board.* Board members must be able to answer the question "Why does this board exist?"

3. *Board members must be aware of and understand their major responsibilities to the Board, to the Department and to the citizens of Georgia.* In this regard, it is especially important to distinguish between board governance and organizational management.

4. *Board members must be competent to fulfill their responsibilities (as individual members of the board and as board committee members).* Board

members must commit appropriate time to do the work and must commit to regular board attendance.

What Board Members Need to Be Effective:

5. *Board members must be given high quality, understandable information at least one week prior to regularly scheduled meetings.* The information (neither too detailed nor too condensed) should focus on major issues and risks faced by the agency. Board members have a responsibility to understand these issues and risks.

6. *The board, agency management, and state auditors must have open lines of communication.* Processes must be put in place to allow and encourage an appropriate level of interaction among these parties.

7. *Boards and board members must be accountable.* Processes must be put in place to allow and encourage *transparent* Board operations. These may take the form of publicly aired minutes of meetings, annual reports, and reports from Board audit committees. Transparency is a vehicle to acknowledge *accountability*.

Posttraining evaluation involved individual surveys of all participants, with a report of findings to the office of the governor.

REFERENCES

Burke, M. (2007, July). Ethics training: New needs, new times. *Chief Learning Officer, 32.*

Caremark International Inc. Derivative Litigation, 698 A. 2d 959, Del. Ch. (1996).

Collins, J. (1996, Summer). *Leader to leader no. 1: Aligning action and values.* New York, NY: Leader to Leader Institute.

Cutler, S. M. (2004, December 3). *Tone at the top: Getting it right.* Remarks to the Second Annual General Counsel Roundtable, United States Securities and Exchange Commission, Washington, DC.

Izzo, G. M., Langford, B. E., & Vitell, S. (2006). Investigating the efficacy of interactive ethics education: A difference in pedagogical emphasis. *Journal of Marketing Theory & Practice, 14*(3), 239-248.

Overton, L. (2007, July-August). Compliance training: Savior and death. *E-Learning Age.*

Tkacs, A. (2008, June). *Ethics and compliance training at AGL Resources.* Presentation at the Center for Ethics and Corporate Responsibility, Georgia State University, Atlanta, GA.

United States Sentencing Commission. (2004, April 13). *Sentencing commission toughens requirements for corporate compliance and ethics programs* (Press release). Retrieved from http://www.ussc.gov/press/rel0404.htm

CHAPTER 12

BEYOND THE CLASSROOM

Business Ethics Training Programs for Professionals

William I. Sauser, Jr.

INTRODUCTION

The corporate "culture of character" has been described as one where "positive moral values are ingrained throughout the organization such that all of its members strive without fail to know what is right, value what is right, and do what is right" (Sauser, 2008a, p. 7). In such a culture, according to Sims (2005):

- There exists a clear vision and picture of integrity throughout the organization.
- The vision is owned and embodied by top management, over time.
- The reward system is aligned with the vision of integrity.
- Policies and practices of the organization are aligned with the vision; there are no mixed messages.

Experiences in Teaching Business Ethics
pp. 247–271
Copyright © 2011 by Information Age Publishing
247

- It is understood that every significant leadership decision has ethical value dimensions.
- Everyone is expected to work through conflicting-stakeholder value perspectives (p. 406).

What steps might the leaders of an organization take to craft such a culture? Sauser (2008a, pp.10-13) suggested the following steps as a starting point: (a) adopt a code of ethics, (b) provide ethics training, (c) hire and promote ethical people, (d) correct unethical behavior, (e) take a proactive strategy, (f) conduct a social audit, (g) protect whistle blowers, and (h) empower the guardians of integrity. It is the second step—provide ethics training—that is the subject of this chapter. Who should provide the training, and how should it be structured? Is there a meaningful role for employees to play in the design of such training programs? What might an effective ethics training program look like? What kinds of programs foster strong employee participation and lead to meaningful learning and implementation of ideas?

This chapter is intended to stimulate further discussion of these important questions among business ethics professors, business leaders, and other interested persons. The chapter describes the importance of ethics training as a step in the creation of such a culture, then briefly reviews research relating to elements of an effective ethics training program. Three examples of ethics training programs designed and provided by the author are then described, one for municipal employees, one for university employees, and one offered at a distance to professional engineers. The chapter concludes with some reflections on the role of the business ethics professor in providing ethics training "beyond the classroom."

BRIEF REVIEW OF RESEARCH

The idea that ethics training is an important component of any corporate effort to instill morality into the fabric of its being—and ethicality into its day-to-day operations—is not new, of course. In 1979, Purcell and Weber presented the concept of "institutionalizing ethics" straightforwardly as "getting ethics formally and explicitly into daily life" (p. 6). Sims (1991) counseled those who seek to institutionalize business ethics into corporate culture to consider a number of actions, including: "Develop a systematic training program (with input from employees at *all* levels of the organization) for all employees explicitly concerned with ethical principles and with relevant cases" (p. 504). Research results on a national sample of 313 business professionals employed in the United States, summarized by

Valentine and Fleischman (2004), "provide significant statistical support for the notion that businesspersons employed in organizations that have formalized ethics programs have more positive perceptions of their companies' ethical context than do individuals employed in organizations that do not" (p. 381). In terms of economic incentive, LeClair and Ferrell (2000) credit—at least in part—the "due diligence" standard of the 1991 United States Sentencing Guidelines for Organizations for turning the ethics training and consulting business into a billion dollar industry. Providing ethics training is widely touted nowadays by experts as a key component in any effective corporate ethics program (see, for example, Ferrell, Fraedrich, & Ferrell, 2011, pp. 228-230; Trevino & Nelson, 2004, pp. 296-299). Sauser (2008b) found that conducting ongoing training and education programs with respect to business ethics is a "best practice" recommended (or mandated) by key legal standards for businesses across the world, and Weber (2007) commented, "Formal business ethics training, often mandatory, is now common in companies around the globe" (p. 61).

Goals of an Effective Ethics Training Program

What should be the goals of an ethics training program for employees? LeClair and Ferrell (2000) provided a straightforward answer to this important question: "An effective program is organization-specific and takes advantage of self-regulatory incentives by developing ethical standards and appropriate communications, controls, and training to ensure employees and other agents understand and abide by these expectations" (p. 313). Kirrane (1990) argued that ethics training should (a) identify situations where ethical decision making is involved, (b) lead to a greater understanding of the culture and values of the organization, and (c) evaluate the impact of ethical decisions on the organization's well-being. Valentine and Fleischman (2004) suggested, "Such training should ideally teach individuals the ethical requirements of the organization, as well as how to recognize and react to common ethical problems experienced in the workplace" (p. 382).

Jones (1988-1989) provided a helpful list of seven possible goals for an ethics training program:

1. provide the tools to help employees understand the ethical decision process;
2. help people assess ethical priorities;
3. provide ways to deal with those who violate ethical standards;

4. enable employees to identify ethical problems with respect to company policy;
5. increase sensitivity to ethical issues;
6. enhance individual reflectiveness; and
7. improve the ethical climate of a business through the creation of ethics support systems and codes.

More recently, Ferrell et al. (2011) provided a similar set of eight key goals for successful ethics training programs:

1. Identify key risk areas that employees will face.
2. Provide experience in dealing with hypothetical or disguised ethical issues within the industry through minicases, online challenges, CD-ROMs, or other experiential learning opportunities.
3. Let your employees know that wrongdoing will never be supported in the organization and that employee evaluations will take their conduct in this area into consideration.
4. Let employees know that they are individually accountable for their behavior.
5. Align employee conduct with organizational reputation and branding.
6. Provide ongoing examples through communication with employees of how employees are handling ethical issues appropriately.
7. Allow a mechanism for employees to voice their concerns that is anonymous, but allows for the provision of feedback to key questions (24-hour hotlines).
8. Provide a hierarchy of leadership for employees to contact when they are faced with an ethical dilemma that they do not know how to resolve (p. 230).

Content of an Effective Ethics Training Program

What should an ethics program for employees contain? Contents should flow directly from the goals of the program, of course. Ferrell et al. (2011) provided a comprehensive menu from which to select relevant content. They stated:

Training can educate employees about the firm's policies and expectations, relevant laws and regulations, and general social standards. Training programs can make employees aware of available resources, support systems, and designated personnel who can assist them with ethical and legal advice.

They can also empower employees to ask tough questions and make ethical decisions. (p. 228)

Weber (2007) conducted a thorough review of learning theory to glean some insights to guide designers of ethics training programs. His summary suggestions include:

- Combine pedagogical approaches and use flexible physical settings to take into consideration various learning styles.
- Leverage organizational influences, such as a statement of values and acceptable patterns of behavior within the organization.
- Use group discussions, particularly among individuals at different levels of cognitive moral development.
- Discuss real life situations, including business cases.
- Integrate stakeholder analysis by considering viewpoints of stockholders, managers, peers, other employees, suppliers, customers, family, friends, industry groups, host communities, and other parties.
- Assign participants an active role in designing the program.
- Use inductive learning (learning by example).

With respect to training methods, LeClair and Ferrell (2000) noted that the most popular methods are videotapes and lectures, while some companies have developed games as a method of ethics training. LeClair and Ferrell provided a strong case for the perspective that experiential training—including behavioral simulation—is a highly effective approach to ethics training.

From a pragmatic standpoint, Aguilar (1994) offered two important suggestions: (1) make certain any training materials and cases are clearly relevant to the audience, and (2) be sure all participants "are given ample opportunity to ask questions, challenge assertions, and generally to engage actively in the learning process" (p. 104). Building on this idea, Sauser and Sims (2007) offered this possibility:

A highly effective way to conduct an ethics training session is to provide "what if …" cases for discussion and resolution. The leader would present a "real world" scenario in which an ethical problem is encountered. Using the organization's code of ethics as a guide, participants would explore options and seek a consensus ethical solution. This kind of training sharpens the written ethical code and brings it to life. (p. 276).

Ethics Training Providers

Who is best suited to provide training in business ethics? Answers to this question vary widely, and are dependent on the purposes of the program, its content, and the skills of the personnel available to provide the training. Possible trainers include moral philosophers, religious leaders, prominent citizens who have a stellar reputation for ethics, members of the organization's training staff, ethics officers, senior consultants (Trevino & Nelson, 2004, p. 297), and company officers and senior executives (Aguilar, 1994, p. 103). Lattal and Clark (2005) endorse the idea of using company managers as trainers, with the following caveat: "Depending on your role in the organization, it may be appropriate for you to conduct such workshops yourself after receiving training that would contribute to your own moral sensitivity and professional development" (p. 341).

No matter who is selected to lead the training, Weber (2007) believes—based on his review of relevant research in learning theory—there are some "desirable traits" that characterize effective trainers. He wrote, "Better facilitators" are effective at:

- Encouraging participants to analyze and modify their views as a result of insights gained from others in group discussions;
- Encouraging participant critical thinking and inquiry skills (for example, critical thinking is likely to emerge when a facilitator encourages participants to consider why their individual views vary from views of others regarding the morality of specific business choice alternatives);
- Supporting development of participant self-confidence by encouraging small participant groups to be independent in managing their discussions and in arriving at conclusions, while simultaneously encouraging individual creativity; and
- Establishing a timetable and stages along the inductive learning process, including a planned close and logical wrap-up, where participants are encouraged to help evaluate their own progress toward learning goals (p. 66).

The present author strongly endorses Weber's (2007) suggestions as presented above, and recommends that the reader look at them carefully one more time. Realistically, given these criteria, who might be a better choice as a facilitator of ethics training workshops for employees than *business ethics professors* who are knowledgeable about moral issues in business; cognizant of learning styles, individual differences, stages of moral development, and the need for critical thinking; skilled in the very techniques Weber recommends; experienced in guiding undergraduate and graduate students through cases, simulations, projects, and discussions; and able to evaluate and develop individual students, teams, and classes as a whole? From this author's perspective, this seems to be an ideal role for the business ethics professor who desires to "make a difference" beyond the classroom.

In a forceful and highly influential essay, Swanson (2004) argued that universities must "reclaim ethics education as part of their broad institutional responsibility" (p. 58). While her essay was designed to convince deans (and provosts, presidents, and trustees) that universities must include courses in business ethics as part of the required curriculum in their colleges and schools of business, the present author believes her argument is equally valid for university programs beyond the classroom. "Anything less," Swanson asserted, "smacks of second-class citizenship for ethics and sets the stage for the next wave of corporate misconduct" (p. 58).

How might business ethics professors draw upon the research summarized above and go about designing and implementing effective ethics programs for professionals? The three examples described below have been produced, offered, and refined by the present author over the past decade; they are provided here as stimuli for readers who wish to build their own programs tailored to meet the needs of the organizations they serve. All three of these programs were most recently offered in newly revised versions during the 6 months preceding the preparation of this chapter, so they are certainly fresh in the mind of the author, whose general reflections on them follow their descriptions.

A PROFESSIONAL ETHICS PROGRAM FOR MUNICIPAL EMPLOYEES

This first example describes an ethics training program the author developed about a decade ago for the city of Auburn, Alabama. The city's website (www.auburnalabama.org) describes this municipality as follows: "The city of Auburn is home to Auburn University. Auburn is a thriving community of approximately 54,000 residents. Auburn is located alongside Interstate 85 in east central Alabama." The city employs over 800 persons working in 13 departments: economic development, environmental services, finance, human resources, information technology, judicial, library, office of the city manager, parks and recreation, planning, public safety, public works, and water resource management. The city conducts a citizen survey every year to gauge citizen satisfaction with city services; the satisfaction tallies remain uniformly high every year (thanks to the good work of the city's employees).

This ethics training program grew from a conversation between the author and the city's human resources (HR) director. The HR director wanted to establish a short (2-hour) workshop on professional ethics that would be suitable for all city employees. The city has a good reputation for ethics and professionalism; the workshop was designed to maintain this reputation and build on it, *not* because there were any ethical problems the city was facing. The HR manager was aware of the author's workshop facilitation skills and interest in professional ethics, and invited the author to partner with the city to develop and lead a series of workshops that would enable as many as possible of the city's employees to participate.

A steering committee for the workshop was appointed representing senior employees from throughout the city. The author presented to this steering committee his existing introductory materials and sought their advice regarding relevant issues, examples, and methods that would appeal to the city's employees. Significantly, the author asked the members of the steering committee to provide to him written examples of ethics issues they had faced, heard about, or observed during their career; these examples were then turned into a series of anonymous minicase materials used in the workshop (see Table 12.1). The author also prepared a 25-item "City of Auburn Ethics Quiz" with items drawn directly from the city's personnel policy manual (see Appendix A). To date over 600 city employees have participated in this workshop, including the city manager and all city department heads. It was most recently offered on June 23, 2010.

Each workshop session includes approximately 30 participants widely representative of the city's workforce in terms of age, gender, racial-ethnic identity, and departmental assignment. The participants are seated at small tables in a city training room designed to maximize participant interaction. The HR director or a member of his staff introduces each workshop, explaining to the participants that the workshop was designed with input from a representative committee of city employees. The author begins the workshop by soliciting discussion using a series of questions regarding the nature of professional ethics. Is "ethics in public service" an oxymoron? Does "professional ethics" represent an (impossible?) ideal, or perhaps a manifestation of a person's value system, or even a way of life? Is ethics something one can learn? How does each person's life experience influence his or her approach to professional ethics? The author allows these questions to be explored in a manner that encourages participant expression of multiple perspectives, thus setting a tone of openness for later discussion.

Discussion then shifts to an examination of various guidelines for professional behavior, including moral codes; professional association stan-

Table 12.1.   City of Auburn Ethics Scenarios

1. You work in the planning department. You have been approved to attend a professional meeting at Fort Walton. The meeting begins on Wednesday and ends on Friday. You would like to take your wife and two children to the meeting and extend your stay to Sunday. However, your travel budget is tight and you have to stay in a budget motel about a block away from the beach. Therefore you are going to the meeting alone and returning home on Friday evening.

    About a couple of weeks before the meeting a developer comes in with a proposal for a large apartment project. During the meeting you mention that it will be your responsibility to review his proposal and prepare a report and recommendation to the planning commission as to whether are not it should be approved; and you note that you will have to draft your report fairly quickly because you are going to attend a meeting in Fort Walton.

    A few days later you get a call from the developer in which he tells you that he owns a condominium right on the beach in Fort Walton; no one is presently using it; and you could use it while you are attending the meeting. You could also take your family and stay through Sunday. He also points out that by using his condo you could be saving the city the costs of the motel.

    How do you respond to this invitation? Would your response vary whether you were going to recommend approval of the developer's project or you were going to recommend delaying or disapproving it?

2. Every month a water service cut off occurs for all customers who have not paid for their water service. While generating the list of customers to be cut off, you recognize the names of three city employees, two of which are at levels higher than your own, and one city council member. What do you do?

3. A patrol officer answers an alarm at a business downtown late one evening and after clearing the building, requests communications to telephone the owner. After a walk - through in the building the owner expresses his appreciation of the police officer's diligence and hands him a bag of candy from the store. The officer politely refuses but the store owner insists. The officer accepts the gift, believing that to refuse would insult the store owner.

4. An out of town vender whom you have done business with in the past learns of your interest to purchase some equipment. He calls and mentions that he will be passing through town around noon on his way to an appointment in a nearby city. Because of the time of his arrival, he asks if you can meet over lunch to discuss your needs. You agree. After lunch, he picks up the check and is going to pay for your lunch. Is it okay for him to do so? Why or why not?

5. You notice other employees are using the city's computers and Internet service for personal reasons such as catching up on the latest in sports, sending personal greetings, browsing through online catalogs, and playing games. In fact, it is quite widespread leading you to believe that the city's Technology Resources Acceptable Use Policy is not really enforced, especially since some supervisors seem to turn a blind eye to this practice. You decide that because so many people are taking advantage of the computers and Internet service, you will too, but only during your breaks. Can this decision be supported from an ethical standpoint? A policy standpoint?

6. Your cousin, E. Lected Offishal, ran for office on the city council and won. You would not consider Lected a "close" relative, but you and he have always been cordial and came to know each other over the years at family reunions and holiday gatherings. Soon after taking office, Lected paged you while you were working with your crew. You have been assigned a full day of work, but felt inclined to return the call in case it was a family emergency. You called him from the field, and he said that there was a very large pot hole on the other side of town that just popped up after the heavy rains. He asked that you and the crew address it immediately since it is a liability and he is now an elected official and it is his sworn duty to take care of such things. How do you handle this situation (1) with Lected? (2) with your crew? (3) with your supervisor/department head?

(Note: The "city" may or may not know of this familial relationship).

dards; the law; city policy, rules and regulations; societal norms; and personal values and beliefs. The author then presents three key ideas, the major "takeaways" from the workshop:

- Never use your public position for private gain.
- Remember—the citizens are your employers, and they are always watching.
- The perception of wrongdoing can be as damaging as actual wrongdoing.

At this point the concept of "an ethical challenge" is presented: An ethical challenge is defined by the author as "a situation with a potential course of action that, although offering potential personal benefit or gain, is also unethical in that it violates one or more of the standards for behavior we have just discussed." A list of examples of typical ethical challenges is then presented (see Table 12.2), and specific actions relevant to the jobs represented among the participants are discussed. (For example, mixing "dark water" with "clear water" would be an example of the provision of an unsafe service by employees in water resource management, as they readily recognize and point out.)

Attention then shifts to a brief discussion of unethical requests bosses sometimes make of subordinates—and how to handle them—followed by

Table 12.2.   Examples of Ethical Challenges

- Providing a product or service you know is harmful or unsafe
- Misleading someone through false statements or omissions
- Using "insider information"
- Playing favorites
- Manipulating and using people
- Benefiting personally from a position of trust
- Violating confidentiality
- Misusing company property or equipment
- Falsifying documents
- Padding expenses
- Taking bribes or kickbacks
- Participating in a cover-up
- Negligence or inappropriate behavior in the workplace
- Substance abuse
- Theft or sabotage
- Violence
- Acts of terrorism

examples of rationalizations for unethical behavior—and how to identify and avoid them. After a short break the larger group is broken into small groups of five or six persons, and each group is assigned one of the ethical scenarios displayed in Table 12.1, with instructions to read and discuss the scenario, identify the ethical issues involved, and decide what action would be appropriate to take. The results of the small group discussions are then shared with the larger group, and all participants are encouraged to join into the discussion. Alternative solutions are examined and the group typically reaches a clear consensus on how to handle the situation. (This allows group norms to be solidified.) During the discussion, the author might change a fact or two about the scenario, and the participants are invited to describe how a change in facts might change the group-accepted normative response. Free discussion is encouraged during this portion of the workshop, and ideas flow readily from the group members.

When this discussion is concluded (and it typically takes a deliberate effort on the part of the author to close this lively discussion), the three lists illustrated in Tables 12.3, 12.4, and 12.5 are presented and discussed. The purpose of this discussion is to provide some tools to the workshop participants they can use when making their own ethical decisions.

At this point in the workshop the "City of Auburn Ethics Quiz" is then discussed as a group. While the answers to many of the questions on this quiz are obvious (thus reinforcing city policy), several of them—different items among different groups—engender considerable discussion. Alternative responses are presented and defended, and city policies are read and interpreted for the group. This helps participants realize that not all cases are black and white, and that standards of reasonable judgment must prevail. The workshop ends with a restatement of the "three key ideas" mentioned above, plus an admonition to "walk the talk" by exhibiting professionalism no matter what one's role within the city.

Table 12.3.   Checklist for Making Ethical Decisions

1. Recognize the ethical challenge
2. Get the facts
3. Identify your options
4. Test each option: Is it legal, right, beneficial? Note: Get some counsel!
5. Decide which option to follow
6. Double check your decision
7. Take action
8. Monitor the results

Table 12.4. Double-Check Considerations

- Your attorney
- Your accountant
- Your boss
- Your coworkers
- Your stakeholders
- Your family
- The newspaper
- "60 Minutes"
- Your religious leader
- Your deity

Table 12.5. Establishing a Strong Ethical Culture

- Adopt a code of ethics
- Provide ethics training
- Hire and promote ethical people
- Correct unethical behavior
- Take a proactive strategy
- Conduct a social audit
- Protect whistle blowers

The workshop has been well received by the participants. Many have mentioned to the author and the HR director how the workshop has "clarified some things," "made me think," or "opened my eyes to important issues." Formal evaluations conducted by the HR manager have also been very positive. Most importantly, the city has maintained its reputation as an ethically managed municipality, a jurisdiction whose citizens are very pleased with the services they receive and the professionalism of city employees. The city's annual Citizen Survey provides clear-cut data to bear out these statements.

A PROFESSIONAL ETHICS PROGRAM FOR UNIVERSITY ADMINISTRATIVE/PROFESSIONAL EMPLOYEES

This second example shares some characteristics with the municipal program described above (on which it was based), but also has some unique features of its own. It grew from a conversation between the author and the director of human resource development (HRD) at Auburn University. Auburn University offers a catalog of no-cost HRD programs to its employees every year so they may continue to grow professionally. The

HRD director was aware of the author's work with the city of Auburn and asked if he might also develop a workshop on professional ethics suitable for University employees. This 3-hour workshop is now offered every semester; it was most recently offered on October 25, 2010. The workshop is offered in a well-appointed training room near the University campus. The classes are typically smaller than those for the municipal workshop; the University workshop draws about eight to a dozen participants per offering, which allows for more individual attention from the author and interactive discussion among the group.

Auburn University is described on its website (www.auburn.edu) as

> a comprehensive land, space and sea grant research institution blending arts and applied sciences.... The main campus had an enrollment during fall of 2009 of 24,602. Auburn University offers degrees in 13 schools and colleges at the undergraduate, graduate and professional levels.

While an occasional faculty member or staff member (hourly employee) participates in this course, it was designed primarily for the university's administrative/professional employees, a group of persons described on the university's website as "all nonfaculty [Fair Labor Standards Act] exempt employees."

The author opens this workshop by exhibiting a list of private sector firms that have made news headlines by taking part in unethical activities; participants are then asked to create a list of similar examples from the field of higher education—and they are readily able to do so! The "three key ideas" are then broached for discussion (note that Auburn University is a public institution):

- Never use your university position for private gain.
- Remember—the citizens are your employers, and they are always watching.
- The perception of wrongdoing can be as damaging as actual wrongdoing.

The guided discussion then shifts to the nature of ethical behavior and the standards that define ethical behavior for University administrators and professionals. The concept of an "ethical challenge" is then defined, and a list of examples similar to that shown in Table 12.2 is displayed, but discussed in the context of higher education; participants are invited to provide specific examples of each type of challenge. At this point in the workshop—immediately prior to a short break—the participants are asked to form small groups (of five or six persons) and given the following assignment: "Share with your group members some ethical concerns/

dilemmas you have faced. As a group, write a brief description of one or two ethical dilemmas your group would like discussed." Participants are counseled not to "name names" or violate any confidences; the purpose of this exercise is not to accuse members of the University community of wrong-doing, but rather to provide some "real life" examples for the (same) groups to consider during a later exercise in the workshop. The author has learned from experience that many of the participants who sign up for this workshop have ethical concerns they are eager to discuss with peers, and this portion of the workshop gives them the opportunity directly to address their concerns.

Following a short break the workshop reconvenes with an exposition by the author on individual and organizational factors that affect the incidence of unethical behavior in any organization (see Tables 12.6 and 12.7). Also presented by the author is a list of "questionable things bosses say to subordinates" (see Table 12.8); these double messages at best create doubt and at worst appear to endorse unethical actions on the part of employees. Supervisors are urged not to make such statements; employees are cautioned to seek clarity from any supervisor giving them such instructions—make certain the supervisor is not asking for unethical action to be undertaken.

An exhortation from the author to show ethical leadership at the university by "walking the talk" is made at this point in the workshop, then "An AU Ethics Quiz" (see Appendix B) developed by the author based on the university's *Administrative & Professional Handbook* is administered individually, then discussed as a group. As with the municipal employee workshop discussed above, this portion of the university workshop typically engenders lively discussion, particularly when "what if?" questions are posed by other workshop participants and the author. Again, this exercise reinforces group norms and University policies in a fun, engaging manner.

At this point in the workshop the three tools illustrated in Tables 12.3, 12.4, and 12.5 are shared with the participants and discussed by the

Table 12.6.   Why Do People Take Unethical Actions?

- Malice—intentional evil
- Sociopathy—lack of conscience
- Personal greed
- Envy, jealousy, resentment
- Will to win or achieve at any cost
- Fear of failure

Table 12.7.   Other Reasons: Organizational Culture

- Indifference
- Lack of knowledge; uninformed
- Poor incentive systems!
- Weak organizational culture
- Poor leadership
- Mixed signals

Table 12.8.   Questionable Things Bosses Say to Subordinates

- "I don't care how you do it, just get it done!"
- "Don't ever bring me bad news!"
- "Don't bother me with the details; you know what to do."
- "Remember, we always meet our financial goals somehow."
- "No one gets injured on this worksite ... period. Understand?"
- "Ask me no questions, I'll tell you no lies."
- "I'm the boss; just do what I say and you'll be okay."

author. Attention then turns to a unique exercise particular to this group: A line-by-line discussion of *The Auburn Creed*. This creed, written by Dr. George Petrie—eminent historian, beloved professor, dean of the academic faculty... *and Auburn's first football coach* (Jernigan, 2007)—is not an official policy statement of the University, but rather an aspirational guide intended to raise the level of moral behavior exhibited by all "Auburn men and women." The Auburn Creed (see Table 12.9) is found in many offices and public gathering places around the University and is known far and wide by "Auburn people." What follows next is an invitation for workshop participants to consider—in their original small groups—the following question: "How would Auburn men and women, using the Auburn Creed as their ethical guide, respond to the ethical issues we identified in our small group discussions?" This sobering assignment typically prompts much discussion on the part of the small group members, and leads to some innovative applications of *The Auburn Creed* to issues relevant in the life and work of the workshop participants. As a "wrap up" comment, the author reminds the workshop participants of the "three key ideas," then concludes the 3-hour session with an admonition to "Go walk the talk!"

As with the municipal employee workshop discussed above, the University professional ethics workshop receives very positive formal reviews

Table 12.9.   The Auburn Creed (by George Petrie, 1945)

I believe that this is a practical world and that I can count only on what I earn.
Therefore, I believe in work, hard work.

I believe in education, which gives me the knowledge to work wisely
and trains my mind and my hands to work skillfully.

I believe in honesty and truthfulness, without which I cannot
win the respect and confidence of my fellow men.

I believe in a sound mind, in a sound body and a spirit that is not afraid,
and in clean sports that develop these qualities.

I believe in obedience to law because it protects the rights of all.

I believe in the human touch, which cultivates sympathy with my fellow men
and mutual helpfulness and brings happiness for all.

I believe in my Country, because it is a land of freedom and because it is my own home,
and that I can best serve that country by "doing justly, loving mercy,
and walking humbly with my God."

And because Auburn men and women believe in these things,
I believe in Auburn and love it.

Source: www.auburn.edu/main/auburn_creed.html

by participants. The author is often told by participants how meaningful the workshop was; many participants recommend it to their fellow employees, and this workshop is subscribed by interested participants every semester.

ETHICS CONTINUING EDUCATION OFFERED "AT A DISTANCE" TO PROFESSIONAL ENGINEERS

The third example differs considerably from the first two. Whereas they were both programs offered face to face by the author to a group of persons in real time, this third example is a continuing education program offered to individuals in an asynchronous manner through distance learning technology. In fact, this third example is a 6-hour professional development course offered at a distance to professional engineers through Auburn University's Engineering Continuing Education office, a unit of the Samuel Ginn College of Engineering. As noted on the unit's website (www.engce.auburn.edu), this organization provides approved continuing education courses for professional engineers, surveyors, architects, business professionals, contractors, and managers in 41 of the 50 United States. Professionals purchase this course—which is delivered either via CD-ROM or online through streaming video, study it at their own pace in whatever location they choose, complete a 10-item examination for each module, and receive credit for a specified number of hours of continuing professional education which can be applied during the license renewal process. This particular course is described as follows on the unit's website:

Business Ethics

Business ethics is a topic of worldwide interest today due to revelations of ethical breaches among some of the world's leading firms. What does an engineer or technical manager need to know and do to ensure ethicality in business practices? These two modules—which may be studied individually or as a comprehensive set—are designed to meet four objectives: (1) To become familiar with issues and terminology related to business ethics. (2) To consider the viewpoints of various experts in areas of business ethics. (3) To help you begin to formulate your own personal code of ethics. (4) To promote ethical behavior in business. Each module features discussions of key issues by Dr. Sauser plus interviews with two prominent organizational leaders in which they present their own beliefs about business ethics.

Module One: Ethical Challenges in Business

In this module Dr. Sauser discusses several recent breaches of business ethics and considers reasons why some individuals make poor ethical decisions. Standards defining ethical behavior are presented, classical theories of business ethics are briefly discussed, and practical ideas for making ethical decisions every day are shared. Examples of a wide range of ethical challenges in business are then explored. The module features interviews with leaders in the information technology and heavy manufacturing industries.

Module Two: Social Responsibility and Corporate Performance

In this module Dr. Sauser reviews personal, organizational and environmental factors that influence ethical decision making; explores four corporate cultures with respect to ethics in business; and discusses steps one can take to establish a strong ethical culture. The concepts of social responsibility and corporate performance are then introduced, the importance of following the law is emphasized, and best practices for business ethics are discussed. Employee theft and ethical practices in human resources management are provided as further examples. This module features interviews with leaders in the chemical and government consulting industries.

While this continuing education program for professionals considers many of the same topics as the two described above, it is packaged much differently. It is an adaptation of the executive MBA distance education course described by the author elsewhere in this volume ("Teaching Business Ethics at a Distance to Executive MBA Students"). While this continuing education program does not include the reading and writing

264 W. I. SAUSER, JR.

assignments that are part of the executive MBA course, it does include much of the lecture material and many of the illustrations—plus four of the interviews—used in that course. Earlier videotaped versions of this continuing education course have been available for several years. The most recent version was produced July 20-21, 2010, in a specially-designed continuing education classroom/studio by media production specialists using proprietary software designed to deliver high-quality video and audio through computer streaming.

Earlier versions of this continuing education course for professionals have been well received. Participant evaluations have been good, as has anecdotal evidence provided by the participants over the years. Importantly, over 90 percent of those taking the course have passed the accompanying examinations on the first try, thus qualifying to receive credit toward their annual licensing requirements for continuing professional education. Business ethics has proven to be an interesting subject for study by these professionals in engineering and technology management.

REFLECTIONS AND LESSONS LEARNED

Having offered versions of these three business ethics training programs for professionals for most of the past decade, this author has learned some lessons that he willingly shares with the readers of this chapter. Consider the following:

- From this author's perspective, it is far more difficult to deliver an on-line lecture-type program (like the third example) than it is to work with a lively group of participants in a face-to-face arrangement (as in the first two examples). Speaking for hours on end to a television camera in an empty room can be a daunting task! Until one gains experience providing continuing education at a distance, it may be better for a business ethics professor to focus on guiding face-to-face discussions in a manner most have experienced daily in the classroom.

- Distance education, though, provides many benefits to busy professionals who cannot always take the time to travel to fixed training locations, or afford the time away from their clients. Distance education programs like the third example described above can be ideal for those who must learn at odd times on an irregular schedule; that is one of the reasons they are so popular.

- It helps, when producing a televised distance education program, to remember that you are sharing information with a single viewer. Seek to speak in a conversational style, be natural, maintain eye contact, vary your voice inflection and speed, and use plenty of examples relevant to the professional you are addressing.

- While face-to-face programs (like the first two examples) may be easier to deliver, it is very important to provide them in a highly professional manner. Mastering the facilitation skills described by Weber (2007; see the brief review of research above) are essential when one is working with discerning professionals. Know how to manage time, foster meaningful group discussion that leads to shared insights, encourage critical thinking, and summarize important points gained through inductive learning. Be certain to explore multiple points of view, and allow positive group norms to become evident. Reinforce important organizational values (like those expressed in *The Auburn Creed*) whenever possible.

- To ensure relevance, use examples and materials that participants would encounter during the regular course of their work. Making use of an advisory committee of representative employees (as in the first example) is an excellent way to gather pertinent information and to test out ideas before they are brought up in the training environment.

- Minicases like those used in the first example typically engender lively discussion and are often remembered by program participants and shared with their peers. It is important to select case examples carefully, edit them for anonymity, and make certain they are discussed thoroughly from multiple perspectives. When there is disagreement within the group on how best to handle a case example, discover the reasons for this disagreement, explore them for insights, and see if a group consensus emerges over time. This is when many seasoned group participants with high levels of moral reasoning have (and take!) the opportunity to provide leadership to the group, thus setting a good example for others to follow.

- The "ethics quizzes" used in the first and second examples have proven over time to be excellent tools for stimulating discussion and maintaining participant engagement. It takes time to review policies and create meaningful "ethics quizzes," but the resulting inductive learning makes the effort worthwhile. Employees are able to "refresh their memory" about organizational policies (and, for some, to encounter them for the first time!) and see how the black and white language of many policies needs to be tempered by interpretation and judgment.

- Having a cross-section of employees from the various functional divisions of the organization has proven very effective in these training programs. Employees get to see things from others' points of view, and to gain a better understanding of the ethical issues encountered across the organization. Having top and middle managers participating in these programs alongside the rank and file sets a good example, demonstrating that this material is important enough to be considered by persons at all levels of the organization. It has been the author's experience that the presence of members of the organization's leadership team rarely stifles discussion; in fact, it often leads to a higher quality discussion of important ethical issues and provides an opportunity for leaders to set a high ethical tone for the organization.

- The author admits that he has not often been called upon to provide ethics workshops for organizations that are in the midst of an ethical crisis or under immoral leadership. These circumstances require exceptional skill on the part of the facilitator. Rather than seeking to use a public workshop as a forum for meaningful ethical change, the business professor might recommend individual consultation with the organization's leadership team first to establish the foundation for an organizational culture of character. Until the organization's leaders are "walking the talk" with respect to business ethics, launching an ethics training program might actually be counterproductive, since hypocrisy would likely be exposed and employee morale could suffer further.

As stated in the introduction to this chapter, a major purpose of this work is to stimulate discussion among business ethics professors, business leaders, and other interested persons about moral issues in business and ways to improve ethicality in business operations. What are the "best practices" for teaching business ethics to professionals? To what extent does past experience and research provide useful guidance in designing effective training programs? Are minicases and "ethics quizzes" like those provided here truly useful devices for business ethics training? Who is best qualified to lead training programs in business ethics, and what skills are essential for effective workshop leadership? Is there an important role here for business ethics professors "beyond the classroom?" Let the discussion begin!

The present author *does* believe that an important purpose of colleges and schools of business—and the professors serving on their faculties—is to elevate the level of moral thought and action in business. Perhaps others who share this perspective can build on the ideas presented in this chapter and make an important difference for society. Let us continue to walk the talk.

APPENDIX 1: CITY OF AUBURN ETHICS QUIZ

Directions: Read each item carefully and decide whether the action described is ETHICAL or UNETHICAL based on the City of Auburn Personnel Policies. Circle E or U next to the item number.

Circle One

E	U	(1)	A friend of yours is looking for a job. You are a city of Auburn employee. You say to your friend, "You ought to apply for a job with the city. They won't tell you so, but I guarantee that if they hire you, you'll have a job for life." (1.03 #6)
E	U	(2)	Your brother-in-law is interested in a job with the city of Auburn. You say, "I can't hire you into the crew which I supervise, but I'll be glad to put in a word for you if a job comes open in another city department." (2.06)
E	U	(3)	One of your best city employees has been invited on an all-expenses-paid 1- week vacation in Hawaii. She only has 4 days of annual leave accrued. You—her supervisor—say, "Go ahead and take your vacation. We'll charge the extra day against next month's accrual." (3.03 #5)
E	U	(4)	You are a city employee and are summoned for a week of jury duty. You request time off with pay for the week you spend on the jury. (3.07)
E	U	(5)	Because you worked a little late last night, you (a city employee) decided to come in a little late today. (5.04)
E	U	(6)	You are cleaning a hallway in city hall during the night shift when a coworker gives you a cigarette. Since you are the only two people in the building, you light up and enjoy a quick smoke. (5.04)
E	U	(7)	By Friday of most weeks you have run out of cash, so you ask your coworkers to give you lunch money. (5.04)
E	U	(8)	Your church has rented chairs for a special event. On your lunch hour you pick up the chairs from the rental agency, load them into your city truck, and deliver them to your church. (5.04)
E	U	(9)	You forgot to stop by the bank on your way to work, so you write out an IOU, take $10.00 from your city office's petty cash fund, then replace the money the next day. (5.04)
E	U	(10)	Your sink is broken, so—after asking your supervisor—you borrow a pipe wrench from your city tool box, take it home and repair your sink, then bring it back the next day. (5.04)
E	U	(11)	You are a city department head. One of your employees refuses to obey a reasonable and necessary order. You fire him on the spot, and tell him never to come back. (5.05)
E	U	(12)	You're having trouble "making ends meet" on your city pay, so you take a second job working nights at a convenience store. (7.02)
E	U	(13)	It is mid-December and you are collecting trash on your regular route as a city sanitation worker. A lady greets you at the curb, says "Merry Christmas," and hands you a $10 gift certificate for lunch at a local fast food restaurant. You thank her as you slip the certificate into your pocket. (7.03)

E U (14) A city council member you admire is running for reelection. After completing your work day for the city, you post his campaign sign in your own front yard. (7.04)

E U (15) You are a city of Auburn employee. You've loaned your daughter $10,000 to start her own business. You are delighted when she obtains a contract to provide supplies to the city. (7.06)

E U (16) You have a romantic interest in your city supervisor and agree to meet after work for a date. (7.07)

E U (17) You are supervising a city work crew. A passing motorist shouts a racial slur at one of your crew members and then drives off. Later the same person repeats this action. You shake your head and look the other way. (7.08)

E U (18) One of your city coworkers gets on your nerves. One day you have an argument over who should put something away. After work you confront the coworker at home and get into a little fight. (7.09)

E U (19) You have a valid permit from the county sheriff to carry a concealed weapon, a pistol which you keep in the closed console of your car. You take your children to a city park on your day off, lock your car, and supervise them while they play. (7.10)

E U (20) While walking through city hall you notice an open confidential personnel file in a basket on a desk. Curious, you flip through the file to see what is says. (13.01)

E U (21) You are a 35-year-old city employee. While watching a football game at a neighbor's house on your day off, you drink a beer while eating some peanuts. (Section 14)

E U (22) It is "Girl Scout Cookie Sales Season." You take your daughter to your city office so she can take orders from your coworkers. (15.03)

E U (23) During your lunch hour you "surf the Internet" using your city office computer in order to find bargains you plan to order later from home. (15.04 #1)

E U (24) You like the word processing program on your city office computer, so you download it onto a zip disk and upload it onto your home computer for family use. (15.04 #5)

E U (25) On your way to another work site, you stop for lunch in your city truck. (policy statement re: city vehicles)

Note: The number in parentheses following each question refers to the relevant section of the city of Auburn Personnel Policies. Revised February 18, 2003.

APPENDIX B: AN AUBURN UNIVERSITY ETHICS QUIZ

Directions: Read each statement below. If you believe it represents an ethical action, circle "E." If you believe it represents an unethical action, circle "U."

E U 1. On the first day of her employment, Susie, an AU employee, was asked by her supervisor to attend a general orientation session conducted by human resources. (5)

E U 2. Clyde, a supervisor at AU, had some concerns about one of his probationary employees, so asked that the probationary period be extended for a second 90-day period. (6)

E U 3. Jack, when he found out that one of the candidates for a job in his work group had served in Viet-Nam, struck the candidate's name from the list of persons to be interviewed. (6)

E U 4. Upon learning that one of her employees had made a visit to the Affirmative Action/Equal Employment Opportunity Office, Joan moved the employee to a smaller desk further from the window. (6)

E U 5. After completing her probationary period, Estelle was placed on a continuing appointment. Tom, her supervisor, told her, "That means you can never be separated from the university." (7)

E U 6. When Joseph, a native of Ghana, reported for work on his first day, he forgot to bring along his completed I-9 form. "That's okay," said his supervisor. "You go ahead and get started on the job, and we'll deal with the paperwork later." (7)

E U 7. During her breaks, Shirley enjoyed reading through the personnel files for the other employees in her unit. (8)

E U 8. Knowing that his next "payday" would fall on a university holiday, Jesse asked if he could pick up his check on the last working day preceding the holiday. (8)

E U 9. Allison was interested in finding out what jobs were open at Auburn University, so she called the human resources job line. (8)

E U 10. John grew tired of his job at Auburn University, so he left his workplace and never came back. (9)

E U 11. Chris did not enjoy conducting performance review sessions with her employees, so refused to do them. (10)

E U 12. Maxine was very impressed with her colleague Jackson's work, so she nominated Jackson for a "Spirit of Excellence" award. (10)

E U 13. When Mike heard on the radio that Auburn University was closed due to a snowstorm, he did not report for his office job that morning. (11)

E U 14. Frustrated because he could not find a parking space near his office, Larry parked in a handicap space, even though he did not have a placard. (11)

E U 15. Linda saw sparks jumping from a frayed power cord in one of the labs and said to herself, "I hope someone from facilities spots that before anyone gets hurt." (11)

E U 16. When one of his employees tripped over a door mat and scraped his arm and cut his forehead, Lou asked the employee to fill out a "First Report of Work Related Injury" form within 3 days. (13)

E U 17. Bill's mother was sick, so he requested a week of annual leave so he could visit her and take care of her. Bill's supervisor asked for written documentation that Bill's mother was really sick before she would approve the request for annual leave. (13, 14)

E U 18. Lizzie was issued a summons to report for a week of jury duty and was granted jury duty Leave. After the first day of court, she was told that her jury panel was released for the rest of the week, so she went home and enjoyed herself for the next 4 days. (15)

E	U	19.	Oscar was having difficulty making ends meet financially, so he sought confidential counseling through Auburn University's Employee Assistance Program. (19)
E	U	20.	Trixie enjoyed three beers during her lunch break, then drove back to her university office. (21)
E	U	21.	Alex broke his stapler at home, so took a new one out of his university supply closet as a replacement. (21)
E	U	22.	Realizing that her supervisor was out for the afternoon, Josephine closed the door to the departmental office and took a nap on the sofa. (21)
E	U	23.	Jerry loved to hunt, so he kept his rifle on a rack in the cab of his truck, which he parked in a B-zone lot while at work. (34)
E	U	24.	Margaret received one those "chain letter" e-mails on her university computer. Amused, she e-mailed it to everyone on her departmental mailing list. (34)
E	U	25.	Wilbur was very impressed with one of the candidates for city council, so he put the candidate's campaign sign in his own front yard at home. (34-35)

Note: The number(s) in parentheses following each question refer to the pages in the Auburn University Administrative & Professional Handbook where policy guidance for the question can be found. Similar policies are found in the Auburn University Staff Handbook.

REFERENCES

Aguilar, F. J. (1994). *Managing corporate ethics: Learning from America's ethical companies how to supercharge business performance.* New York, NY: Oxford University Press.

Ferrell, O. C., Fraedrich, J., & Ferrell, L. (2011). *Business ethics: Ethical decision making and cases* (8th ed.). Mason, OH: South-Western Cengage Learning.

Jernigan, M. (2007). *Auburn man: The life & times of George Petrie.* Montgomery, AL: The Donnell Group.

Jones, T. M. (1988-1989). Ethics education in business: Theoretical considerations. *Organizational Behavior and Teaching Review, 13*(4), 1-18.

Kirrane, D. E. (1990, November). Managing values: A systematic approach to business ethics. *Training and Development Journal,* 53-60.

Lattal, A. D., & Clark, R. W. (2005). *Ethics at work.* Atlanta, GA: Performance Management Publications.

LeClair, D. T., & Ferrell, L. (2000). Innovation in experiential business ethics training. *Journal of Business Ethics, 23,* 313-322.

Purcell, T. V., & Weber, J. (1979). *Institutionalizing corporate ethics: A case history.* [Special Study No. 71] New York, NY: The Presidents of the American Management Association.

Sauser, W. I., Jr. (2008a). Crafting a culture of character: The role of the executive suite. In S. A. Quatro & R. R. Sims (Eds.), *Executive ethics: Ethical dilemmas and challenges for the C-suite* (pp. 1-17). Charlotte, NC: Information Age.

Sauser, W. I., Jr. (2008b). Regulating ethics in business: Review and recommendations. *SAM Management in Practice, 12*(4), 1-7.

Sauser, W. I., Jr., & Sims, R. R. (2007). Fostering an ethical culture for business:
The role of HR managers. In R. R. Sims & S. A. Quatro (Eds.), *Human resource
management: Contemporary issues, challenges and opportunities* (pp. 253-285).
Greenwich, CT: Information Age.

Sims, R. R. (1991). The institutionalization of organizational ethics. *Journal of
Business Ethics, 10,* 493-506.

Sims, R. R. (2005). Restoring ethics consciousness to organizations and the workplace: Every contemporary leader's challenge. In R. R. Sims & S. A. Quatro
(Eds.), *Leadership: Succeeding in the private, public, and not-for-profit sectors* (pp.
386-407). Armonk, NY: M. E. Sharpe.

Swanson, D. L. (2004). The buck stops here: Why universities must reclaim business ethics education. *Journal of Academic Ethics, 2,* 43-61.

Trevino, L. K., & Nelson, K. A. (2004). *Managing business ethics: Straight talk about
how to do it right* (3rd ed.). New York, NY: Wiley.

Valentine, S., & Fleischman, G. (2004). Ethics training and businesspersons' perceptions of organizational ethics. *Journal of Business Ethics, 52,* 381-390.

Weber, J. A. (2007). Business ethics training: Insights from learning theory. *Journal
of Business Ethics, 70,* 61-85.

ABOUT THE AUTHORS

Christopher Adkins earned his PhD in education from the College of William & Mary, his MA in philosophy from Boston University, and his BA from the College of William & Mary. In his research, Chris explores the educational implications of research in cognitive neuroscience and social psychology, particularly in the areas of ethical decision making, sustainability, and experiential learning. As an educator, he has worked with the Giving Voice to Values program to adapt their MBA-level initiative for undergraduate ethics courses. With sustainability consulting firm Saatchi S, Chris led the first personal sustainability program at a university. In 2010, he cofounded the Corporate & College Collaborative for Sustainability, a new partnership of business leaders, faculty and students for innovation in undergraduate sustainability education.

Achilles Armenakis is the James T. Pursell, Sr., Eminent Scholar in Management Ethics and director of the Auburn University Center for Ethical Organizational Cultures at Auburn University. Achilles has been on the faculty at Auburn since 1973 serving in administrative as well as professorial capacities. Achilles is a fellow in the Southern Management Association and the International Academy of Management. His research efforts have concentrated on organizational change and management ethics. Detailed biographical information can be obtained at http://business.auburn.edu/nondegreeprograms/ethics.

Johannes Brinkmann, PhD, is a professor of business ethics, BI Norwegian School of Management BI, Oslo, Norway. He has taught business ethics for almost 20 years. His main research interest is empirical business ethics research, more recently risk and insurance ethics research. Johannes has published more than 30 refereed journal article publications, mainly within business ethics, and nine books, mainly textbooks in Norwegian. For further information, see websites http://home.bi.no/fgl92025/ and http://www.bi.no/roff. Contact email: johannes.brinkmann @bi.no.

John C. Knapp, PhD, is a university professor and Mann Family Professor of Ethics and Leadership at Samford University, where he serves as founding director of the Frances Marlin Mann Center for Ethics and Leadership. He previously was professor and director of the Center for Ethics and Corporate Responsibility at Georgia State University's Robinson College of Business. Educated at the University of Wales, U.K., (PhD), Columbia Theological Seminary (MA), and Georgia State University (BS), his books include *Worlds Apart: How the Church Fails Businesspeople (and What Can Be Done About It)* (Eerdmans, in press), *The Business of Higher Education, Three Volumes* (Praeger, 2009), *Leaders on Ethics: Real-World Perspectives on Today's Business Challenges* (Praeger, 2007), and *For the Common Good: The Ethics of Leadership in the 21st Century* (Praeger, 2007). A fellow of Caux Round Table, Knapp was awarded the 2001 Georgia Governor's Award in the Humanities for his work promoting ethics in business and government.

Steven Olson, PhD, is an assistant professor and the director of the Center for Ethics and Corporate Responsibility at the J. Mack Robinson College of Business, Georgia State University. He earned his BA in philosophy and history from Calvin College, his MA. in religion from Yale University Divinity School, and his PhD in ethics and society from Emory University, where his doctoral dissertation, "The Ethics of Leadership," received the International Leadership Association's Frederic M. Jablin Award for Best Dissertation in Leadership (2007). He was director of business and professional ethics at Emory University's Center for Ethics in Public Policy and the Professions (1994-1999) and instructor of management at Emory's Goizueta Business School (1992-1999). He cofounded The Southern Institute for Business and Professional Ethics. His interests include leadership and its development, organizational development, professional and clinical ethics, and environmental sustainability. He received the Outstanding Professor award from the Global Partners MBA program of Coppead (Brazil), Robinson (United States), and IAE/Sorbonne (France) and the Crystal Apple MBA Teaching Award from the Robinson College of Business.

William I. Sauser, Jr., PhD, is a professor of management and higher education at Auburn University. He earned his BS in management and MS and PhD in industrial/organizational psychology at the Georgia Institute of Technology. His interests include organizational development, strategic planning, human relations in the workplace, business ethics, and continuing professional education. He is a fellow of the American Council on Education and the Society for Advancement of Management, a former president of the Alabama Psychological Association and the Society for Advancement of Management, and a former chair of the Alabama Board of Examiners in Psychology. Sauser was awarded the 2003 Frederick W. Taylor Key by the Society for Advancement of Management in recognition of his career achievements.

Ronald R. Sims is the Floyd Dewey Gottwald Senior Professor in the Mason School of Business at the College of William & Mary, where he teaches leadership and change management in the Executive, Residential and Flex-Masters in Business Administration Programs, and business ethics, organizational transformation/change management, human resource management and organizational behavior in the undergraduate program. He received his PhD in organizational behavior from Case Western Reserve University. His research focuses on a variety of topics to include business ethics, leadership and change management, HRM, employee training, and management and leadership development (i.e. human resource development), learning styles, and experiential learning. Sims is the author or coauthor of 30 books and more than 80 articles that have appeared in a wide variety of scholarly and practitioner journals.